The Impact of the Military

Stephen Pickard | Michael Welker | John Witte, Jr. (Eds.)

The Impact of the Military

on Character Formation, Ethical Education, and the Communication of Values in Late Modern Pluralistic Societies

WIPF & STOCK · Eugene, Oregon

Wipf and Stock Publishers
199 W 8th Ave, Suite 3
Eugene, OR 97401

The Impact of the Military
On Character Formation, Ethical Education, and the Communication
of Values in Late Modern Pluralistic Societies
By Pickard, Stephen and Welker, Michael
Copyright © 2022 Evangelische Verlagsanstalt GmbH All rights reserved.
Softcover ISBN-13: 978-1-6667-8075-8
Hardcover ISBN-13: 978-1-6667-8076-5
Publication date 5/23/2023
Previously published by Evangelische Verlagsanstalt GmbH, 2022

Table of Contents

Acknowledgments 7

Preface to the Series 9

Stephen Pickard
Introduction 13

Part One: Combatants, Ethics, and Society

Jochen Cornelius-Bundschuh
The Military Defense System and the Public Soul in Germany: A Protestant Perspective 27

Angelika Dörfler-Dierken
Inner Leadership, or The Soldier's Responsibility for Humanity and Peace 39

Gerd Theißen and Sylvie Thonak
The Complementary Path to Peace: On Peace Ethics in German Protestantism 49

Part Two: Virtues: Re-Evaluating the Military Context

Hartwig von Schubert
Which Morals Society Should Learn from the Military, and Which Decidedly Not 61

Marco Hofheinz
The Indispensability of Virtues in the Military: Virtue Ethical Considerations Following the Guiding Concept of the *Miles Protector* 79

Keith Joseph
Different Missions, Different Virtues? 93

Martin Elbe
From the Playing Field to the Battlefield: Does Sport in the Military Promote the Formation of a Specific Character? 105

Torsten Meireis
After Chivalry 123

Part Three: Moral Injury and Character

Seumas Miller
Moral Injury, Moral Character, and Military Combatants 141

Isolde Karle and Niklas Peuckmann
In the Shadow of the Operation: Moral and Spiritual Injuries as New Challenges for Pastoral Care in the German Armed Forces 153

Justin Bronson Barringer
Communal Responses to the Business of War 167

Contributors 185

Acknowledgments

A consultation leading to this volume had been planned to take place at the Forschungszentrum Internationale und Interdisziplinäre Theologie (FIIT) at the University of Heidelberg in 2020. Due to the COVID-19 pandemic, however, the consultation had to be canceled. We are grateful to the Public and Contextual Theology Research Centre, Charles Sturt University, Australia, for the generous support of this publication.

Stephen Pickard, Michael Welker, and John Witte Jr.

Preface to the Series

Five hundred years ago, Protestant reformer Martin Luther argued that "three estates" (drei Stände) lie at the foundation of a just and orderly society—marital families, religious communities, and political authorities. Parents in the home; pastors in the church; magistrates in the state—these, said Luther, are the three authorities whom God appointed to represent divine justice and mercy in the world, to protect peace and liberty in earthly life. Household, church, and state—these are the three institutional pillars on which to build social systems of education and schooling, charity and social welfare, economy and architecture, art and publication. Family, faith, and freedom—these are the three things that people will die for.

In the half millennium since Luther, historians have uncovered various classical and Christian antecedents to these early Protestant views. Numerous later theorists have propounded all manner of variations and applications of this three-estates theory, many increasingly abstracted from Luther's overtly Christian worldview. Early modern covenant theologians, both Christian and Jewish, described the marital, confessional, and political covenants that God calls human beings to form, each directed to interrelated personal and public ends. Social-contract theorists differentiated the three contracts that humans enter as they move from the state of nature to an organized society protective of their natural rights—the marital contract of husband and wife; the government contract of rulers and citizens; and, for some, the religious contracts of preachers and parishioners. Early anthropologists posited three stages of development of civilization—from family-based tribes and clans, to priest-run theocracies, to fully organized states that embraced all three institutions. Sociologists distinguished three main forms of authority in an organized community: "traditional" authority that begins in the home, "charismatic" authority that is exemplified by the church, and "legal" authority that is rooted in the state. Legal historians outlined three stages of development of legal norms—from the habits and rules of the family, to the customs and canons of religion, to the statutes and codes of the state.

Already a century ago, however, scholars in different fields began to flatten out this hierarchical theory of social institutions and to emphasize the foundational role of other social institutions alongside the family, church, and state in shaping private and public life and character. Sociologists like Max Weber and Talcott Parsons emphasized the shaping powers of "technical rationality" exemplified especially in new industry, scientific education, and market economies. Legal scholars like Otto von Gierke and F. W. Maitland emphasized the critical roles of nonstate legal associations (*Genossenschaften*) in maintaining a just social, political, and legal order historically and today. Catholic subsidiarity theories of Popes Leo XIII and Pius XI emphasized the essential task of mediating social units between the individual and the state to cater the full range of needs, interests, rights, and duties of individuals. Protestant theories of sphere sovereignty, inspired by Abraham Kuyper, argued that not only churches, states, and families but also the social spheres of art, labor, education, economics, agriculture, recreation, and more should enjoy a level of independence from others, especially an overreaching church or state. Various theories of social or structural pluralism, civil society, voluntary associations, the independent sector, multiculturalism, multinormativity, and other such labels have now come to the fore in the ensuing decades—both liberal and conservative, religious and secular, and featuring all manner of methods and logics.

Pluralism of all sorts is now a commonplace of late modern societies. At minimum, this means a multitude of free and equal individuals and a multitude of groups and institutions, each with very different political, moral, religious, and professional interests and orientations. It includes the sundry associations, interest groups, parties, lobbies, and social movements that often rapidly flourish and fade around a common cause, especially when aided by modern technology and various social media. Some see in this texture of plurality an enormous potential for colorful and creative development and a robust expression of human and cultural freedom. Others see a chaotic individualism and radical relativism, which endangers normative education, moral character formation, and effective cultivation of enduring values or virtues.

Pluralism viewed as vague plurality, however, focuses on only one aspect of late modern societies—the equality of individuals, and their almost unlimited freedom to participate peaceably at any time as a respected voice in the moral reasoning and civil interactions of a society. But this view does not adequately recognize that, beneath the shifting cacophony of social forms and norms that constitute modernity, pluralistic societies have heavy normative codes that shape their individual and collective values and morals, preferences and prejudices.

The sources of much of this normative coding and moral education in late modern pluralistic societies are the deep and powerful social systems that are the pillars of every advanced culture. The most powerful and pervasive of these are the social systems of law, religion, politics, science/academy, market, media, family, education, medicine, and national defense. The actual empirical forms of each of these powerful social systems can and do vary greatly, even in the relatively homogeneous societies of the late modern West. But these deeper social systems in one form or another are structurally essential and often normatively decisive in individual and communal lives.

Every advanced society has a comprehensive legal system of justice and order, religious systems of ritual and doctrine, a family system of procreation and love, an economic system of trade and value, a media system of communication and dissemination of news and information, and an educational system of creation, preservation, and application of knowledge and scientific advance. Many advanced societies also have massive systems of science, technology, health care, and national defense with vast influence over and through all of these other social systems. These pervasive social systems lie at the foundation of modern advanced societies, and they anchor the vast pluralities of associations and social interactions that might happen to exist at any given time.

Each of these social systems has internal value systems, institutionalized rationalities, and normative expectations that together help to shape each individual's morality and character. Each of these social spheres, moreover, has its own professionals and experts who shape and implement its internal structures and processes. The normative network created by these social spheres is often harder to grasp today, since late modern pluralistic societies usually do not bring these different value systems to light under the dominance of just one organization, institution, and power. And this normative network has also become more shifting and fragile, especially since traditional social systems, such as religion and the family, have eroded in their durability and power, and other social systems, such as science, the market, healthcare, defense, and the media, have become more powerful.

The aim of this project on "Character Formation and Ethical Education in Late Modern Pluralistic Societies" is to identify the realities and potentials of these core social systems to provide moral orientation and character formation in our day. What can and should these social spheres, separately and together, do in shaping the moral character of late modern individuals who, by nature, culture, and constitutional norms, are free and equal in dignity and rights? What are and should be the core educational functions and moral responsibilities of each of these social spheres? How can we better understand and better influence the complex interactions among individualism, the normative binding powers of these social systems, and the creativity of civil groups and institutions? How can we map and measure the different hierarchies of values that govern each of these social systems, and that are also interwoven and interconnected in various ways in shaping late modern understandings of the common good? How do we negotiate the boundaries and conflicts between and among these social systems when one encroaches on the other, or imposes its values and rationalities on individuals at the cost of the other social spheres or of the common good? What and where are the intrinsic strengths of each social sphere that should be made more overt in character formation, public education, and the shaping of minds and mentalities?

These are some of the guiding questions at work in this project and in this volume. Our project aims to provide a systematic account of the role of these powerful normative codes operating in the social spheres of law, religion, the family, the market, the media, science and technology, the academy, health care, and defense in the late modern liberal West. Our focus is on selected examples and case studies drawn from Western Europe, North America, South Africa, and Australia, which together provide just enough diversity to test out broader theories of character formation and moral education. Our scholars are drawn from across the academy, with representative voices from the humanities, social sciences, and natural sciences as well as the professions of theology, law, business, medicine, and more. While most of our scholars come from the Protestant and Catholic worlds, our endeavor is to offer comparative insights that will help scholars from any profession or confession. While our laboratory is principally Western liberal societies, the modern forces of globalization will soon make these issues of moral character formation a concern for every culture and region of the world—given the power of global social media, entertainment, and sports; the pervasiveness of global finance, business, trade, and law; and the perennial global worries over food, health care, environmental degradation, and natural disasters.

In this volume, we focus in on the role of the military and defense systems in shaping character development, ethical education, and the communication of values in late modern pluralistic societies.

Michael Welker, University of Heidelberg
John Witte Jr., Emory University
Stephen Pickard, Charles Sturt University

Introduction

Stephen Pickard

Pluralistic societies have heavy normative codes that shape their individual and collective values and morals, preferences and prejudices. The sources of much of this normative coding and moral education in late modern pluralistic societies are the deep and powerful social systems that are the pillars of every advanced culture. As stated in the preface to the volumes in this series, the aim of the overall project is "to identify the realities and potentials of these core social systems to provide moral orientation and character formation in late modern societies." While the actual empirical forms of each of these powerful social systems can and do vary greatly, nonetheless such systems remain structurally essential and often normatively decisive in individual and communal lives. To date, volumes have appeared interrogating a number of these social systems, including law, religion, the family, education, the economic market, and the academy, with new volumes soon to appear on the media and health care.

This volume focuses on the role of the military and defense systems in shaping character development, ethical education, and the communication of values in late modern pluralistic societies. In some respects, this particular volume highlights the ambiguous nature of the underlying societal structures that energize individual, social, and institutional life. In the first instance, it is not immediately obvious, let alone believable, that a system devoted to the exercise of force and its consequences (violence and even war) might at the same time offer insights and clues about character development, ethical education, and the communication of values. It seems entirely antithetical to such aspirations. Yet it is precisely in the domain of military defense that significant and important ethical inquiry and reflection have been undertaken and continue to occur in order to assess the significance, potential, and threat that this social system provides to the well-being, safety, and even flourishing of human society.

There exists a long and well-known tradition of ethical, philosophical, and theological reflection on the military and the conditions under which war might be fought. This important theme emerges in some of the essays in this volume. The conflicts of the twentieth century have generated significant ethical reflection on the nature of virtue and its relevance for military defense systems. Moreover, soldiering within the context of modern warfare and the recognition of what is termed in shorthand PTSD (posttraumatic stress disorder) has provided the conditions for more sustained focus on the experience of moral injury, and associated concerns for spiritual damage and pastoral care. These various interrelated streams in ethical reflection on military defense as a powerful social (and economic) system provide the framework for this present volume.

The book is divided into three parts. Part One, "Combatants, Ethics, and Society," examines some critical developments in post–World War II Germany with respect to the military's role and responsibility in society: soldiering, the relationship between the military and a values-based society, the concept of inner guidance (*Innere Führung*), peace ethics, deterrence, and pacifism. These chapters represent the mature reflections of those who, by virtue of their national context, have had to examine, perhaps more deeply than others, some of the important ethical issues that arise for the military, soldiering, and the host society. Part Two, "Virtues: Re-Evaluating the Military Context," focuses on the nature of virtue and its ambiguities within a military defense system, and raises important questions about the moral status of agents of force. Part Three, "Moral Injury and Character," examines the logic, nature, and power of moral and spiritual injury in the military; articulates some of the challenges for pastoral care in the armed forces; and addresses some of the ethical issues that arise from the business of war. This section locates the military defense system within a wider social and economic horizon, even as it probes new ways forward of a communal and pacific nature.

The essays highlight some of the significant tensions we have to learn to navigate as communities and societies acutely aware of the need for safety as a condition for human flourishing and the priority of peacemaking, yet alive to the realities of conflicts, violence, and the persistent unregulated human drives that make for war. An ethics of peace, it seems, has to be able to give an account of both realities. It is precisely in this mix that this volume presses the question as to whether and under what conditions military defense systems might contribute to character formation, ethical education, and the communication of values in late modern pluralistic societies.

The majority of contributors come from Germany, though contributions also come from Australia and the United States. The underlying framework for the volume, as for the series more generally, is informed by the values and orientation of Christian traditions of the West. However, the academic and professional backgrounds of contributors are varied and include theology and the church, the social sciences, philosophy, ethics, the military, and business.

Part One, "Combatants, Ethics and Society," begins with a chapter by Jochen Cornelius-Bundschuh ("The Military Defense System and the Public Soul in Germany: A Protestant Perspective"). Cornelius-Bundschuh draws attention to the fundamental reconsideration of the military in post–World War II Germany in relation to the "public soul of Germany." The basis for this reconsideration was the development of the concept of *Innere Führung* (inner leadership or inner guidance). This concept had a twofold significance: (a) setting out the ethical framework for the military as an essential and accountable component of a democratic society; and (b) making actors within the military personally responsible ethically for their actions. The role of the military was thus narrowly defined in terms of contributing to a more just peace. Cornelius-Bundschuh notes that this framework, with the concept of *Innere Führung*, is now under serious threat in a complex global network of failed states, powerful authoritarian actors, the advent of autonomous weapons systems, and changing warfare.

He asks the critical questions: "Can the military system find the means to deal with these transformations in such a way that it does not fall back into authoritarian and violent forms of action? Can it contribute to the development of the 'public soul' which, critical of power, strengthens the commitment to the constitution, to international law, and to human dignity?" These questions inform the background to the development by the churches of chaplaincy as a civilian institution embodying a peace ethic within the armed forces. This way of locating chaplaincy "reflects the indissoluble tension into which military action moves under the perspective of a Protestant peace ethic." There are no easy answers for the crisis of responsibility in the military, which is increasingly under pressure to support short-term political and economic interests in national and international affairs and sacrifice an "intelligent love of the enemy."

The importance of *Innere Führung* with respect to the responsibility of soldiers for their actions is examined in more detail by Angelika Dörfler-Dierken ("Inner Leadership, or The Soldier's Responsibility for Humanity and Peace"). The concept covers a range of meanings: "leadership development and civic education concept," "leadership philosophy," or even "internal leadership" or "inner guidance." Dörfler-Dierken notes that "the concept is unique, because it is value-based and strengthens the virtue and responsibility of each soldier. It is the normative basis of personality development and the guideline for the training of military personnel." The development of *Innere Führung* was based on the view that "soldiers have rights as citizens of a democracy, and human dignity, freedom of religion, and freedom of conscience have to apply to them even during their military service." As such, the idea of soldiers as "citizens in uniform" was born.

Among many things, this development signaled an important reciprocity between a top-down role model for soldiers, via politicians and defense agencies, and a traditional bottom-up approach, by which soldiers understood themselves as geared to fight. In the context of nuclear armaments, this latter approach constituted an ever-present threat, because soldiers fighting against enemies would inevitably endanger their own people, on whose behalf they fought. Soldiers now had to learn a new way of engagement, wherein a soldier "had to fight in order not to have to fight[,] ... preparing for an emergency in order to prevent exactly that; never implementing what one practices." In short, combat readiness with an orientation toward peace. This constituted a new ethical horizon for the soldier and made a claim upon the combatant as an agent responsible for the furtherance of a peaceful humanity. This is the inner attitude aligned with the politics of peace. It presumes a close bond between soldiers (and by extension the military system) and the broader community to which they belong. Accordingly, Dörfler-Dierken shows that the core concepts of Inner Leadership "are not military, but civil and humane." It is an effort in the second half of the twentieth century, not uncontroversial, yet intended to recover the communal and social embeddedness of military ethos and action in order to sustain a politics of deterrence.

The concept of *Innere Führung* has been associated with modern initiatives for peace, a focus on deterrence, and more recent challenges regarding the ethical imperatives required to navigate the complexities and threats of modern global military conflicts. These themes are addressed by Gerd Theissen and Sylvie Thonak ("The Complementary Path to Peace: On Peace Ethics in German Protestantism"). The authors take their point of reference from the "complementary peace ethic" proposed in the *Heidelberg Theses* of 1959. This document represented an attempt to maintain Protestant unity in Germany as the country examined the contentious issue of rearmament. The framers of the theses recognized that the path of peace required holding two quite different, even opposing positions—that is, pacifist nonviolence and military defense policy. Theissen and Thonak note that these two positions are "asymmetrical: nonviolence is the clearer sign on the way to a future peace order, but military defense readiness is indispensable to secure the existing peace." The result was a commitment to "cooperation in the interest of peacekeeping." This complementary ethic of peace had an analogy in democratic political life, wherein "the ruling party and the opposition secure freedom through their opposition."

Theissen and Thonak traverse the rich biblical traditions regarding peace and the way in which peace and war have been handled in the history of Christianity. The authors point to Saint Paul's comments on the role of the state as an earlier echo of a complementary ethic of peace. However, the authors note that over the course of the past quarter century, global conflicts and developments in modern military capability have placed increasing strain on the aforementioned idea of complementarity. A military ethic of responsibility and political realism is often at odds with pacifism, which views military operations abroad as covert forms of the remilitarization of politics—for example, where peacekeeping missions end up becoming the catalyst for greater conflicts. The fact is that peace operations are extremely risky and, moreover, do not always succeed. Military chaplaincy has become isolated, a church within or beyond the church. Pacificism can likewise become disconnected from the world of military operations, and soldiering can be easily devalued. On all three counts, the complementary peace ethic has eroded. The authors express a concern that the complementary peace ethic is morphing into a militarily focused ethic of responsibility and discrediting of pacifist protest as an unrealistic ethics of conscience. The authors argue that both pacifist and military approaches to peace are required for a full account of an ethic of responsibility.

Part Two, "Virtues: Re-Evaluating the Military Context," examines an area of military life that has come under increasing focus, if not scrutiny. This can be observed, for example, in government inquiries into often questionable actions of soldiers in combat zones. Hartwig von Schubert ("Which Morals Society Should Learn from the Military, and Which Decidedly Not") sets the scene by identifying the military defense system in terms of security-sector institutions. This connection is significant because, among other reasons, it de-privatizes the military and opens it up for scrutiny into the legitimacy of the use of political force in the institutions of the security sector, including the military and the police. Schubert examines the relationship between security-sector institutions and society under the criterion of the common good. His concerns are multilayered and include the key "normative functions, value hierarchies, and spheres of action of security-sector institutions" and "conflicts between the security sector and society."

In his analysis, Schubert identifies primary and secondary virtues with respect to armed forces. Primary virtues are those associated with the right and duty to conduct combat, including the consideration of collateral damage, such as the lives of uninvolved persons. In this context, Schubert refers to the tension between the "specific character constellation" necessary for training combatants to kill and, on the other hand, the knowledge that they will remain unpunished as long as they do so within the "the limits of the law of armed conflict." Schubert notes that "compliance with this paradoxical duty demands a high degree of voluntary self-restraint from every soldier and the armed forces as a whole. The danger of excess is present at all times, and the risk is very high, given the enormous potential for damaging effects."

Secondary virtues (for example, initiative, fidelity, loyalty to legitimate order, and solidarity with the vulnerable and protected) are transferable to other systems beyond the security sector. Schubert notes, however, that "in view of the relationship between the military and society, even more important than the cultivation of secondary virtues is the common awareness associated with the term 'strategic culture.'" The reason for this focus is that historically, the most significant level of warfare on earth is within states (civil wars), and therefore strategic thinking cannot be reduced to military capabilities. The key to overcoming and pacifying conflicts is the role played by "'brave' civilian actors." Schubert concludes, "Hardly anyone demands this more emphatically and passionately than soldiers returning from missions. The state and civil society should listen to them and, above all, learn this insight from them."

Marco Hofheinz ("The Indispensability of Virtues in the Military: Virtue Ethical Considerations Following the Guiding Concept of the *Miles Protector*") asks somewhat provocatively whether we really need virtues. For example, on one account steadfastness, loyalty, duty, diligence, and obedience might be regarded as indispensable virtues, albeit of a secondary kind. Yet such virtues can easily degenerate into vices when associated with torture and retaliatory acts that are criminal and constitute war crimes. Hofheinz reminds readers of Oskar Lafontaine's retort to German Chancellor Helmut Schmidt that such virtues as loyalty, duty, and so on can also be used to run a concentration camp. Hofheinz raises the fundamental problem for a virtue ethics in the context of cultural pluralism, subjectivized convictions, and complex authority structures. The military and defense system is not immune from this problem. However, he argues for a reimagined virtue ethics. Beyond a duty ethics that seeks normative rules, and a "good ethics" focused on the effects of moral action, a reimagined "virtue ethics" is concerned with the performers of an action and asks, "How should I/we *be?*" "This brings into focus the person who acts well and their characteristics, abilities, and skills. Those who ask only rule- or result-oriented questions will lose sight of the person and the force determining the person's actions." A virtue ethics needs to be brought into relation with a duty ethics and an ethics of the good in order to develop a new integrative military ethics that can also draw upon the long history of the doctrine of ethics and the "soldiery ethos."

In particular, Hofheinz discusses the appeal in more recent times to the concept of the *miles protector* (Latin for soldier protector), wherein the focus is on the soldier of the twenty-first century to protect, help, and save. Hofheinz draws attention to another ethicist (Gustav Däniker) regarding the *miles protector:* "His mission statement is to make an increasingly targeted and effective contribution to peacekeeping, peacebuilding, and securing a livable existence for the people." Such a soldier is "one who provides protection through his efforts but is also capable of aid and rescue with the same energy and competence with which he masters combat tasks." In this sense, modern soldiers become "cosmopolitan guardians of the law" and "citizens in uniform" who exhibit "vigilant-critical loyalty and a sense of responsibility." Hofheinz proposes a broader framework for soldierly virtues, in which military ethics are more fully integrated with broader community ethics and values, such as concerns for justice and human rights. This approach gives particular significance to the development of military ethics for those institutions and agencies that embody such societal ethics. The church has an important role to play here in inculcating an open spirit (Barth's "skylight") to the transcendent spiritual realm of the Kingdom of God.

Keith Joseph ("Different Missions, Different Virtues?") comments that when military ethics is considered, it is applied in the form of traditional symmetric warfare—such as the World Wars. Clearly, these wars dominate our views of military conflict, and the laws applicable to armed conflict (such as the Geneva Conventions of 1949) and the development of military ethics result from this style of warfare between large, roughly equal sovereign states.

However, Joseph notes that since World War II most Western liberal democracies have not engaged significantly in traditional symmetric warfare. For example, Australia has been involved in long periods of asymmetric warfare (as in Vietnam and Afghanistan), various peacekeeping missions, and assistance to the civil authorities. Joseph poses two pertinent questions: "are the military virtues different in war as compared to peace? Does military ethics apply differently between warlike operations and peacekeeping?"

Joseph's chapter probes these questions and argues that the traditional military virtues, and the traditional framework of just-war theory, can be extended to these varying types of operations and missions. He takes the example of the military virtues of courage and prudence. Courage might be more noted in symmetric warfare than prudence, and vice versa on peacekeeping operations—but both are still necessary. He notes that while principles of necessity and proportionality in just-war theory also apply to peacekeeping, nonetheless in asymmetric warfare and policing much greater discrimination between combatants and noncombatants is required. He also observes that more recently, "the idea of *jus post bellum* (justice after war) has also been posited: this is the idea that there needs to be a moral transition from war to peace. The lack of a workable exit strategy from a conflict would be an example of a breach of *jus post bellum*." Joseph concludes that "the general framework of military virtues and military ethics, if applied with some nuances, still remains an overall framework capable of guiding thought and decision-making."

Martin Elbe ("From the Playing Field to the Battlefield: Does Sport in the Military Promote the Formation of a Specific Character?") examines the extent to which sport in the military is capable of imparting values and fostering a certain set of character traits, values, and behaviors. It is an interesting and unusual approach, and Elbe's discussion is driven by three questions: To what extent does sport in the military help foster a particular set of character traits, values, and behaviors? Is sport a means of seducing youth—toward military docility? To what extent is sport suitable to convey values?

The starting point for his discussion is the prevailing conviction in the military that sport can have an educational effect on adults, but then too, of course, sports training is also suitable for building the character of soldiers. However, there is much to be said for the fact that sports training primarily achieves physical effects. There is no doubt that targeted sports psychology training can also improve cognitive performance and promote mental strength—but this is not usually what is meant when we talk about character building through sports. However, the analysis of the personality of former officers indicates that it is not so much a specific character that is imparted through sport, but rather that competencies are developed that the former officers want to match with general societal expectations, and the officers themselves do not want to be considered character stereotypes of officer-typical secondary virtues. The teaching of values in relation to sport and the military is "less about individual character building and the socializing effect, and more about creating opportunities to experience community."

Torsten Meireis ("After Chivalry") notes that "despite the industrialization and the ongoing robotization of warfare in the late modern nation-state, there is a need for a value-based self-image of agents of force, who include not only military personnel but also the police." This need has become even more urgent, given that the "image of the agent of force in society has become strangely ambivalent." Whereas on-duty soldiers might be lauded as "chivalrous heroes," on return from conflicts they often can quickly become liabilities. In short, Meireis suggests that "the moral status of agents of force has become problematic." Meireis reframes the question thus: "not in which way the values of organizations of force influence society, but rather how society deals with the normative insecurity in its armed forces, whether military or police." At this point he invokes Bonhoeffer's concept of responsibility and the acceptance of guilt.

Meireis outlines some developments in the military and police as organizations of force. In doing so, he examines some empirical findings regarding the ethos of military and police personnel. This sets the groundwork for a discussion of the "ethical dilemmas that agents of force face from a theological and philosophical point of view." Meireis's discussion picks up themes in earlier essays in this volume when he draws attention to important relationships between the values, ethos, and human rights accorded to people in civil society, and the codes of behavior and ways of acting appropriate for those who have a special task to provide protection, help, and safety to people. In this context, Meireis notes that "the normative images of the agents of force are also changing. The soldier becomes a *miles protector*, the police person the neighborhood mediator in community policing." This leads to an interesting juxtaposition stated thus: "the constabularization of the military and the militarization of the police." This transformation not only changes the task and image of agents of force but also bridges the gap between "a civil society that cherishes nonviolence, on one hand, and the organizations of force, on the other," in which the latter are "integrated in a concept of nonviolent conflict resolution that provides robust criteria for the use of force as a means of last resort." This understanding clearly has implications for education and training for those in organizations of force. It also presents another way of imagining the complexities of modern society and conflict, and what constitutes genuine chivalry.

Part Three, "Moral Injury and Character," opens up an important discussion that underlies those social systems designed to protect, help, and save people.

While this purpose is not restricted to organizations of force (for example, caring and health professions also bear the same charge) the military defense system has become, in recent decades, the location for a new awareness of the injuries both moral and spiritual that are associated with involvement in modern conflicts and war.

Seumas Miller ("Moral Injury, Moral Character, and Military Combatants") notes the well-established fact regarding the traumatic effect of war on military combatants and the impact of what has become known as posttraumatic stress disorder (PTSD) among veterans. Miller's focus is directed to the post-Vietnam War phenomenon referred to as moral injury. He notes that "military combatants are held to be especially vulnerable to moral injury" and notes the standard medicalized view that moral injury is considered a species of PTSD wherein "moral injury is held to be PTSD in which the moral values of the sufferer have been violated by himself or by others." Miller takes a contrary view, arguing that moral injury is not a species of PTSD, but rather that PTSD is a species of moral injury. He notes that his alternative approach allows the constitutive moral features of PTSD to come into view. Such features "are obscured or even denied on the standard view in favor of what might be referred to as an implicit medicalized conception." Miller frames both PTSD and moral injury in terms of a "moral-psychological conception."

Miller's approach makes use of the notion of caring deeply about something or someone worthy of being cared deeply about. Accordingly, he proffers a care-based account of moral injury (and, therefore, of PTSD). On his care-based account, "one's moral identity—that is, what one most deeply cares about, including one's autonomy and, in the case of military combatants, one's honor—can be undermined or substantially diminished by traumatic events beyond one's own control." When combatants suffer moral injury, their moral character and moral identity can be undermined, not only if they engage in war crimes but also if they suffer enemy assaults in which combatants on both sides are following the generally accepted moral principles of war.

Isolde Karle and Niklas Peuckmann ("In the Shadow of the Operation: Moral and Spiritual Injuries as New Challenges for Pastoral Care in the German Armed Forces") take up their discussion where Miller's paper concludes. While generally following the more familiar approach of treating moral injury as a variant of PTSD, the authors distinguish moral injuries that "can be traced back to a lasting shaking of the moral-value orientation" from posttraumatic stress disorder, which "is a physiological reaction to an extreme situation." They note that "in PTSD, *anxiety states* are in the foreground, whereas in moral injuries, *feelings of shame* and *guilt* dominate," the latter playing an important role in Christian anthropology. In this latter perspective, moral injury can be examined in terms of its religious implications, wherein *spiritual injury* constitutes a disruption of "the value orientation" familiar in moral injury.

Karle and Peuckmann's extension of the concept of moral injury to matters of spiritual damage—"hidden wounds of war"—provides a theological perspective where spiritual injury is interpreted in terms of a damage "to the relationship between human and creation or between human and God." In this context, they introduce the concept of the "soul wound" and "soul repair." The key question is "to what extent these mission-related stress reactions represent a topic for military pastoral care, and how pastors in the Bundeswehr can make room for these experiences in pastoral care." The chapter examines in detail exactly how spiritual injury and its repair are diagnosed and attended to through the ministry of military chaplaincy. Karle and Peuckmann raise questions about a new culture of the heroic for combatants, the dangers this generates for returning "invisible veterans," and the challenges such a culture creates for military chaplaincy. The authors endorse the idea that military chaplains "learn to cultivate a kind of 'second-order heroism' that maintains an appreciative-critical distance not only from the heroism of the soldiers but also from their own 'heroic parts.'" Karle and Peuckmann remind the reader that pastoral care in the shadow of deployment requires a high degree of personal self-awareness of the dynamics of moral injury and spiritual injury and a clear sense of the often-ambiguous place of military chaplaincy within the armed forces.

The final chapter in the volume, by Justin Barringer ("Communal Responses to the Business of War"), offers a more radical approach to war and explores what might be entailed in a genuine communal and Christian response. His premise is clear: "Warmaking is also a unique sort of business because of the way it relies on destruction of lives and property; social infrastructures and economic systems; morality and decency. Thus, for Christians this ought to raise questions about how the church can offer a response to the economic, violent, and moral aspects of war, preferably at the same time. What might be appropriate and distinctly Christian responses to the business of war?"

Barringer writes from the context of the modern U.S. military-industrial complex (MIC). He invites readers to think about the moral aspects of the MIC. In doing so, he disrupts the conventional wisdom about the necessity of the military for peace by revealing that war has been always a lucrative profit-making business. He notes that Christians have employed a number of tactics to demonstrate opposition to war, including public protest, destruction of military property, prayer services outside weapons-manufacturing sites, draft dodging, and signing petitions.

With the face of modern warfare changing, Barringer asks how Christians might adapt peace witness in response. He engages with key texts in the Acts of the Apostles and "delineates four practices in which the earliest Christians participated together: simplicity, community, charity, and spirituality." Such practices, he argues, "are deeply relevant for Christians who seek to resist, subvert, or provide prophetic critiques of the MIC." These distinct practices provide patterns for disciples "to refuse, as much as possible, to participate in the systems—economic, political, and philosophical—that perpetuate war and its requisite moral deformation, oppression, and isolation." By combining insights from the work of scholars such as James William McClendon and Andrew Bacevich, and the example of activists such as the Berrigan brothers and Bayard Rustin, the chapter maps possible Christian responses to the increasingly complex business of war. These possible Christian responses include the Christian virtues and practices of simplicity, community, charity, and spirituality.

Barringer's chapter offers a view from below, so to speak, on the business of war and agencies of force in the modern world. In doing so, his essay resonates with earlier chapters on peace ethics and societal values, and more recent re-evaluations.

Part One:
Combatants, Ethics, and Society

The Military Defense System and the Public Soul in Germany: A Protestant Perspective

Jochen Cornelius-Bundschuh[1]

"An influential church, a tangible saber, strict obedience, and rigid customs."[2] In Heinrich Mann's novel *Professor Unrat*, the professor uses these words to describe the social situation in Germany before World War I. Not until the end of World War II was there a fundamental reconsideration in society as well as in the church as to what contribution the military should make to the "history of the public soul in Germany."[3]

The basis of this reconsideration was the concept of *Innere Führung* (inner leadership or inner guidance), which rigorously views the Bundeswehr, or armed forces, as an essential component of democratic society and demands accountability for military actions by all actors involved before the forum of democratic institutions. At the same time, "inner leadership" means that anyone who acts militarily within the Bundeswehr must take personal ethical responsibility for their actions.

This departure from an earlier ethos was widely echoed in the Protestant church and theology. It corresponded to the revision of the church's own position on military conflict resolution in the twentieth century: military action can be ethically justified only within narrow limits, provided it serves the goal of a "more just" peace. To this end, it must be grounded in state or international law, limited in time, and directed toward a legitimate goal; it must help to preserve life and stabilize or open up possibilities for achieving sustainable solutions in

---

[1] Thanks to Pastor Eleanor McCormick, of Karlsruhe, who has translated the German version into English.
[2] Heinrich Mann, *Professor Unrat oder Das Ende eines Tyrannen* (Frankfurt, 1997), 45. The novel was filmed in 1930 under the title *The Blue Angel*, by Joseph Sternberg, and is one of the most important films of the Weimar Republic.
[3] That was the originally planned subtitle to Heinrich Mann's novel *Der Untertan*, which was serialized in a magazine beginning in January 1914, then was published in a small private edition in 1916, and appeared as a widely available book only after the lifting of censorship in 1918.

political, social, or ecological conflicts. On this basis, Protestant Pastoral Care in the German Armed Forces came into being, which since then has helped to shape the formation and communication of values within the military system through, among other things, the *Lebenskundlicher Unterricht* (life lessons), the code of professional ethics that specifically instructs soldiers in ethical formation and personal responsibility.

Since the 1990 s, the Bundeswehr's situation has changed drastically. It increasingly operates in global contexts and in asymmetrical conflict constellations that are shaped by political and economic special interests. It encounters "failed states" and a differentiated, global civil society, which, on one hand, is steadily gaining importance and, on the other, is massively threatened by powerful authoritarian actors. Autonomous weapons systems also are changing warfare. All of these changes threaten the concept of *Innere Führung*, because they call its very foundation into question: without an ethically founded acceptance of responsibility, there is no justification for military force!

Can the military system find the means to deal with these transformations in such a way that it does not fall back into authoritarian and violent forms of action? Can it contribute to the development of the "public soul" which—critical of power—strengthens the commitment to the constitution, to international law, and to human dignity?

God's Peace Movement and the Limited Role of the Military System

The Protestant peace ethic is aligned with the peace movement of God, expressed in the powerful and multiform urge of Christ's love (2 Corinthians 5) for reconciliation.

As a movement, it is more than a guiding principle: it wants to sweep away the evil and encourages participation in this movement, which takes small and large steps. It distinguishes between God's action and our commitment to peace, which always remains particular and conflictual and sometimes stands against the Triune God's action for peace. It nurtures skepticism about clear-cut friend/foe classifications and endures tensions in situations of conflict.

God's peace changes our world comprehensively. It aims at a life in dignity and at the individual, collective, and international protection against violence, the preservation of the environment and the livelihood of future generations, the reduction of injustice and hardship, the recognition of cultural diversity, the strengthening of justice and freedom, and an economic system that knows and shapes its limits and serves the lives of all.

Within this logic, military action has a narrowly defined ethical right to contain the violent assertion of interests and to strengthen sustainable solutions to civil conflict. To this end, the military system must be self-critically aware of the vested interests behind its own actions and must resist any instrumentalization. The perspectives of the opposing side must be perceived realistically and soberly, but also taken seriously.

After the end of the Second World War and the shock over the participation of the Wehrmacht in the crimes committed during the reign of National Socialism, military action appeared to be ethically justifiable only with such a demanding ethical concept, which relies on continuous learning processes in reflection, decision-making, and action.

Innere Führung: An Ethical Awakening after World War II

"Whoever wanted to kick had to let himself be kicked."[4] With these words, Heinrich Mann sums up the authoritarian-minded mentality that characterized the German military until the end of World War II.

The attitude of the newly emerging Bundeswehr was to differ markedly from this. To safeguard the new army against a "relapse into the spirit of the Wehrmacht,"[5] the concept of *Innere Führung*[6] was developed. Soldiers (and, beginning in the mid-1970s, female soldiers as well) were to see themselves as functionaries of the state in a democratically constituted society and to locate themselves at the center of this society: "The rights guaranteed in the Basic Law also apply to them. But as citizens in uniform, they are particularly committed to the values and standards of the Basic Law."[7]

The concept drew on the tradition of German resistance around Claus Schenk Graf von Stauffenberg[8]:

> To prevent the danger of a repetition of the crimes [of the Wehrmacht], the special historical and political situation in which the founding of the Bundeswehr was carried out had to be taken seriously, and the relationship between the state and the

---

[4] Heinrich Mann, *Der Untertan* (Leipzig: Kurt Wolff, 1918), 434.
[5] Claus von Rosen, "Baudissins dreifache politisch-militärische Konzeption für den Frieden," in *Wolf Graf von Baudissin, Grundwert: Frieden in Politik-Strategie-Führung von Streitkräften* (Berlin: Hartmann, Miles Verlag, 2014), 9–36.
[6] "Staatsburger in Uniform" (Citizen in uniform), https://www.bmvg.de/de/themen/verteidigung/innere-fuehrung/staatsbuerger-in-uniform.
[7] Die Innere Führung—das Wertegerüst der Bundeswehr.
[8] See Bundesministerium der Verteidigung (Federal Ministry of Defense), *Die Tradition der Bundeswehr. Richtlinien zum Traditionsverständnis und zur Traditionspflege* (2018), 4.

armed forces had to be redefined. This could only be done through a reformist concept that, under the name of "Innere Führung," tied the military to the values and norms of the Basic Law. The central tenet of the value-based security policy to which the Federal Republic of Germany has committed itself since its founding is therefore human dignity, which claims to apply not only for Germans but for all people in the world. From the military reform program emerged the "citizen in uniform," who protects the liberal democratic basic order. For him or her, too, human dignity is the supreme value. This includes the fundamental right to freedom of conscience. Not only does the soldier protect this value, but it also protects him or her in the event of conflict, as the Federal Administrative Court unequivocally established in 2005 when confirming the ethical principles of Innere Führung. Conscience establishes the limitations to the duty to obey.[9]

In this sense, "the Bundeswehr ... does not know unconditional obedience. The ultimate decision-making authority remains the conscience of each individual. Training this conscience is the task of historical and political education, life skills instruction of the *Lebenskundlicher Unterricht*, and of leading by example.... The principles of Innere Führung guide [the soldiers] and give them orientation."[10] The principles provide members of the armed forces with "the moral support to meet the special demands their profession places on them."[11] "Soldiers in the Bundeswehr fulfill their mission when, out of inner conviction, they actively stand up for human dignity, freedom, peace, justice, equality, solidarity, and democracy as the guiding values of our state."[12]

This concept of *Innere Führung* sets out the value framework of the Bundeswehr and the ethical basis for its military action. The values are those

- against which the specific service, including in deployment abroad, must legitimize itself;
- which ensure the integration of military action into society; and
- which oblige soldiers to an obedience guided by their conscience and to an assumption of personal responsibility.

---

[9] Markus Thurau, "Innere Führung—Normative Grundlage der Persönlichkeitsbildung in der Bundeswehr," *Ethik und Militär: Kontroversen in Militärethik & Sicherheitspolitik*, 2019, no. 2, http://www.ethikundmilitaer.de/de/themenueberblick/20192-ethik-fuer-soldaten/doerfer-dierken-thurau-innere-fuehrung-normative-grundlage-der-persoenlichkeitsbildung-in-der-bundeswehr/ (translation by the author).
[10] "Staatsburger in Uniform."
[11] Die Innere Führung—das Wertegerüst der Bundeswehr.
[12] Zentrale Dienstvorschrift (ZDv) A-2600/1: *Innere Führung. Selbstverständnis und Führungskultur der Bundeswehr*. Bonn, Ziffer 106 (emphasis in original).

Strengthening Personal Responsibility through the *Lebenskundlicher Unterricht*

The concept of personal responsibility places high demands on the actors in the military system, ties them closely to the democratic practice of society, and expects them to represent that society in a distinctive way.[13] In order to promote this link between the military and civilian spheres, civilian actors, such as the churches, should also be involved in the values formation of soldiers.[14]

In the 1950 s—and again during the debates surrounding the reunification of Germany in the 1990 s—the Protestant churches engaged in groundbreaking debates on peace ethics about whether they should take on this task. In the end, they decided to establish the Protestant chaplaincy in the Bundeswehr. Their understanding of the chaplaincy "as a civilian [organized] institution within the armed forces, independent of the military hierarchy, which sees itself in critical solidarity with the Bundeswehr,"[15] reflects the indissoluble tension into which military action moves under the perspective of a Protestant peace ethic.

The particular interest of the chaplaincy lies in accompanying soldiers in a pastoral, but also in an ethical-educational, way, attaching special importance to participation in shaping the *Lebenskundlicher Unterricht*[16] as a "professional ethics qualification measure." The chaplaincy focuses on the soldiers' reflective competence and ethical judgment. The goal is to enable them to justify their own

---

[13] "The education of the soldier in the political and ethical sense must be given the greatest attention from the outset in the context of general service teaching. It does not have to be limited to the purely military." Heiner Timmermann, ed., *Die Himmeroder Denkschrift vom 9. Oktober 1950* (Nonnweiler: Dewies, 2013), section 5, D.

[14] Dirck Ackermann, "Ethische Bildung in der Bundeswehr auf neuen Wegen?," in *Seelsorge in der Bundeswehr*, ed. Isolde Karle and Niklas Peuckmann (Leipzig: Evangelische Verlagsanstalt, 2020), 250.

[15] Ibid., 236. See also Angelika Dörfler-Dierken, "Militärseelsorge in der Bundeswehr," in Karle and Peuckmann, *Seelsorge in der Bundeswehr*, 146–65. More critical: Jens Müller-Kent, *Militärseelsorge im Spannungsfeld zwischen kirchlichem Auftrag und militärischer Einbindung. Analyse und Bewertung von Strukturen und Aktivitäten der ev. Militärseelsorge unter Berücksichtigung sich wandelnder gesellschaftlicher Rahmenbedingungen* (Hamburg: Steinmann & Steinmann, 1990). With a view to the debate on whether military pastoral care should also be extended to the eastern federal states, see Ines-Jaqueline Werkner, *Soldatenseelsorge versus Militärseelsorge. Evangelische Pfarrer in der Bundeswehr* (Baden-Baden: Nomos, 2001).

[16] For *Lebenskundlichen Unterricht in Bundeswehr*, see also Meike Wanner, "Lebenskundlicher Unterricht in der Bundewehr," in Karle and Peuckmann, *Seelsorge in der Bundeswehr*, 245–56.

actions responsibly, to become sensitive to possible misjudgments,[17] and to become aware of the attitude with which they perform their service.[18] This third aspect has acquired greater importance because of foreign deployments.[19]

Through the continuous confrontation with external ethical perspectives, the lessons not only legitimize military action but also challenge it: military intervention has a right only as *ultima ratio*, provided it serves to secure peace.[20] By pointing this out, the military chaplaincy sharpens consciences in the Bundeswehr and keeps alive the realization that whoever uses military force has already crossed a line. At the same time, the chaplaincy ensures that the church does not lose sight of the reality of the violent handling of interstate conflicts.[21]

A Concept in Crisis?

The uncovering of right-wing extremist tendencies in some military units, but above all the reports of many soldiers facing a discrepancy between their expectation of participating in a great, ethically sound mission and their personal experiences of the ambivalence of concrete military actions, show that the concept

---

[17] Rainer Anselm, "Sensibilisieren, nicht legitimieren," in Karle and Peuckmann, *Seelsorge in der Bundeswehr*, 230 f.

[18] See Rainer L. Glatz, "Führen im Einsatz—Verantwortung über Leben und Tod—eine berufsethische Annäherung," in *Am Hindukusch—und weiter? Die Bundeswehr im Auslandseinsatz: Erfahrungen, Bilanzen, Ausblicke*, ed. Rainer L. Glatz and Rolf Tophoven (Bonn: Bundeszentrale für Politische Bildung, 2015), 187–202, at 192.

[19] Friedrich Lohmann, "Ethische Bildung—ein zentraler Bestandteil der Aus- und Fortbildung in der Bundeswehr," Ethik und Militär: Kontroversen in Militärethik & Sicherheitspolitik, 2019, no. 2, http://www.ethikundmilitaer.de/de/themenueberblick/20192-ethik-fuer-soldaten/lohmann-ethische-bildung-ein-zentraler-bestandteil-der-aus-und-fortbildung-in-der-bundeswehr/. An exemplary question is: "Should the mission in Mali be ended? Develop the ethical arguments for and against the continuation of the mission."

[20] Fred van Iersel, "Militärische Praxis zwischen Ethik und Tragik: Moralische Dilemmata im Kontext der Friedensbildung für Streitkräfte," Ethik und Militär: Kontroversen in Militärethik & Sicherheitspolitik, 2019, no. 2, http://www.ethikundmilitaer.de/de/menueberblick/20192-ethik-fuer-soldaten/van-iersel-militaerische-praxis-zwischen-ethik-und-tragik-moralische-dilemmata-im-kontext-der-friedensbildung-fuer-streitkraefte/.

[21] See, in this regard, Jelena Beljin and Ralf Karolus Wüstenberg, eds., *Verständigung und Versöhnung. Beiträge von Kirche, Religion und Politik 70 Jahre nach Kriegsende* (Leipzig: Evangelische Verlagsanstalt, 2017).

of *Innere Führung* is in crisis.²² This situation has intensified after the first major military defeat of the Bundeswehr, in Afghanistan.

Here, as in many other current theaters of war, it is evident that well-formed and practiced ethical judgment can hardly do justice to the complex constellation of military conflict. New elements of warfare—such as the fluid transition between terrorist and military actions, the rather softening distinction between civilian and military actors, the use of mercenary troops, the use of autonomous weapons, and differences between those politically responsible for the conditions of deployment and the guiding principles and basic values in military action, even within one's own alliance—seem difficult to map onto the concept of *Innere Führung*.

How can military action under these conditions still be justified within the framework of a Protestant ethic? Does the concept of "conscience-led obedience" (ZDv A 2600/1, no. 401) ascribe a responsibility to persons in a system that they cannot fulfill—to consciously exercise discretion in a highly complex field under real space-time conditions and to act in an ethically well-founded manner, up to and including the responsible decision to use lethal force?²³

The Limitations of the Military System and the Power of Civil Conflict Resolution

In the view of Protestant ethics, war can be justified only as a last resort. The instance to which this justification must be made is one that encompasses a "whole-of-society"²⁴ perspective. In the twenty-first century this must be global and includes the ecological system and the future generations, as we see in the actual war in Ukraine. It affects not only people in Europe but also millions of people in Africa, who depend on wheat and oil from Ukraine or Russia; it undermines the chance to stop climate change, and weakens the influence of civil society and the perspective on human rights. Until the world wars of the twentieth century, war constituted

> the state of emergency and the normal circumstances of modernity ... the state of emergency because it attempts to make the mechanism of differentiation temporarily invisible, and normal circumstances insofar as war has been not only a techno-

---

[22] Ackermann, "Ethische Bildung in der Bundeswehr auf neuen Wegen?," 247.
[23] See "Service in the Bundeswehr therefore places high demands on the personality of the soldiers. Above all, they make decisions of conscience that find their ethical bond in the basic values," ZDv A 2600/1, no. 105.
[24] Armin Nassehi, *Unbehagen. Theorie der überforderten Gesellschaft* (Munich: C. H. Beck, 2021), 84.

logical and organizational modernizer, but also a social one. War has been able to relate the centripetal forces of the economic, the religious, the legal, the educational, the medial, the artistic, and, not least, the political to one another in such a way as to produce temporary forces of integration.[25]

Three main factors have led to a structural change in military action in the present[26]: the transformation of political structures, the constraints of civil society, and the dynamics of the development of autonomous weapon systems.

Military Action in Fragmented Political Systems

Military force and strength play an important role in public perceptions of current global developments. They stand for the possibility of defending or enforcing positions of power. Accordingly, the pressure is high for nations and individual actors to secure their own political and economic interests by military means. This applies at all levels: Those who, like the European Union, want to play an influential role in world politics believe they must increase spending on defense and their own military potential. Those who want to exert influence within a "failed state" need their own military capabilities. Those who want to secure their criminal actions or economic and political interests against control by the state or by civil society resort to (para-)military force in many countries.

Following Zygmunt Baumann, George Dimitriu shows in the *Journal of Strategic Studies* how power has become increasingly fragmented and detached from political structures and institutions ("politics") in recent decades.[27] "The political logic of war is defined here as the convergence of the interrelating factors of power struggles and policy objectives within a given polity that restrains and enables these political forces."[28] Political bodies and leaders are coming under pressure; supranational, intergovernmental, and nonstate actors, including mercenary armies, are gaining power and access to weapons of the latest technology and to the media in unexpected ways. "The fragmentation of state-level political

---

[25] Ibid.
[26] See Herfried Münkler, "Politik und Krieg. Die neuen Herausforderungen durch Staatszerfall, Terror und Bürgerkriegsökonomien," in *Der Begriff des Politischen*, ed. Armin Nassehi and Markus Schroer (Baden-Baden: Nomos, 2003), 471–90.
[27] Herfried Münkler, in *Über den Krieg. Stationen der Kriegsgeschichte im Spiegel ihrer theoretischen Reflexion* (Weilerswist: Velbrück Wissenschaft, 2002), 220 ff., mentions, among other things, "denationalization" and an increasing asymmetry in warfare.
[28] George Dimitriu, "Clausewitz and the Politics of War: A Contemporary Theory," *Journal of Strategic Studies* 43, no. 5 (2020): 645–85, https://www.tandfonline.com/doi/epub/10.1080/01402390.2018.1529567?needAccess=true, (1.6.2021).

power has decreased the effectiveness of force."²⁹ "Wars are fought without a clear beginning and without a clear end, a permanent state of conflict involving a fluctuating variety of militaries, non-governmental organizations, private military companies and civilians."³⁰

The conflicts of the twenty-first century are global disputes within the framework of multilateral alliances; however, political actors in the West base their actions primarily on their internal political audiences. They respond in the short term with military action to events such as the terrorist attacks of September 11, 2001, or looming humanitarian catastrophes, such as the attack on the Yezidi population in Syria; they seek to minimize the political costs of controversial military interventions.

"In addition, the fluidity of politics and the decline of power in state-level politics have caused politicians who contemplate war to become increasingly occupied with electoral considerations at the expense of crafting sound policy objectives." "What we see in Afghanistan, Iraq and Syria today is not *New War* but rather a mirror of contemporary Western politics, attempting to tame, mould and utilise wars abroad in order to win wars at home." "One of the consequences is the growing disconnect between the bureaucracy and the political leadership when it comes to understanding the utility of force."³¹

The long war in Afghanistan, with its antecedents in the Soviet invasion of the country from 1979 to 1989, has shown how the military system has been instrumentalized to varying degrees on all sides for limited and small-scale internal and external political-economic interests and power constellations. A long-term perspective aiming at common security of the parties to the conflict, minimizing violence and strengthening human rights, was no longer discernible. Instead, there was an increase in power for special interests and population groups that profited from the war economy.

From the point of view of the concept of *Innere Führung*, military action lost the power to perform its specific function within the framework of a coherent, overarching perspective. This would have consisted precisely in limiting the violent nature of conflicts, protecting human rights, and enforcing international law against powerful particular interests.

The Justification of Military Action before Civil Society

The concept of *Innere Führung* not only assigns the military system to the state but also locates it in the middle of society: soldiers are citizens in uniform! They

---

[29] Ibid.
[30] Ibid.
[31] Ibid.

act on the basis of orders but are simultaneously able to justify to themselves and society what they do or, in the case of foreign missions, can justify their actions to the population in the countries concerned. This principle can be well illustrated by the Afghanistan mission. In the debates about the mission, the focus was not only in parliament but also, in particular, in discussions with soldiers of the German armed forces about prospects for economic development, promotion of political participation, and above all, education and women's rights. In their military practice, many soldiers experience that they can contribute little to such developments in concrete terms. In order to provide for its own security, the military must depend on a demarcation of matters, but also on a "politics of enmity" (Achille Mbembe) that sorts groups and persons into good and evil, friend and foe. This sorting settles into minds and hearts and determines concrete actions.

Christ's love contradicts this logic and pushes us into empathy and into the in-between: away from unambiguousness that tempts us to follow the logic of violence, and instead into the ambivalence and conflicts of everyday life and politics, which we approach—trusting in Christ's reconciling action—"civilly," that is, nonviolently and participatively, in search of a solution acceptable to all. In the struggle for sustainable solutions to conflict, it should be the task of the military system to establish links with civil society, to protect it from violent encroachment, and to promote its power to organize itself.

There were attempts to do this in Afghanistan, but they could be successful only if military action did not serve its own political or economic interests, but strengthened people in taking responsibility for themselves and their lives. This also included, in particular, holding responsible those criminally accountable for unlawful use of force.

Autonomous Weapons and the Crisis of Responsibility

The technological development of weapons has repeatedly called into question the ethical justification of military action. This is still true today with regard to nuclear, biological, and chemical weapons; it is particularly true at present with regard to the question of the use of so-called lethal autonomous weapon systems. In these systems, it is no longer one or more humans who decide on the selection of targets and the use of weapons, but an algorithm.[32] The result is an interaction between human and machine that fundamentally calls into question the concept

---

[32] See Anja Dahlmann, Elisabeth Hoffberger-Pippan, and Lydia Wachs, "Autonome Waffensysteme und menschliche Kontrolle. Konsens über das Konzept, Unklarheit über die Operationalisierung," in SWP-*Aktuell 2021*, A 31, Apr. 14, 2021, https://www.swp-berlin.org/publikation/autonome-waffensysteme-und-menschliche-kontrolle.

of *Innere Führung*, which is based on clearly ascribed personal responsibility. Already, reports of mental illness among drone pilots show how stressful the new constellation is. With these weapons, they can be highly effective in destroying military targets and killing enemies. This effect remains abstract at first—a "digital experience," barely distinguishable from a computer game. However, the very real stories of suffering hidden beneath do not remain behind the screen but penetrate the psychosocial and emotional experiences of the individuals involved.

Behind every military action with autonomous weapons are highly sensitive ethical decisions which are, according to the previous logic of *Innere Führung*, the responsibility of the person acting: Is it possible to distinguish combatants from noncombatants, not to reduce the "enemies" to data sets, and to maintain the principle of proportionality? How can soldiers cope with the speed and unambiguity with which machines arrive at decisions that are significantly faster and clearer than humans are capable of? Does reciprocal use of autonomous weapons systems still allow for intervention in de-escalation of conflicts? Will a pause remain possible in which civilian forms of conflict resolution can come into view?

The development of autonomous weapon systems reinforces the crisis of the concept of *Innere Führung*. This is because the actors involved within the Bundeswehr "know" that they will have to answer for their actions as citizens in uniform "in the end," not only within the framework of the German constitution but also to the world community and its legal framework. At the same time, they experience their personal effectiveness and responsibility becoming less important with the development and use of autonomous weapon systems, as these systems are "built into" the logic of a machine. How can a "conscience-led obedience" take shape in such a human-machine interaction?

With the concept of *Innere Führung*, German policy after the end of World War II deliberately and proactively positioned the military system in the center of society. Democratic values, ethical education, and personal responsibility were to shape the actions of the Bundeswehr. Soldiers should internalize this attitude as citizens, act accordingly in their professional environment, and even assume, in an exemplary manner, responsibility for the democratic constitution governed by the rule of law.

The political, economic, and technological changes alluded to threaten the effectiveness of this concept. In favor of short-term and particularistic political and economic interests and successes, they call into question the orientation toward a long-term and sustainable ethic of responsibility that includes the interests of all actors involved in the conflict. In favor of the security of their own side, but also of the speed and unambiguity of automated decisions, the new context pushes back the responsibility of actors.

The Protestant faith offers freedom and encourages us not to go along with this return to particularity. On the contrary, it relies on an "intelligent love of the enemy,"[33] which reliably establishes communication with enemies in the run-up to conflicts, and practices procedures for interrupting conflict dynamics, such as those most recently experienced between Russia and Ukraine, in order to arrive at solutions to civil conflicts.

The concept of *Innere Führung* has made it clear that the ethical education of soldiers plays a central role in this approach to resolving conflicts. Soldiers are called upon to assume responsibility on the ground at all levels for themselves and others in complex conflict constellations. A Protestant peace ethic promises them that, in the power of the Holy Spirit, they will be freed from fear and encouraged to walk uprightly, in order to orient themselves, time and again, toward the path of peace. The central criterion for any form of military action is precisely not the ability to assert one's own interests, as presently demanded by political actors in many current declarations, but the conscious limitation of power—one's own power and that of others—and its subordination to the law.

In this way, and only in this way, can military action contribute in an independent and helpful manner, under changed circumstances, toward a sustainable resolution of civil conflict.

---

[33] Carl Friedrich von Weizsäcker, "Die intelligente Feindesliebe," in *Der bedrohte Friede. Politische Aufsätze 1945–1981* (Munich: Carl Hanser Verlag, 1994), 533–38 (first published in November 1980 in *Deutsches Allgemeines Sonntagsblatt*).

Inner Leadership, or The Soldier's Responsibility for Humanity and Peace

Angelika Dörfler-Dierken

Instead of an Introduction: The Break with the Wehrmacht of the Third Reich

After the crimes of the Wehrmacht in the war of extermination in the vastness of Eastern Europe, it was clear to the thoughtful among the soldiers that in the future, the task of the soldier had to be rethought. It could no longer be acceptable to leave the decision for war and peace, for the deployment of human beings and of lethal, ultimately world-destroying weapons to those in power, and to demand nothing but loyalty and obedience from the single soldier. The German expression *Innere Führung* means a twofold reality: on one hand, the inner spirit of the military organization and, on the other, the inner spirit of the single soldier. Officially, *Innere Führung* is translated for joint-service regulations of the Bundeswehr as "leadership development and civic education concept," "leadership philosophy," or even "internal leadership" or "inner guidance." This concept is unique, because it is value-based and strengthens the virtue and responsibility of each soldier. It is the normative basis of personality development and the guideline for the training of military personnel.

Soldier for Democracy

As early as 1947, individual former Wehrmacht soldiers were thinking about the postwar order. One of them was Wolf Stefan Traugott Graf von Baudissin (1907–93), a Protestant[1] officer who had spent July 20, 1944—the date of the attempted

---

[1] The Protestant impact on Baudissin and his relation to the Lutheran religion and church is explained by Angelika Dörfler-Dierken, *Ethische Fundamente der Inneren Führung. Baudissins Leitgedanken: Gewissensgeleitetes Individuum—Verantwortlicher Gehorsam—Konflikt- und friedensfähige Mitmenschlichkeit* (Strausberg: Sozialwissenschaftliches Institut der Bundeswehr, 2005). The best biography is Dagmar Bussiek, *Dem Frieden ver-*

assassination of Adolf Hitler by German officers—in British captivity in Australia. His memorandum *Ost oder West—Gedanken zur deutsch-europäischen Schicksalsfrage* (East or West—Thoughts on the German-European question of fate) was a clear-sighted geopolitical study that saw a legally fixed and thus pacified order as imperative for Western Europe. There was no other way to secure the Western European "appendix" to the huge Euro-Asian continental plate against the advance of Stalinist communism. It was a matter of securing a space of freedom against the space of totalitarianism.

> Deployment and training [of soldiers and troops] happen today in the midst of a confrontation between the totalitarian and the freedom principle of life. It [this confrontation] has led to the permanent civil war without borders in space and time; in it, each of us is, at the same time, a carrier, a means, and a goal. Neutrality is not possible. The attempt to "stay out of it" means the option for the totalitarian.[2]

The long inner-German border between the Russian-dominated East and the U.S.-dominated West made it necessary, only a few years after the end of World War II, for West Germans to participate in the defense of West Germany. Konrad Adenauer offered the American high commissioner for German, John J. McCloy, German troop contingents to work together with the occupation troops to secure the border. At the same time, the chancellor commissioned studies from experienced German generals on how such troops could be deployed most effectively. The planning conference in the Eifel monastery of Himmerod became particularly well known because many later high-ranking Bundeswehr generals were involved. Baudissin, then still a major, pushed through the formulation for the final paper that "fundamentally new things" had to be created, because soldiers have rights as citizens of a democracy, and human dignity, freedom of religion, and freedom of conscience have to apply to them even during their military serv-

---

pflichtet. Wolf Graf von Baudissin (1907-1993)—Die Biografie (Baden-Baden: Nomos, 2021. There is no English translation of the writings of Baudissin, although he was a very important German general in NATO. From April 1962 until December 1967, he served as the first German deputy chief of staff (DCOS) for Operations and Intelligence at the AFCENT Headquarters in Fontainebleau, as commander of the NATO Defense College in Paris, and as DCOS for Plans and Operations at SHAPE. See *Wolf Graf von Baudissin. 1907-1993. Modernisierer zwischen totalitärer Herrschaft und freiheitlicher Ordnung*, ed. Rudolf Schlaffer and Wolfgang Schmidt (Munich: Oldenbourg, 2007).

[2] Baudissin, "Ost oder West—Gedanken zur deutsch-europäischen Schicksalsfrage," translation from the manuscript in Baudissin-Dokumentationszentrum (BDZ) Führungsakademie der Bundeswehr Hamburg. The full text does not exist in print. Partial publication is available in *Wolf Graf von Baudissin: Grundwert: Frieden in Politik- Strategie—Führung von Streitkräften*, ed. Claus von Rosen (Berlin: Miles, 2014), 37-41.

ice.³ Cadre obedience and command necessity, terms used to describe the conditions in the Wehrmacht, should no longer exist.⁴ Moreover, Baudissin realized very early on that technical developments—obviously, after the atomic bombs dropped on Hiroshima and Nagaski—demanded that new wars be avoided. After all, he said, any military conflict could quickly escalate to nuclear war. Thus, after the USSR had developed hydrogen bombs on its part, deterrence had to be more important than traditional offensive power.⁵

This understanding, however, changed the theoretical role model defined in a top-down manner by politicians and defense agencies for soldiers as well as the soldiers' self-image grown from their experiences (bottom-up). The role model differs from the self-image, because the fighter cannot be allowed to fight in the age of nuclear warfare. That might be too dangerous for the attacked region and perhaps for the whole world. The first step to calm aggression in this situation is the understanding of the idea of the soldier's profession as a "citizen in uniform."⁶ Soldiers will be trained to keep peace and to defend freedom and self-responsibility—in short, the Western way of living. In fact, the technical and military situation changed the role model. The soldier is no longer the one who is fighting against enemies in the battlefield. Nowadays the soldier is the one who has to avoid fighting if he does not want to destroy his own country and the world. This means that the soldier has to both train like a traditional fighter and,

---

3   Markus Thurau, "Warum Werte für Soldaten wichtig sind," in *Militärseelsorge* 58 (2020): 55–71; Angelika Dörfler-Dierken and Markus Thurau, "Innere Führung—Normative Basis of Personality Development in the German Armed Forces," in *Ethics and Armed Forces* 2019, no. 2 (2019): 38–45; Wilfried von Bredow, *Demokratie und Streitkräfte. Militär, Staat und Gesellschaft in der Bundesrepublik Deutschland* (Wiesbaden: Westdeutscher Verlag, 2000); *Military Ethics and Leadership*, ed. Peter Olsthoorn (Leiden: Brill/Nijhoff, 2007). The Potsdam Professor of Military History, Sönke Neitzel, denies the newness of this concept. He is convinced that the Bundeswehr has integrated a lot of Wehrmacht knowledge in its fighting traditions and less philosophy of inner guidance. See Sönke Neitzel, *Deutsche Krieger. Vom Kaiserreich zur Berliner Republik—eine Militärgeschichte* (Berlin: Prophyläen, 2020).
4   Christian Hartmann, *Unternehmen Barbarossa. Der deutsche Krieg im Osten 1941–1945* (Munich: Oldenbourg, 2009), 469–788.
5   The best-known German document, born out of these discussions on the nuclear-based revolution in military affairs, is titled "Heidelberger Thesen" ("The Heidelberg Theses"). See Günter Howe, *Atomzeitalter, Krieg und Frieden* (Witten: Eckart-Verlag, 1959), 226–36. The "Heidelberg Theses" were written by Carl Friedrich von Weizsäcker for an interdisciplinary commission working at the Forschungsstätte der Evangelischen Studiengemeinschaft (FEST) in Heidelberg.
6   See Angelika Dörfler-Dierken and Gerhard Kümmel, eds. *Identität, Selbstverständnis, Berufsbild. Implikationen der neuen Einsatzrealität für die Bundeswehr* (Wiesbaden: Verlag für Sozialwissenschaften, 2010).

at the same time, avoid warlike situations. It was now: "To be able to fight in order not to have to fight." Thus, soldiers are forced to endure and shape a paradoxical situation: preparing for an emergency in order to prevent exactly that; never implementing what one practices. This is where the "inner attitude" becomes important, for "swaggering" must be avoided and prevented just as much as excessive aggressiveness. Combat readiness with simultaneous peace orientation of the soldiers "can, under certain circumstances, decide on winning and losing the conflict." Soldierly action is thus aligned with the highest degree of political action. The soldier must therefore be "authentic" to the highest degree.

> Only those who affirm a community, are rooted in it, and know that their own existence depends on the continued existence of this order can stand up for it. If an "against what" remains the only common thing, then hatred and fanaticism become the last resort, binding and at the same time disintegrating. The common "for," on the other hand, is only felt by those who have a concrete share in it; responsibility for something is only felt by those who feel called upon to help shape it. Only that which is consciously experienced seems worth defending.[7]

This principle of Baudissin's military theory is fundamental, for it sees the soldier in full possession of all those rights "which he is to protect outwardly." As a "citizen in uniform," he is part of the political life of his people, possesses the right to vote and to stand for election, has the right to free information and free expression of opinion, has the right of coalition and petition, and enjoys freedom of faith and conscience. Any restriction of fundamental civil rights must be specifically justified.[8]

Thus, the Bundeswehr has a guiding principle that is not constructed by soldier subjects on the basis of their particular experiences (bottom-up), but which is given to them (top-down). One can grow into such a guiding principle. This guiding principle is designed for the future. It should help one to "grow" individually. War and military attack become an intellectual challenge. The guiding principle is deterrence. In the social sciences, guiding principles are understood to be

---

[7] *Handbuch Innere Führung. Hilfen zur Klärung der Begriffe*, ed. Bundesministerium für Verteidigung, Führungsstab der Bundeswehr – B. September 1957 (Schriftenreihe Innere Führung), 141 (my translation).

[8] Wolf Graf von Baudissin, "Der Staatsbürger in Uniform," in *Wolf Graf von Baudissin, Grundwert*, 139–53, here at 141 f., emphasis omitted.

socially shared, mentally anchored, and internalized patterns of orientation that are fed by ideas of a future that is both desirable and considered feasible. They shape the perception, thinking, and actions of those who share the guiding principle... . Thus, the shared orientation pattern does not have to be fully conscious to the model bearers in order to unfold its perception-, thinking- and action-directing effect.[9]

The guiding principle of leadership development and civic education persists in the Bundeswehr to this day. This is because the major goal of civilizing soldiers internally continues to apply—even when they take on tasks that can lead to their killing people. It is in line with the guiding principle to check orders received for their legality and to contradict superiors. Reflective acceptance of responsibility is therefore the goal of soldierly education and training.

Oath and Pledge

In September 1957, under defense minister Franz Josef Strauß (1915–88) and his inspector general, Adolf Heusinger (1897–1982), who had been present in Himmerod, the graphically elaborate handbook *Innere Führung: Hilfen zur Klärung der Begriffe* (Leadership development and civic education: Aids to clarifying terms) was published. The authors were Baudissin and his staff. Until 1972, "the yellow book," as it was called because of its mustard-yellow linen cover, was issued to all officers of the Bundeswehr for self-study. Officers, who were to develop into the nucleus of the new spirit, were to take the oath to "bravely defend the law and freedom of the German people." The other soldiers were to take a "vow," but not to swear. The very first chapter of the manual elaborates on the difference between the oath to the Führer required of Wehrmacht soldiers and the oath in the Bundeswehr. The following chapters then deal with the soldierly tradition and the significance of July 20, 1944; they develop "guiding principles for human leaders," emphasize the importance of "group self-work" based on the fact that superiors "trust" subordinates, and explain "troop information" as the "opposite of propaganda." The newness is already clear in the chapter on the oath. In taking his oath, the soldier should know that he is "before the final authority" that accompanies and evaluates all his actions. This reflects the Christian character of West German postwar society. In East Germany, Christianity was already being aggressively suppressed at that time.[10] "Already once—in a

---

[9] Katharina D. Giesel, *Leitbilder in den Sozialwissenschaften. Begriffe, Theorien und Forschungskonzepte* (Wiesbaden: Verlag für Sozialwissenschaften, 2007), 246 f.

[10] Thomas Friebel, *Kirche und politische Verantwortung in der Sowjetischen Zone und in der DDR, 1945–1969. Eine Untersuchung zum Öffentlichkeitsauftrag der evangelischen Kirchen in der DDR* (Gütersloh: Gütersloher Verlagshaus, 1992). See also *Die Kirchenpo-*

much clumsier unspiritual guise—the totalitarian gained power over us. This could happen because too few individuals felt the obligation to stand uncompromisingly by the basic values of Western humanity."[11]

Readers of the handbook on inner leadership could feel confirmed in their anti-Bolshevism when they looked at the events in Korea (1950/51) and Hungary[12] (1956). For they confirmed the antitotalitarian orientation of the Bundeswehr. But restrictively, they said: "The defense of law and freedom does not authorize us to engage in crusades, or in enterprises that lead to the enslavement and destruction of others or even of the whole world." Right and freedom are at risk at all times; their defense "demands a constantly alert conscience, an open eye, and a compassionate heart for one's fellow men; it presupposes a whole man who knows himself responsible to the principle of humanity in the interest of those entrusted to his care." Here basic concepts of Inner Leadership emerge, which in their deepest sense are not military, but civil and humane. As an example for men (women joined the Bundeswehr first in 2001 and are thus addressed only since that date), the men of July 20, 1944, are recalled, for they recognized "where right loyalty, right obedience, right responsibility, the oath taken before God, carries them. They sacrificed their existence for freedom, justice, and human dignity. Those who take our oath of service and its mandate seriously can only look to these men as their role models with deep gratitude and admiration."[13] Even if many of the terms used here come from the intellectual arsenal of the 1950 s and seem old-fashioned today, a modern way of thinking about the soldier and his task is evident. For social change, technical innovations, and their consequences for soldiers are considered. The central demands for the citizen in uniform still apply today:
- The soldier in democracy is fundamentally different from the one in the totalitarian system.
- He is in a "permanent civil war"—a permanent struggle—for the liberal and constitutional order, even if he is not in a "hot battle."

In addition:
- Europe shall be an area of peace.

---

litik von SED und Staatssicherheit: Eine Zwischenbilanz, ed. Clemens Vollnhals (Berlin: Ch. Links, 1996).
[11] Handbuch Innere Führung, 11 (my translation).
[12] Peter Gosztony, "Der Volksaufstand in Ungarn 1956," in Militärgeschichtliche Beiträge: Sammelband der Zeitschrift Militärgeschichte 1988, no. 2: 55–70; and Erich Lessing and Michael Gehler, Ungarn 1956: Aufstand, Revolution und Freiheitskampf in einem geteilten Europa (Innsbruck: Tyrolia, 2015).
[13] Handbuch Innere Führung, 10–12; see Baudissin, Wolf Graf von: Grundwert, 37–41 (Baudissins Anmerkungen zu Emil Brunners Gerechtigkeit, 1943).

- The human dignity of every soldier, as well as that of the enemy, must be respected at all costs.

In 1972, under defense minister Helmut Schmidt, the *Innere Führung* manual was transformed into a standing order and issued as Central Service Regulation (ZDv 10/1) Leadership Development and Civic Education. Thereafter, this regulation was adapted several times to current political and social developments, and a new system of regulations was introduced (A 2600/1). Subordinate to it are the Central Service Regulations on Political Education (A 2620/2) and Historical Education (A 2620/4).

Human and Peace-Building Influence on the Military by Christian Churches

The Bundeswehr does not know the system of military chaplains that the Wehrmacht did and that the U.S. Army knows today. After World War II, the system of ministering to German soldiers was totally changed. The pastor is no longer a military officer with a special order and is not subordinated to a high-ranking officer. The minister to German soldiers in the Bundeswehr is a civilian minister, invited to serve the soldier's soul. Thus, spiritual care is no longer a military order but a spiritual offering for military personnel. The main interest of the Protestant churches was to strengthen the influence of the regional churches and their ethical freedom in the military organization. The bond between the civilian churches and the military organization should be very strong. The responsibility of officers for religious matters should be avoided. The Protestant churches in Germany are historically rooted in the different regions (*Landeskirchen*). Their historical traditions are not only submission to the governor because he is to be seen as a representation of God (right-wing Lutheran tradition) but also resistance against tyranny (left-wing Lutheran and Reformed tradition). This left-wing tradition is the one that had to be strengthened in the post-Nazi era.

The planners of the Bundeswehr identified a second problem: the strong identification of pastors with military ideals and military life. The planners preferred ministers who preached in the military environment the same gospel as in civilian churches. Therefore, the Catholic Church and the Protestant churches send pastors to the military organization only for a limited number of years, between six and ten. Afterward, the pastors leave the military service and return to service in a civilian church. This permeability between the military and the civilian community ensures that a special kind of militarized church cannot arise. The chaplaincy is not assigned to officers, and the pastor does not have any military rank or authority. This arrangement strengthens the influence of civilian virtues in the Bundeswehr.

Since the formation of the first units of the Bundeswehr, the pastors have been teachers of the soldiers. Their lectures train the soldiers to develop their personality. The (military) lessons on *Innere Führung* are supplemented by *Lebenskundlicher Unterricht* (life skills lessons) (ZDv A 2620/3 Lebenskundlicher Unterricht).[14] These civilian lectures follow those on character guidance, which was implemented in the U.S. Army and in the labor service (former German soldiers working for the U.S. Army). This, too, is characteristic of the concept of Inner Leadership: ethically educated civilians are responsible for teaching professional ethics to uniform wearers. Connected with this mission is the expectation of the mainline Christian churches—and, since December 2019, the Central Council of Jews in Germany[15]—that their understanding of freedom, law, and peace as well as of conscience and responsibility for fellow humanity can be heard in the military organization. Apparently, the military does not trust the finest declarations of intent of its own leadership and seeks sparring partners and "watchdogs" closely related to the ethics of the churches. The military chaplaincy contract (1957) is a unique contract between the German Protestant Church (Evangelische Kirche in Deutschland, EKD) and the German government. The military chaplaincy of the Catholic Church depends on a contract from 1933. By the measures outlined, a new kind of military would grow in the Bundesrepublik Deutschland. The message of peace and humanity is thus made doubly loud: through Inner Leadership and through life skills lessons. "In the thinking of the European and thus also of the German soldier, peace has always been considered the normal state and thus constitutes the goal for the sake of

---

[14] Dirck Ackermann, "Ethische Bildung in der Bundeswehr auf neuen Wegen? Militärseelsorge als Gesprächs- und Kooperationspartner in der Persönlichkeitsbildung von Soldatinnen und Soldaten," in *Seelsorge in der Bundeswehr. Perspektiven aus Theorie und Praxis*, ed. Isolde Karle and Niklas Peuckmann (Leipzig: Evangelische Verlagsanstalt), 235–44; Meike Wanner "Lebenskundlicher Unterricht in der Bundeswehr," in Karle and Peuckmann, *Seelsorge in der Bundeswehr*, 245–56. For education in the Bundeswehr, see Kai Uwe Bormann, *Erziehung in der Bundeswehr. Konzeption und Implementierung militärischer Erziehungsgrundsätze in der Aufbauphase der Bundeswehr 1950–1965* (Berlin: De Gruyter, 2021).

[15] Military chaplaincy contract (*Militärseelsorgevertrag*) was concluded between the Evangelische Kirche in Deutschland and the German government under the presidency of Konrad Adenauer in 1957. For the original text of this contract, see *Glauben Leben. Evangelische Militärseelsorge in der Bundesweh*, ed. Evangelisches Kirchenamt für die Bundeswehr (Leipzig: Evangelische Verlagsanstalt), 114–26.

which alone war can be justified. It is from peace that warfare gets its mission and its limits."[16]

It may be useful to remind ourselves of this principle, especially in times of foreign deployments. This also applies to the principle of compassion, with an undertone of love of one's neighbor (see the double commandment of love: Mark 12:21–31).

> Compassion is not divisible. If it is to be reserved only for certain groups, it will be lost altogether. The soldier who has no respect for his fellow man—and even the enemy is his fellow man—is tolerable neither as a superior nor as a comrade or fellow citizen. Objectivity toward the enemy, that is, hate-free clarity even in battle, was an essential part of chivalric tradition.[17]

The Transcendence of the Military

The concept of Inner Leadership has deeply permeated and shaped the Bundeswehr to the present day—particularly in that it has repeatedly invited debate. It is suitable for pluralistic societies and can also withstand a great deal of diversity: women, queer people, people with non-German parents, young mothers and men with disabilities—they can all commit to the supratemporal principles of Innere Führung. Those who talk about the Bundeswehr as having passed the Cold War but failed in the hot battle in Afghanistan would have to be reminded that the very moment of coming to combat shows that the concept of engaging the enemy with his opposing interests has not been adequate to the circumstances. After all, securing peace is a spiritual task that requires many civilian skills and virtues.[18]

---

[16] Reflective acceptance of responsibility must therefore be the goal of military education and training. See the chapters on the "paradox war" of the Bundeswehr in Afghanistan in *Einsatz ohne Krieg? Die Bundeswehr nach 1990 zwischen politischem Auftrag und militärischer Wirklichkeit. Militärgeschichte, Sozialwissenschaften, Zeitzeugen*, ed. Jochen Maurer and Martin Rink (Göttingen: Vandenhoeck & Ruprecht, 2021); and *Friedensethik und Sicherheitspolitik. Weißbuch 2006 und EKD-Friedensdenkschrift 2007 in der Diskussion*, ed. Angelika Dörfler-Dierken and Gerd Portugall (Wiesbaden: Verlag für Sozialwissenschaften, 2010).

[17] *Handbuch Innere Führung*, 64, my translation.

[18] Franz-Josef Overbeck and Alexander Merkl, "Konstruktive Konfliktkultur," *Militärseelsorge* 58 (2020): 45–54. See *Handbuch Friedensethik*, ed. Ines-Jacqueline Werkner and Klaus Ebeling (Wiesbaden: Springer, 2017).

The Complementary Path to Peace: On Peace Ethics in German Protestantism[1]

Gerd Theißen and Sylvie Thonak

In the 1950 s, faced with diverging perceptions about the wisdom and direction of German rearmament, German Protestantism overcame the threat of a split in the church with the "complementary peace ethic" proposed by the "Heidelberg Theses" of 1959. The most important thesis of the document is that, on the path to peace, opposing attitudes are necessary, both pacifist nonviolence and military defense policy. The relationship of these attitudes is asymmetrical: nonviolence is the clearer sign on the way to a future peace order, but military defense readiness is indispensable to secure the existing peace. This combination of deterrence and pacifism was a message to potential adversaries abroad, saying to them: "We want peace. We want to prevent a world war." By this complementary peace ethic, the Protestant churches were able to transform the conflict between advocates of deterrence, on one hand, and conscientious objectors to military service, on the other, into cooperation in the interest of peacekeeping. What we successfully practice in politics in a democracy found an analogy in defense policy: just as the ruling party and the opposition secure freedom through their opposition, so peace is stabilized through the opposing stance of soldiers and pacifists.

For a while, after the end of the Cold War, in 1989, there was confidence that an international peace order could permanently prevent international wars. At the same time, asymmetrical wars in unstable areas of countries without formal declarations of war increased. In this situation, the Protestant peace ethic continued to develop. Today, the "complementarity principle" links not only military defense readiness and conscientious objection to military service, but also military peacekeeping operations and pacifist peace work. Here, too, the principle of complementarity applies: both peace work and military defense are more successful when they work together. Civil peace work promotes social structures that secure peace. However, it can often be effective only where military oper-

---

[1] See Sylvie Thonak and Gerd Theißen, *Militärseelsorge. Das ungeliebte Kind protestantischer Friedensethik? Konzepte und Probleme* (Münster: LIT, 2020).

ations minimize local conflicts. Soldiers protect peace work, while peace workers create conditions under which peacemaking military operations can succeed.

In this new situation, military pastoral care and pacifist peace work should actually respect and recognize each other. However, this is now, more than sixty years later, difficult for both. Those who consider military operational capability to be necessary not infrequently claim a realistic "ethic of responsibility" (*Verantwortungsethik*) for themselves and criticize pacifist peace work as an "ethic of attitude" (*Gesinnungsethik*), far removed from political realism. Pacifists, on the other hand, criticize the increasing military missions abroad as a clandestine remilitarization of politics. In fact, some peacekeeping operations very quickly become wars. The catalyst for this new polarization was the Afghanistan mission of the German Bundeswehr under a UN mandate, which failed to secure peace but perhaps was able to reduce the danger of terrorist attacks, such as the destruction of the World Trade Center on September 11, 2001.

The complementary path to peace is, in principle, independent of such changing situations. The Protestant peace ethic is based in a long tradition and can refer to the Bible. In the Old Testament, in the midst of a history marked by many wars, we find the vision of a nonviolent world brought about by God alone; in the New Testament, on the other hand, we find an ethic of nonviolent human action as a possible way to this goal—together with an acceptance of soldiers. The Protestant peace ethic combined these two traditions. However, this was possible only after two terrible world wars.

The Old Testament Vision of Peace

We find the aim of every peace ethic in the Old Testament as a prophetic vision of peace. Isaiah 2:1–5 and Micah 4:1–5 contain the same prophecy of a pilgrimage of nations to Zion. In an international legal order created by God, people beat swords into plowshares. God himself enforces peace. The basis of this peace is justice.

According to another prophetic saying, in Isaiah 32:15–20, peace comes about because the "Spirit of God" is poured out on all nature: "And the fruit of righteousness shall be peace; and the fruit of righteousness shall be everlasting quietness and safety; and my people shall dwell in peaceable pastures, in a sure habitation, and in a proud rest" (Isaiah 32:17 f.). Who is to realize this justice, however? Some texts name God and the king as the peacemakers.

According to Psalm 85, God alone brings about peace. This peace is characterized by the fact that "goodness and faithfulness meet, justice and peace kiss each other" (85:10 f.). In Psalm 46, God establishes peace by abolishing weapons. This cosmic peace is in contrast to the chaos of the primeval flood. Here it becomes clear that the comprehensive concept of peace in the Old Testament means more than the absence of war, but a just cosmic and social order. Human beings are involved in this peace through their actions, but only to a very limited extent.

Among human beings, the king above all is the peacemaker who, according to Psalm 72, enforces peace. Under him, justice and peace shall flourish. This justice is not a neutral justice above contending parties but protects and upholds the weak. This peace includes an economic and social balance: the king of peace will stand up for the poor and the miserable. Military features that appear in other royal Psalms (for example, Psalm 2) are absent. The question remains unclear: Are we dealing with poetic exaggerations during the feasts of inauguration, when the court installs a new king? Or is this peace a messianic dream of a king of salvation, as in other prophetic texts (Isaiah 9:1–6 and 11:1–10)? In Zechariah's prophecy, this future king has, at all events, nonmilitary features and combines peace and justice:

> You, daughter of Zion, rejoice greatly, and you, daughter of Jerusalem, exult! Behold, your king comes to you, a righteous man and a helper, poor and riding on an ass, on a colt of the ass. For I will destroy the chariots in Ephraim, and the horses in Jerusalem; and the bow of war shall be broken. For he will command peace to the nations, and his dominion will be from sea to sea and from the river to the ends of the earth. (Zechariah 9:9–10)

It is to the Old Testament that we owe the vision of peace among nations based on law and justice. Since law and justice are the basis for this peace, they oblige all people to work for peace. For the Old Testament requires all people to do justice, though it mentions only the king specifically. Sometimes this king enforces his rule by might (Psalm 110), but often he is a prince of peace. If human beings were involved in enforcing peace, their participation would inevitably take on warlike characteristics. It is precisely the fact that God alone is effective that has made these visions of a future peace without war possible. If God alone brings about universal peace, this peace can come about without military victories. God integrates all peoples into a universal community of law. Therefore, this is not a political peace program but a utopian dream of peace. What people can contribute to this peace through their actions remains open.

Nonviolent Action in the New Testament

Was the vision of nonviolence in the New Testament possible only because early Christianity did not have much experience of military state violence in wars? Under the protection of the Pax Romana, secured by others, a small group of people without political responsibility perhaps was able to develop peaceful dreams. It is true, indeed, that the New Testament originated in a relatively peaceful time, but the Gospels and other New Testament writings reflect the Jewish-Roman War of 66–70 CE. Both Jesus and Paul lived in the shadow of this threatening war.

Jesus formulated his message on the periphery of the Roman Empire, in Galilee and Judea, where Romans acted as foreign rulers. Jesus's teaching of a demonstrative renunciation of violence has a political dimension: renunciation of violence was used in his time by Jews against Pilate (ca. 26 CE) and shortly after his time against the Syrian governor Petronius (39/40). Both actions of protest were a success through demonstrative renunciation of violence. In the second case, peaceful protests even prevented a war. Therefore, Jesus's proclamation had political relevance at that time. When Jesus taught to give to Caesar what is Caesar's and to God what is God's (Mark 12.13–17), he called for the payment of taxes. Refusal to do so would have been a declaration of war. In fact, the Jewish revolt against the Romans began with the cessation of tax payments and sacrifices for Caesar. The Gospel of Luke clearly states that if Jesus had been listened to, the Jewish-Roman war would have been avoided (Luke 19:41–44).

Paul formulates his thoughts on violence and peace in his letter to the Roman congregation, which lived in the center of Roman power. In this letter, he demands of all people, not only of Christians, that they submit to the "superior authorities" (Romans 13:1). He is conspicuously silent about the emperor, although Caesar ruled in Rome. The "superior authorities" (plural) are republican offices of the Republic of Rome. The office of the emperor was only a combination of republican offices. Therefore, Paul indirectly means the emperor as well. We can therefore say that for Paul, the political power that is legitimate is republican controlled.

In the city of Rome, the praetorians exercised state power. Their police duties in the city of Rome were clearly distinguished from the duties of the legions in the provinces. Only in exceptional cases did the authorities allow the legions to enter the city of Rome. Anyone who resisted this political order, formally organized as a republic, brought judgment upon himself. Here Paul is thinking not only of rebels from below but also of emperors, who provocatively violated the republican order from the top of the state. Paul may therefore also be thinking of Emperor Gaius Caligula, whom a prefect of the praetorians killed because he did not respect the traditional order.

What is relevant for a theology of peace is that Paul also represents a complementary ethic in his thoughts on the state. He surrounds the general admonitions for all people concerning the state authorities with admonitions only to Christians (12:9–21; 13:8–10). In doing so, he contrasts the coercive order of the state with the Christian community of love. On one hand, the state must take "vengeance" on evildoers (13:4). People owe taxes and customs to the state

(13:7). Christians, on the other hand, are to renounce "vengeance," which is reserved for God alone (12:19-21). They should owe nothing to anyone (13:8). Paul also serves peace through his activity. His last journey to Jerusalem had the aim of opening the temple to Gentiles and thus reducing tensions between Jews and non-Jews, which later led to the outbreak of the Jewish War. Paul was not successful.

Jesus and Paul both advocated the reduction of political tensions that led to real war in their day. Jesus formulated a complementary ethos in the provinces that both recognized the state and advocated nonviolent action. Paul developed a complementary ethic for Christians in Rome, where violence, controlled by law, and the congregation's ethos of love complemented each other.

Our interim conclusion, then, is that in the Old Testament we find the utopian goal of a nonviolent legal order, and in the New Testament a nonviolent praxis that corresponds to this goal. However, the New Testament does not link these two approaches to violence. It was only in modern times that the Old Testament's dream of peace became a politically envisaged goal, which we should achieve in various ways with patterns of behavior of the New Testament, through a combination of the demonstrative nonviolence of pacifism, on one hand, and military power controlled by law on the other hand. At the same time, the New Testament accepts soldiers who keep up the order in this passing world.

The Coexistence of Peace and War Ethics in the History of the Church

The Old Testament formulated the political aim of every peace ethic as a prophetic dream: a world free of wars. The New Testament shows a way of nonviolent action, but does not link it to a politically realizable goal. Christian churches first combined both approaches after 1945, when the nonviolent path to political peace became part of a complementary peace ethic that considers defensive military deterrence to be also necessary to maintain peace. The prehistory of this complementary peace ethic developed in five stages.

First, before Constantine, most Christians rejected military service for themselves. Since military service was not compulsory, this rejection was not a problem. People behaved according to the maxim that Christians should not become soldiers, but soldiers can become Christians. At the same time, the peace function of the army was respected and recognized: Christians prayed for the emperor and his military victory. Origen (185-254) interprets this activity as "complementary" behavior: "While others go to war, we take part in the campaign as priests and servants of God, keeping our hands pure and praying for the right cause, the rightful king and his victory.... We form by our prayers an army of our own, an army of piety, which thereby serves the emperor better than all the visible soldiers."[2]

While Origen defended the rejection of military service for all Christians, a different solution prevailed in the second stage of development, the Middle Ages. Only monks followed the *consilia evangelii* for the perfect Christians—that is, the commandments of the Sermon on the Mount on nonviolence—but laypeople followed the *praecepta* for all, which permitted military service of Christians. These were also complementary decisions.

A third period began in the Reformation under the influence of humanism. Small groups within the alternative Reformation and individual humanist writers called for all Christians (not just monks) to work for peace through action. Erasmus of Rotterdam (1469–1536) and Sebastian Franck (ca. 1499–1542) combined Christian and humanist motifs. According to Erasmus, all Christians should orient themselves toward Christ, the great Prince of Peace. When they engage in wars, they continue the suffering of Christ. Parallel to Erasmus, Mennonite and Brethren congregations, and later the Quakers, demanded a consistent rejection of war and violence. This was the turning point from a longing for peace to an obligatory peace ethic. Of course, this was only the special ethic of small groups, most of which did not go so far as to demand that their peace ethic apply to the whole state. The Quakers, however, succeeded temporarily in founding a state organization in Pennsylvania in 1681, through William Penn (1644–1718). This became a refuge for many religious minorities from Europe. However, as early as 1756, the Quakers withdrew from government responsibility at the outbreak of the Seven Years' War. They did not want to be responsible for any acts of war. Nevertheless, peace churches like the Quakers still play a decisive role in the history of modern peace ethics.

During a fourth stage, the Enlightenment, Immanuel Kant (1724–1804) outlined a fascinating secular program for political peace in his essay *Zum ewigen Frieden* (On Eternal Peace [1795]). He expects peace not from "rulers of peace" but from republican states and societies. All people, and not just small peace groups, must be active and participate in the realization of peace. Kant was thus far ahead of his time. In his day, the longing for peace was still the hope for a great prince of peace. The followers of Napoleon expected that he would bring this peace, but he plunged Europe into bloody wars. After their end, people founded the first peace societies, which advocated human rights, social improvements, free trade, abolition of slavery, and the rejection of military force: the American Peace Society (1815), the London Peace Society (1816), and the Geneva Peace Society (1830). It was not until 1892 that the German Peace Society was founded. Even though these peace societies were small, they kept alive the peace ethic in a century marked by an increasing nationalist readiness for war.

---

[2] Origen, *Contra Celsum* VIII 73.

The new development was that in the nineteenth century, new secular peace groups worked for the peace beside the traditional Christian peace churches.

Finally, the threat of nuclear war after World War II made the preservation of peace a general and urgent political obligation in the second half of the twentieth century. Before this time, war was a legal extension of politics, but now the legitimacy of war became the subject of a controversial debate. It was in the threat of a nuclear conflagration that theological ethics combined the Old Testament longing for peace as a goal with the New Testament ethics of peace as a way to that goal. This combination was brought about by the ecumenical movement and, especially, the discussion about rearmament of Germany. The nuclear stalemate between East and West changed the military logic of international conflicts. There was a complementary relationship between the decision to build up defensive missiles in the 1980 s and the protests of the peace movement at the same time. The Eastern Bloc states received a double message, signalling to them a willingness of the Western societies to defend themselves and, at the same time, a readiness for peace. Probably the combination of these two messages overcame the Cold War and the East-West antagonism in 1989.

Complementarity of an Ethic for Pacifists and Soldiers

Since 1989, however, the political situation has changed. For a time, it was not the East-West antagonism that became a problem, but the unstable situation in many countries with asymmetrical wars between rebellious groups and governments without a formal declaration of war—often with the covert support of foreign great powers. Since 1991, the German armed forces have been involved in missions abroad. These are missions to establish or secure peace. Here, too, the principle of complementarity applies in a new way: for without civilian peace work, we cannot secure peace anywhere in the long term.

As in the 1950 s, our situation still requires opposing decisions of conscience. At the same time, however, the perspectives of pastoral care within the military and of pacifism within the church are moving away from each other, while military and civil peace operations continue to complement each other. It is worth asking why a new split within German Protestantism is threatening Here are a few reasons for this development.

The most important reason is probably that peace operations do not always succeed. The peace mission in Afghanistan was legitimized by a UN mandate, but it was problematic from the start. Germany's involvement compensated for its refusal to take part in the second Iraq war, but the chances for real success were limited from the outset. A German general warned against the Afghanistan mission. In any case, one has to respect the deployment of the soldiers in Afghanistan, even if it was controversial. They succeeded in ensuring that the mission in Afghanistan made room for social pacification in that country for a while, even if everything that they achieved is now uncertain. A democratic society, such as Germany, that maintains a parliamentary army and sends it on missions abroad is, in any case, obliged to support the soldiers in such peace missions. Nobody should expect that soldiers would be willing to die for a cause that society and the church devalue as highly questionable.

Precisely for this reason, however, there is a duty to voice criticism and concerns when such peace operations have no chance of success. Margot Käsmann did this in 2009. In a sermon, she responded to a Christmas card motto that "Everything will be all right" and changed it rhetorically to the verdict, "Nothing is all right in Afghanistan." Even if this was certainly a hasty generalization, it was a necessary wake-up call. In retrospect, this call seems justified. Nevertheless, there is in German pacifism too little recognition that there have been military peace operations that succeeded, such as the mission in Kosovo, which no UN mandate secured. The mission in Kosovo was justified as humanitarian intervention.

The second reason for an erosion of the complementary peace ethic is that military spiritual care has isolated itself within the general church. Military chaplaincy became an *ecclesiola in ecclesia*, with the danger of becoming an *ecclesiola extra ecclesiam*. The suspension of compulsory military service in 2011 promoted the emergence of special military cultures both within the Bundeswehr and in the military chaplaincy. In the area of military chaplaincy, we should mention one important development. Since 2014, the military bishop no longer holds two ecclesial part-time offices as leader of a regional church and of the military chaplaincy. Since he is no longer at the same time the leading clergyman of a regional church, he has a much weaker ecclesiastical connection to the general church than in the past, but unfortunately also a much weaker "house power" within the Evangelische Kirche Deutschland and in negotiations with the military administration.

Two incidents serve as small signs of this development. First, a military bishop advocated that the church should cede domiciliary rights[3] to the Bundeswehr at funeral services for fallen soldiers. Second, the inauguration of the first full-time military bishop did not take place in a public worship service. The military chaplaincy legitimizes itself primarily through its proximity to the troops, and less through its proximity to the peace ethic of the church. Consequently, the peace ethic of the church plays only a marginal role in the work of the military chaplaincy. Those who want to change this must be aware of institutional limits. There is no grassroots representation in military chaplaincy in the sense

---

[3] The domiciliary right or the "Hausrecht" is the competence and power to decide who can enter a house and, in this case, to participate in worship. In a church the domiciliary rights are exercised only by church authorities.

of Protestant church orders, and there is no effective and real synodic accompaniment and control of the military chaplaincy. Although there is an advisory board for the Protestant military chaplaincy, its members legitimize themselves not by election but by appointment, and the public does not know their names. The military chaplaincy shelters itself from criticism by institutional barriers.

A third reason for the erosion of the complementary path to peace is that a pacifism that is widespread in the church sometimes forms its own world in which soldiers are devalued across the board. The problem is not so much the politically reflected pacifism of small groups in the church, but a Protestant "national pacifism," which is understandable because of German history, but which sometimes discriminates against soldiers in the everyday life of the church; moreover, this national pacifism seems often to be very naïve. For example, the theologian and ethicist Johannes Fischer criticized a rally of the Twelfth Synod of the Protestant Church in Germany on December 13, 2019, calling the "church on the path of justice and peace" an expression of a narrow *Gesinnungsmilieu* (an inner moral attitude that does not care about real consequences). A peace ethic that gives priority to nonviolent peace work is truly complementary only if it also takes seriously the commitment to an operationally capable Bundeswehr. It is realistic only if it recognizes the dilemmas faced by both pacifist and military deployments for peace.

A fourth reason is that the public is not sufficiently aware that civilian peace service is also dangerous. The spread of asymmetric and subversive wars makes peace work risky for all participants. Future peace projects are likely to be even more dangerous than current ones. They are as dependent on the support of civil society as the soldiers. We should acknowledge that they represent the long-term goal of peace more clearly than the military. The church must promote pacifist peace services. Today, many believe that we cannot do away with wars. The establishment of lasting peace is undoubtedly a great goal, as the abolition of slavery once was. For a long time, many believed that it was not possible to abolish slavery; but it was possible, even if new forms of inhuman dependency have arisen.

The characteristic feature of the contemporary Christian peace ethic continues to be the complementarity of military service and pacifist nonviolence with the common goal of peace. We are concerned that the complementary peace ethic is turning into a so-called ethic of responsibility, which mistakenly considers the juxtaposition of military defense readiness and military peace operations as a full realization of the complementary ethic of Protestantism. At the same time, we fear that this ethic of responsibility is discrediting pacifist protests against rearmament and nonviolent peace operations as an unrealistic "ethics of conscience." Today, responsibility for the world requires everyone to work toward overcoming war and transforming military force into internationally controlled police power. A complementary peace ethic that takes its responsibility for peace seriously encompasses both: the readiness for controlled military response and the necessity for pacifist activities. Both are expressions of an ethic of responsibility. Both can lead to moral dilemmas. Both have their base in an ethics of conscience as a compass that points in the direction of peace.

This complementary peace ethic does not derive directly from the Bible, but follows from an overall biblical view of the Old and New Testaments that emerged only in modern times. It combines Old Testament visions of a cosmic peace with patterns of practical behavior in the New Testament. These patterns in the New Testament comprise, on one hand, the pacifist ethic of loving one's enemies and, on the other hand, the military practice of peacekeeping as a matter of fact. The New Testament accepts soldiers as part of the existing world. The connection of the Old Testament vision of peace as a goal with a New Testament practice as a way to achieve it became a necessity only in our era of nuclear armament. Since then, nonviolence and military service have been complementary on the path to peace. The primary goal of peace is consensus, but the path to it has become more complicated. We must seek this path in many limited and complex conflicts in a new way. There is no guarantee of success. One should always remain aware that both complementary paths to peace can lead to dilemmas. Both can fail, both are realistic, both are expressions of an ethic of responsibility. We work for a climate in the church in which people on both paths can communicate, understand, and respect each other.

Part Two:
Virtues: Re-Evaluating the Military Context

Part Two:

Which Morals Society Should Learn from the Military, and Which Decidedly Not

Hartwig von Schubert

In Plato's dialogue *Laches*, two respected Athenian aristocrats are concerned about the education of their sons and the continuation of their power.[1] They turn to two commanders with the request to train the boys for high offices in the army and, beyond that, in the entire leadership of the state. They also suggest involving Socrates, who is present. All, including the sons, agree and follow Socrates's suggestion to first decide on a concrete educational goal. Since the fathers have turned to military experts, it would be best if this goal were bravery.

In this volume, the project on Character Formation, Ethical Education, and the Communication of Values in Late Modern Pluralistic Societies pursues a similar goal, using the example of the "impact of the military/defense system." Relying on the concept of system, this essay illuminates systems of norms—sketchily, given the limited space available—in which the functions of security-sector institutions are mapped. First, this approach can help to deprivatize, deghettoize, and open up to an interdisciplinary, perhaps even societal critique the discourse on the legitimacy of political force in the institutions of the security sector. Second, a possible spillover into other social spheres can be identified. As a result, the insights gained should not lead to a plea for complete demilitarization, let alone remilitarization of society, but should rather contribute to a critical ethical orientation and a correspondingly enlightened internal differentiation according to the scheme of a triangle of duties, commodities, and virtues.

The following steps are planned: After an introductory clarification of the concept of system, a methodological-terminological grounding will clarify, first, how orders oriented to the common good must be understood in societies with a liberal-egalitarian constitution, so that, second, the special influence of the guiding differences and behavioral codes that are characteristic of institutions of the security sector can be recognized in them. Subsequently, the relationship between security-sector institutions and society is analyzed under the criterion of

---

[1] Plato, *Laches* 190d–200c.

the common good. First, what are the central normative functions, value hierarchies, and spheres of action of security-sector institutions; second, what are the interactions between the normative binding forces in security-sector institutions and those of other social systems; third, where are conflicts between the security sector and society, and how are they managed; fourth, what are the weaknesses and strengths of security-sector institutions in the concert of social subsystems; and finally, what is the conclusion?

Regarding the Term "System"

According to Niklas Luhmann, modern societies are functionally differentiated into subsystems, such as politics, law, economy, and science. And these systems are ideally organized and grasped less by listing and compiling their components than along specific guiding differences, including normative codings, such as "healthy vs. sick" (medicine), "powerful vs. powerless" (politics), "immanent vs. transcendent" (religion), "solvent vs. insolvent" (economy), "true vs. false" (science).[2] Such differentiations are consequently structurally and normatively essential for the personal and communal life of individuals as well. However, no one lives in only one of these systems but is always more or less strongly determined by and determining all systems. An individual member of a pluralistic society may have his or her own preferences, principles, habits, abilities, and possessions, no matter how special they may be, but he or she will always be questioned by a certain social subsystem as to how he or she stands concerning the guiding difference in question. Someone falls ill, for example. Although the medical system sees itself as basically responsible for everyone who can "scientifically" (!) prove a "finding with disease value," the insolvent and uninsured among the sick have a problem. Their problem is then possibly solved by recourse to other systems, such as institutions of politics, religion, or civil society, from whose reserves the costs are reimbursed. This process succeeds to the extent that provisions—that is, rules and resources—are already contained in the normative frameworks and statutes of that state, those religious communities, or those civil associations, or are rapidly generated to legitimize and enable those substitute services. For example, a religious community takes over the costs for the medical treatment of a refugee for half a year, because this has long been laid down in its religious rule.

In the course of ethical verification and updating of such rules and resources, it has proven useful to differentiate them into duties, commodities, and vir-

---

[2] See Niklas Luhmann, *Soziale Systeme: Grundriss einer allgemeinen Theorie*, 5th ed. (Frankfurt am Main: Suhrkamp, 1994); and Walter Reese-Schäfer, *Niklas Luhmann zur Einführung*, 6th ed. (Hamburg: Junnius 2011), 75 ff., 186 f.

tues.³ All participants thus find a net in which they can orient themselves the better, the more they know and understand the ensembles of dominant duties, commodities, and virtues in the institutions of their society. Not all members of society, however, are equally familiar with all subsystems. Those who have never been ill, or who are so wealthy or so well insured privately that they can obtain any medical service quickly, will not have had any experience with state, church, or nonprofit solidarity funds; they do not need them. And this unfamiliarity often also applies to social coping with experiences of violence. To put it bluntly: members of largely stable societies have fewer experiences with diplomacy, justice, police, and the military than members of societies where a high level of violent conflict prevails. In stable zones of the world, people are less familiar with the duties, commodities, and virtues needed in the so-called security sector of their environment than people in unstable zones. People who live in a country heavily affected by drug trafficking, for example, will pay attention to the news when choosing a mode of transportation to see where a gang war is currently raging and where it is not. However, it would be a mistake to believe that the potential for and risks of violence have disappeared in the stable zones; the risks are simply kept in check, so that the vast majority of society does not come into contact with them, although members of the security sector very much do. As a result, familiarity with the norm scaffolding of a societal subsystem is not evenly distributed across all members of a society. People who rarely go to a clinic, for example, may have no idea what goes on in a vascular or brain surgery department, how it is organized, and what can go wrong there. They may experience a real culture shock during the first visit. And anyone coming from a sheltered environment who approaches a packed stadium for the first time on the occasion of a popular sporting event or a disaster-control exercise in an area at risk of fire or flood will have to cope with a heightened adrenaline level, given the massive deployment of police and the deafening noise of helicopters landing and taking off.

However, one does not have to address the extremes first; for an awake and participating contemporary society, it is natural to assume a general co-responsibility for the kind of society we want to live in. For the level of political enlightenment and moral maturity of a society, it is therefore crucial that, especially in the education system, access to the subsystems is made so permeable that the adult members of society have at least the minimum degree of familiarity with the respective sets of norms that is appropriate for being able to orient and move sufficiently, and above all *critically*, in the network of highly differentiated legitimacies. Those who do not want to close their eyes to the internal and external violent conflicts in their immediate and wider environment should get an idea of

---

3   See Hartwig von Schubert, *Nieder mit dem Krieg. Eine Ethik politischer Gewalt* (Leipzig: Evangelische Verlagsanstalt, 2021), 78–83.

the duties, commodities, and virtues that should be available, or perhaps are dramatically lacking, to be able to counter escalating conflicts professionally.

In the countries of the European Union (EU), for example, societies today are no longer under such dominance by the organs of the security sector as was still widely the case in the first half of the twentieth century. It is futile at this point to discuss whether, for example, militarism was more pronounced in the Wilhelmine German Empire than in the Victorian British Empire. In the course of industrialization and capitalization, the formation of nation-states, political revolutions and, not to forget, the spread of totalitarian regimes, not only were all European societies massively exposed to the dynamics of military mass organization, but all traditional ties of religion, region, family, and so on came under pressure, and the new mass-organized systems of industry, media, market, parties, and science gained ascendancy. And the counter-movement against the dominance of "organized modernity" in the second half of the twentieth century did not lead back into the world of traditional ties, nor into the diffusiveness of a social atomization, but into increased but finite differentiations.

Methodological-Terminological Foundations

Understanding the Common Good in Liberal-Egalitarian Societies

How does the "common good" come into being, and how can it be ascertained with certainty? If normative orders are to be oriented toward the common good, then this is done in liberal-egalitarian societies by binding them to human rights. Human rights, determined by the principle of human dignity, do not so much impose a pre-state individual right on a state power conceived of as superior, as they draft the idea of a reasonable state in the form of a constitution with a majority-fixed core of inalienable and incalculable fundamental rights, declaring every citizen to be a powerful participant in the political will-forming and legislative process. It is not the state that graciously, generously, and in paternally just omnipotence grants rights, but the united will of the people that establishes a state of law, in which it gives itself laws to which all state action is then subject. The human right not only forbids setting state purposes according to particular interests, but also forbids, in general, any moral or ideological dictate for the common good, no matter how well-meaning. According to Kant, political freedom is "the privilege to lend obedience to no external laws except those to which I could have given consent. Similarly, external (juridical) equality in a state is that relationship among the citizens in which no one can lawfully bind another without at the same time subjecting himself to the law by which he also can be bound."[4]

A necessary element of a rational constitution is the separation of powers. Since not all citizens can be equally involved in the same question at the same time and in the same place, law-making, law enforcement, and jurisdiction are not conceivable otherwise than by way of representation. The represented citizens, however, do not want to lose the common decision-making process to the representatives but want the representatives to care well for it. The principle of sovereignty is, therefore, to be distributed among all three powers. Each power is independent of the others, rules unrestrictedly in its sphere of competence according to original principles, confronts the others in an ultimately binding and irresistible manner, and is in turn effectively and inescapably subject to them within its specified limits. The legislature says irrefutably what is valid in all conceivable cases, the executive brings the law in the concrete case effectively and irrefutably to validity and effect, and the judiciary judges bindingly and irrevocably whether the execution agrees with the legislation.

The conformity of a law and a governmental measure executed according to law with justice in the sense of the general will or common good is guaranteed by the process of its production. The process never stands still; each of the three powers can, at any time, by its original means and within the limits of its authority, act on any of the others and on political life as a whole. Citizens develop, form, and exercise their convictions and will, which are as strong as possible politically, in the associations and institutions of civil society (clubs, families, churches, professions, schools, foundations, associations, etc.) and bring them to the political parties. The parliamentarians, organized and elected, pass the laws according to which governments must act and courts must judge; the courts judge the constitutionality of laws and the conformity of government action to the law; governments and administrations enforce laws and legal judgments—including, if necessary, against parliaments and judicial authorities. Citizens encounter the entire state in every force; they are required to regard it as their state. The armed forces, in particular, are their armed forces.

On Guiding Differences and Behavioral Coding in Security-Sector Institutions

The organs of the executive may exercise their sovereign power only within the limits set by the legislature and the judiciary in their respective sovereign pow-

---

[4] Translated from http://fs2.american.edu/dfagel/www/Class%20Readings/Kant/Immanuel%20Kant,%20_Perpetual%20Peace_.pdf; the German original: Kant, *Zum ewigen Frieden*, AA VIII, 350 Anm.

ers. Within the executive branch, the army of a nation is, as a rule, the most highly staffed, best-equipped, and most expensive institution of armed state power. Every soldier is accordingly charged with duty: "I swear to serve the Federal Republic of Germany faithfully and to defend the law and the freedom of the German people bravely, so help me God." According to Section 9 of the Soldiers' Act of the Federal Republic of Germany, this is the oath formula for professional and temporary soldiers. Why does this obligation require the increased weight of an oath? One reason lies in an external threat, another in an internal threat.

First, the external threat: As soon as an attack by an armed force is capable of threatening the entire right and freedom—that is, the common good par excellence—of an entire people, there is sufficient reason to repel this attack by suitable, necessary, and appropriate means, including military means, and thus by risking one's own life, and this for no other purpose than to preserve and restore that right and freedom. To what degree of such threats does this apply? Under the criterion of the common good of all states, the use of armed forces is legitimate under international law only in armed conflicts. But how can we be sure whether an armed conflict is imminent or already taking place? Whose responsibility is it to gather this information and to determine with all consequences the case of defense and to send the army into mortal combat?

Second, it is obviously not the state that is to be defended, but the state, through its organs, is to defend the law and the freedom of the citizens as their highest political good. Law and freedom are the end, and the state and its armed forces are the means to their realization and defense. But the means can also be directed against the end, and thus inward. Therefore, with the establishment of state power in general, and with the creation of a standing army in particular, citizens are faced with the decision between republic and despotism. In an organ of state that is constitutively based on the principle of command and obedience and operates with the highly problematic category of "military unity," this decision becomes especially important. For the state and its soldiers can "coup"—they can turn against the citizens in a coup d'état. For this reason, too—and not only because of a possible lack of bravery in the face of the external enemy—the citizens place their citizen-soldiers under sworn affirmation and assurance. So how does one gain certain knowledge as to whether a coup d'état is imminent or already taking place and to be averted? Whose responsibility is it to ascertain these findings and, with all the consequences, to determine and ward off an internal state of emergency?

The principles and virtues that are important for coding the conduct of members of armed state organs are laid down in democratic constitutional states in the provisions—using Germany as an example—of their soldier laws, their military disciplinary regulations, and their military criminal jurisdiction in the operational regulations of the military police in particular, and now also in the statutes of international criminal jurisdiction. All of this fits into the framework of the rules and regulations of international humanitarian law of armed conflicts. What is now specific to military armed state power, what guiding difference could identify it as an irreducible system in the Luhmannian sense, and for what classes of conflict is it needed? Police and military force differ in their basic principles in that the disparity in armed strength between the forces and the targets is structurally much higher in the case of the police than in the case of the military. Under conditions of a stable monopoly on the use of force, the security organs are vastly superior to all other violent actors in terms of their escalation dominance, so that they can assert their sovereign function under peace law restrictions, that is, without fighting and without collateral damage considerations. The situation is different in conflicts in which not this or that legal title is at stake, but the monopoly on the rule of law and the use of force as a whole. There, the opponent can escalate to the same level.

Here, then, is the answer to the two open questions. For such conflict classes —that is, first and foremost for the international armed conflict between states— international law makes the highly problematic concession of granting state armed forces the combatant privilege and the collateral damage assessment. *Conflict classification on the basis of careful and comprehensive situation assessment is the most responsible judgment a state leadership has to make in terms of international law ethics.* And only a high intensity registered by parastate armed forces, for example, justifies classification as a noninternational armed conflict. Only then may the state send armed forces into an armed conflict if it considers itself willing and able to fight through to the restoration of the common good.[5]

If the state, as a monopolist of force, is far superior to the opponent who is prepared to use violence, it sends the unarmed "constitutional protection" as an observing early warning system, the armed police for preventive defense against danger, for repressive prosecution, and for legal protection in a largely pacified society. If a situation is not pacified, and if the state is not far superior, it sends heavily armed military to fight. A region may be described as more civilized the lower the tendency to commit crimes and the more the monopolists of force succeed in separating internal and external security and preventing military defense from occurring in the first place. This distinction leads to a significant conclusion from the point of view of the ethics of law. Although the police fight against criminality is also directed at groups in operational *profiling* and access, it is legally strictly oriented toward the individual and must always prove the crime to be committed by an individual criminal and, above a certain level of intensity of crime, is also commissioned and controlled by the judiciary on a case-by-case basis.

Military combat, on the other hand, is based on the law of armed conflict and is fought by combatants, who, as units, fight the enemy collectively and indis-

---

[5] Von Schubert, *Nieder mit dem Krieg*, 442 ff.

criminately. An enemy's membership in the opposing armed forces is sufficient as a reason to fight him; an individual hostile act does not have to be proven. Any further distinctions between military, border guards, national or civil guards, coast guards, gendarmes, special operations forces, criminal and protective police, tax and customs investigators, or between internal and external security, or between prevention versus reaction, or distinctions among legal framework, command structure, degree of training, equipment and armament, hierarchization, formalization and ritualization, and feedback to society are arbitrary, evolved, and variable, and do not change the basic distinction mentioned above.

Thus, in the case of severe domestic violent conflicts, there can be fluid transitions—a militarization of the police, or a policization (constabularization) of the military. What terminological distinctions, then, should apply? The following are suggested as key differences: "armed monopoly on the use of force" versus "unarmed monopoly on the use of force" and, within the armed monopoly on the use of force, "authorized to wage war" versus "not authorized to wage war." The weight of these provisions becomes particularly impressive when applied to military medical services. Again, most of the characteristics of medical service missions also apply to disaster medicine—for example, extreme stress and environmental conditions; mutually intense loyalty relationship between principal and agent; high demands on care, loyalty, and comradeship; command and obedience; resilience to the threat of *esprit de corps*; mass casualties and deaths; frequent triage situations; high likelihood of trauma sequelae, etc. The uniquely specific characteristic of the medical service of armed forces consists in the standard situation for which the MMS (Mobile Medical Squad) is trained—*it also operates under massive enemy fire.* Nevertheless, the medical soldier is not supposed to take part in combat operations, but to protect only himself and his patients from violence with light armament.

The initial methodological questions have thus been answered. *In liberal-egalitarian societies, normative orders under the guiding concept of the common good are legitimized by procedure; they are the result of electoral law and parliamentarism and the resulting process of permanent law-making, law enforcement and law review, especially with regard to the armed forces.* The influence of the guiding differences and codes of conduct characteristic of security-sector institutions on these orders results, on one hand, from the ethical quality of this law and, on the other hand, from the fact that law, especially in its execution, takes the form of dense legality. Here, nothing is to be left to arbitrariness or chance; on one hand, everything is to be laid out so closely meshed and free of contradictions that no doubt can arise about the spirit and letter of the laws and the commands and operations derived from them. On the other hand, all of this takes place in the medium of individual and contingent experiences and language and is therefore always in need of interpretation, open to consideration and to a high degree subject to justification.

This tension is carried to extremes in military "drill." Drill—psychologically formulated as operant conditioning—as an exercise for the use of individuals and collectives as "units," in the extreme as an "instrument" and "weapon," if not even as "ammunition," threatens to nip any humanity in the bud; at the same time, however, it is the prerequisite for the freedom of moral judgment and the confident execution of a morally required order to have any chance at all, even under the extreme stress of combat. Only those who can competently "lead" combat can also decide when to begin it, why, for what purpose, and how to lead it and when to end it, and then reflect on all this ethically.[6] But this in turn presupposes that all those involved really know what they are doing and regard their office and its functions as a "role" and "representation" rather than as the core of their identity.[7]

Results of the Further Analysis

What ideal-typical picture emerges from the above findings, particularly for the formation of virtue and character, ethical education, and the teaching of values in the relationship between the institutions of the security sector and the rest of society under the criterion of the common good?

Central Normative Functions, Value Hierarchies, and Spheres of Action of Institutions of the Security Sector

According to the provisions of international humanitarian law on armed conflicts, the right and duty to conduct combat, including the consideration of collateral damage, including the lives of uninvolved persons, is exclusively the "privilege" of members of the armed forces of states recognized under international law. This restriction has consequences concerning permissible and impermissible means and methods of combat, prisoner-of-war status, etc. Consequent-

---

[6] Shimon Naveh, *In Pursuit of Military Excellence* (London: Frank Cass, 1997); Dietrich Ungerer, *Der militärische Einsatz* (Potsdam: Miles, 2003); Rupert Smith, *The Utility of Force: The Art of War in the Modern World* (London: Penguin, 2006); Dietrich Ungerer, *Militärische Lagen. Analysen, Bedrohungen, Herausforderungen* (Berlin: Miles, 2007); and Robert J. Art and Kelly M. Greenhill, eds., *The Use of Force: Military Power and International Politics*, 8th ed. (Lanham, MD: Rowman & Littlefield, 2015).

[7] On ethics in the police and correctional system, see the literature in von Schubert, *Nieder mit dem Krieg*, 418n740; on military ethics, see ibid., 449n795.

ly, this unique feature *does not allow any transfer from the military to* any other social subsystem and the formation of character, ethical education, and transmission of values there.

This nonderivation does not apply, however, to many secondary virtues, which are not specific to the institutions of the security sector. In the fire department, in team and combat sports, and in every disaster situation, duties, goods, and virtues are needed that are not usually needed in the everyday life of a private household, a school, a doctor's office, a hotel complex, or an industrial plant. Since transitions can be fluid, however, it is plausible that it is also useful and morally required in everyday civilian life to line up in a crowd, to group around the victim in the event of harassment in a means of transport, to follow the instructions of the stewards at a mass event, and to train oneself in the much-maligned memorization and "cramming" when learning foreign languages and musical instruments. All this may have proximity to "police" and "soldierly" virtues; some learn such things in the course of their military service, and others just as well in disaster control, the fire department, or the school orchestra.

Based on the following table of soldierly virtues from a seminar on soldierly professional ethics, it would be possible to discuss what can be transferred to other areas of society, such as a hospital or an airport. The result of a review of this catalog might be that, with certain modifications, everything is actually transferable to all areas in which something has to be organized in compliance with moral and legal norms.[8]

1. *Legitimate Authorization: Command and Professional Responsibility*
- Initiative, fidelity, and clarity of command
- Acceptance of the indivisible responsibility and steadfastness in bearing all consequences up to liability
- Setting an example
- Careful attention to legitimate authorizations at all levels

2. *Viable Justification of the Initial Reason: Assessment of the Situation*
- Solidarity with the vulnerable and protected
- Realistic assessment of one's own situation
- Realistic assessment of the opponent's situation

3. *Viable Justification of the Intended Final Reason: Determination of the Purposes and Goals*
- A sense of proportion in setting realistic purposes and goals
- Reliability in the provision of all necessary measures
- Loyalty to the legitimate order

---

[8] Von Schubert, *Nieder mit dem Krieg*, 354–58.

4. Proportionality: Use of Means

- Bravery as a product of courage and readiness to fight, prudence and willingness to make sacrifices in view of one's own danger and that of one's comrades
- Persistence and patience in overcoming resistance
- Moderation in the sense of limiting the action to that which is appropriate for effecting the objective, necessary for the defense against the adversary, and appropriate for the welfare of all those affected as a whole

Excluded is only the specific character constellation that is suitable, necessary, and appropriate for training combatants, on one hand, to perform professional acts of killing, and, on the other hand, informing them that they will remain unpunished in doing so as long as they exercise these powers strictly within the framework of sovereign mandate, authorized command, and the limits of the law of armed conflict. Compliance with this paradoxical duty demands a high degree of voluntary self-restraint from every soldier and the armed forces as a whole. The danger of excess is present at all times, and the risk is very high, given the enormous potential for damaging effects.

Interactions Between the Normative Binding Forces in Institutions of the Security Sector and Those of Other Social Systems

After the "last German war" (Rolf-Dieter Müller),[9] the highly controversial debate about the rearmament of Western Germany within the framework of NATO resulted in the concept of *Innere Führung* (inner leadership) as a set of principles and rules for the conscience commitment of all members of the Bundeswehr.[10] Never again should a German soldier give himself up as a willing instrument for a war of aggression, robbery, and extermination of a moreover totalitarian regime.[11] If other countries want to ensure this self-restraint for their armed forces as well, then their governments must develop a similar "corporate philosophy" with them and for them. In Germany, moreover, this conception has been linked to the Prussian tradition of *Auftragstaktik*, which makes the delegation of responsibility from the strategic to the operational and tactical levels the rule without relinquishing overall responsibility. A further push for the ethical reorientation of Western armed forces was triggered by the "change in values" often

---

[9] Rolf-Dieter Müller, *Der letzte deutsche Krieg 1939–1945* (Berlin: Klett-Cotta, 2005).
[10] Elmar Wiesendahl, ed. *Führung für das 21. Jahrhundert. Die Bundeswehr und das Erbe Baudissins* (Paderborn: Schöningh, 2007).
[11] Müller, *Der letzte deutsche Krieg*; and Christian Hartmann, *Wehrmacht im Ostkrieg: Front und militärisches Hinterland 1941/42*, 2nd ed. (Munich: Oldenbourg, 2010).

announced by the year 1968. This particularly affected the relationship between the sexes in the everyday life of the troops. The soldierly professional ethos experienced a further boost from the change in images of conflict after the end of the Cold War. The bloc confrontation was replaced by foreign deployment, and the conventional mass army was replaced by the highly differentiated operational army, a change that was accompanied by a general leveling of the importance of the military in society but, unfortunately, not by the now all the more important development of a "strategic culture." Following the Russian invasion into Ukraine, the German chancellor, Olaf Scholz, already initiated another epochal shift in the strategic culture of Germany by significantly strengthening the German armed forces.

The result of this multiple change can be indicated on the part of the military with two keywords.[12] The "scientification" of the military operation is exemplified by the individual and organizational psychological penetration of armed combat as well as by the enormous professionalization of medical and hospital services. Soldiers are to receive services in the field and the rescue chain on the level of a district hospital at home. Another keyword is "social competence." Given the focus of "out-of-area" missions, there is a particular emphasis on training cultural competence concerning the respective country of deployment. In Germany, the armed forces may even have become a model of successful integration of different population groups. A relationship between superiors and subordi-

---

[12] Lawrence Freedman, *The Future of War: A History* (New York: Public Affairs, 2019); Sabine Mannitz, ed., *Democratic Civil-Military Relations: Soldiering in 21st Century Europe* (London: Routledge, 2017); Nina Leonhard, "Über den (Wesens)Kern des Soldatseins: Professionssoziologische Überlegungen zur gegenwärtigen Debatte um soldatische Berufs- und Selbstbilder im Bereich der Bundeswehr," in *Professionskulturen–Charakteristika unterschiedlicher professioneller Praxen*, ed. Silke Müller-Herrmann et al. (Wiesbaden: Springer, 2018), 7–29; Marina Nuciari, "The Study of the Military: Models for the Military Profession," in *Handbook of the Sociology of the Military*, ed. Giuseppe Cardio and Marina Nuciari (Cham: Springer, 2018), 35–60; Nina Leonhard, "Towards a New German Military Identity? Change and Continuity of Military Representations of Self and Other(s) in Germany," *Critical Military Studies* 5, no. 4 (2019): 304–21; Tessa op den Buijsetal, "Warrior and Peacekeeper Role Identities: Associations with Self-Esteem, Organizational Commitment and Organizational Citizenship Behaviour," *Journal of Military Studies* 8 (2019): 3–15; Timo Graf, "Zur Integrationsfunktion der Inneren Führung: Eine Betrachtung der öffentlichen Meinung zur gesellschaftlichen Einbindung der Bundeswehr von 2005 bis 2019," in *Jahrbuch Innere Führung 2020: Zur Weiterentwicklung der Inneren Führung*, ed. Uwe Hartmann et al. (Berlin: Miles, 2020), 105–22; Nina Leonhard, "Soldat sein. Sozialwissenschaftliche Debatten über den Wandel des Soldatenberufs," *Aus Politik und Zeitgeschichte* (APuZ) 70, nos. 16–17 (2020): 18–24; and Sönke Neitzel, *Deutsche Krieger. Vom Kaiserreich zur Berliner Republik. Eine Militärgeschichte*, 5th ed. (Berlin: Propyläen, 2020).

nates, which for a long time was purely hierarchical, has also been significantly supplemented by new provisions and instruments of welfare and also by guaranteed appeal and grievance procedures. The professionalization of individual functionaries brought about by technological progress often put them on an equal footing with their military superiors. Today, troop leaders, who have long been academically trained, rely on a staff that also brings practical scientific training and skills to the table. Finally, societal change has not stopped at the general formation of the habitus; this applies to the gender relations already mentioned, including the recognition of same-sex partnerships, the way religious diversity is dealt with, clothing styles, food, stimulants, and addictive substances, as well as the presentation and role of the armed forces and their members in the media.[13]

Conflicts Between the Security Sector and Society, and Their Resolution

The adaptation of the soldierly habitus to society as a whole, as described above, nevertheless results in strong differences, even latent and open conflicts, between the military and society.[14] The contradictions are reflected in the entire habitus formation and, as already explained, affect not only the military but all areas in which people work and live under extreme conditions. A recent example is the implementation of the European Working Time Directive 2003/88/EC in the armed forces of the EU member states, which requires the use of civilian timekeeping and limitation to the military area.[15] Such a strong orientation to the standards of the civilian working world may make sense and be possible in basic military operations. But since it is already there that people gradually learn what is then essential in the field, such a directive tears open a chasm not only between the types of operations but between the units of the armed forces where it can be implemented and those where it cannot. "Imagine it's war, and the weekend begins!" This example may suffice to only hint at further fields

---

[13] Evangelisches Kirchenamt für die Bundeswehr, ed., *Friedensethik im Einsatz. Ein Handbuch der Evangelischen Seelsorge in der Bundeswehr* (Gütersloh: Gütersloher Verlagshaus, 2009), 272 ff.

[14] Maja Apelt, "Das Gewaltdilemma moderner Streitkräfte," in *Krieg und Zivilgesellschaft*, ed. Dierk Spreen and Trutz von Trotha (Berlin: Duncker & Humblot, 2012), 219–37.

[15] *Wissenschaftliche Dienste des Deutschen Bundestages, Die Umsetzung der Europäischen Arbeitszeitrichtlinie 2003/88/EG in den Streitkräften der EU-Mitgliedstaaten. Erfahrungen und Herausforderungen* [WD 2-3000-082/16] (Berlin: Deutscher Bundestag, 2016), https://www.bundestag.de/resource/blob/438620/3ccb67f2fb8352fae6 c26ae2243fc98b/wd-2-082-16-pdf-data.pdf.

here. Despite all the changes in the image of the soldier in recent decades, tensions and conflicts arise from the contradictions between institutional and lifeworld social forms, between reform pedagogy and military drill, between civilian medicine and military medical service, between everyday social life in the sending country and the conditions in the area of deployment, with the subsequent increased risk of trauma sequelae as a result of sudden and unexpected losses of control or changes in the political framework conditions. Particularly challenging is the commitment to the law of armed conflict in combat with adversaries who systematically break this law.

At the root of all these conflicts lies a tension that, as shown, can best be grasped in terms of the ethics of law, even if it must then be dealt with in a differentiated manner at the individual, institutional, and societal levels. For even if armed forces are deployed not on the basis of a supposedly free right of states to wage war but following international law in concepts and systems of common security to preserve and restore peace, it might be obvious to abandon the framework of human rights altogether and instead refer exclusively to the peacekeeping law of the UN Charter and the Hague and Geneva law of armed conflict. However, such a dichotomy of two bodies of law for two supposedly completely separate areas of application—domestic peace here and armed conflict there—is ethically untenable. The Universal Declaration of Human Rights of 1948 and the UN Charter of 1945, together with the Geneva Conventions of 1864 and the Hague Regulations on Land Warfare of 1899, form the umbrella documents of the law of armed conflict, based on a consistent legal ethic and an ethic of law-making, law-preserving, and law-working force.

Nevertheless, there are strong contrasts and tensions. They arise from the differences between peaceful and warlike conditions. However, there is never the one spatial or temporal caesura oriented either only to peace or only to war. Just as human rights conventions include provisions for catastrophic situations in their emergency clauses, the unified corpus of Hague and Geneva law also includes provisions obligating respect for basic standards of human rights. In this respect, the law of armed conflict is a *lex specialis*, which may override provisions of human rights law in the case of armed conflict, but only because and insofar as it more appropriately realizes the basic intention of the one legal idea in the specific case. The social perception of armed conflicts leads from this insight to a self-obligation of responsible citizens for the formation and maintenance of the "strategic culture" of their country.[16]

---

[16] Germany has had some catching up to do in this respect: "Debate about what can and should be done in German foreign and security policy will only find real resonance if it can make Germans understand that this is about their immediate and very personal future, not about far-away problems. This has happened successfully in the case of the climate crisis. The reason for this is partly the grave danger involved, but also the prom-

Weaknesses and Strengths of Security-Sector Institutions in the Concert of Societal Subsystems with Regard to Their Typical Duties, Commodities, and Virtues

Notorious weaknesses of the military system result from inadequate management of the tensions and conflicts described above. The experience of permanent barracking and unreflective drills, for example, can strengthen a yearning for authoritarian regimes among the troops and make them susceptible to cadre obedience, a subject mentality, and military sports training in remote recreational facilities. Without universal conscription, armed forces are much less integrated into society. So it is only too natural to view them as service providers competing with private mercenary firms in the security "market." If the troops adopt this politically irresponsible view, then the step is not far for members of military units to come together in closed enclaves with an isolated special ethos and bizarre traditions.[17] Soldiers' honor and pride in arms in public then turn into a clandestine weapons cult, which in extreme cases prepares the ground for serious human rights violations within the troops, but also against the civilian population in the country of deployment.[18]

Classic strengths lie in the "Prussian" virtues from the period after 1812, which are still proverbial in Germany: decisiveness, comradeship, clarity of language, willingness to suffer and sacrifice, loyalty, punctuality, respect especially

---

ise of salvation, the idea that the problem is 'solvable,' given sufficiently radical action. In the case of climate policy, what is supposedly 'right' is clearer than in most foreign policy crises. Unease and discontent with the ways of the world have grown since it no longer conforms to German expectations that flourished after the fall of the Berlin Wall. However, the reactions of most people in Germany have remained strangely unaffected by this change. But global crises and conflicts concern us, not just because they disturb our normative perceptions of the world, but because many of these directly affect our security, our prosperity, and the future of our democracy." Thomas Bagger, "Germany, We Need to Talk," *Internationale Politik Quarterly* 3 (2021), https://ip-quarterly.com/en/germany-we-need-talk; see also Heiko Biehl et al., eds., *Strategische Kulturen in Europa. Die Bürger Europas und ihre Streitkräfte* (Strausberg: Sozialwissenschaftliches Institut der Bundeswehr, 2011); Heiko Biehl et al., eds., *Strategic Cultures in Europe: Security and Defence Policies across the Continent* (Wiesbaden: Springer, 2013); and Heiko Biehl and Harald Schoen, eds., *Sicherheitspolitik und Streitkräfte im Urteil der Bürger. Theorien, Methoden, Befunde* (Wiesbaden: Springer, 2015).

17 Donald Abenheim and Uwe Hartmann, eds., *Tradition in der Bundeswehr. Stimmen zum Erbe des deutschen Soldaten und zur Umsetzung des neuen Traditionserlasses* (Berlin: Miles, 2014).

18 See, for example, the Australian *Inspector-General of the Australian Defence Force Afghanistan Inquiry Report* (Brereton-Report), https://afghanistaninquiry.defence.gov.au/sites/default/files/2020-11/IGADF-Afghanistan-Inquiry-Public-Release-Version.pdf.

for the enemy, steadfastness, bravery, loyalty, reliability. All these virtues are needed in many areas of society—for example, in art. A virtuoso concert pianist could not have his score not only in his head but in his entire body if he had not spent an entire musical life on his "drill," namely, practicing for several hours every day.[19] An example of the use of a military image in the realm of religion is the "spiritual armor" in Ephesians 6:10–17. Virtuosity, piety, and liturgical competence do not fall from heaven but must be lived and practiced in order to endure when the going gets tough and uncomfortable. And because this need for habituation applies to all human skills and abilities, it also applies to the entire spectrum of military combat. Largely pacified societies, in particular, are well-advised not to ridicule, marginalize, or even demonize their armed forces because of their job-typical discipline.[20]

Conclusion

The army is not the "school of the nation," but it is one of the many organizations of society in which people are generally prepared for the assumption of responsibility in the public sphere and especially for extremely exceptional situations.[21] These situations can suddenly affect everyday life, while normal life already challenges us morally. The militarily untalented civilian Socrates is the only really brave one in a dispute of experienced strategists about the military virtue of bravery. For he is the only one who is not satisfied with the enumeration of external examples and cases from the world of objects and phenomena but invites his interlocutors to introspection and self-comprehension—in modern terms, specific leading differences—and does not stop there, but untiringly proceeds, unperturbed by disinterest and contradiction, to ethical principles, which he in turn tests for general validity. And even the most solemn plea for compre-

---

[19] Ana-Marija Markovina, *Glücks-Spiel* (Düsseldorf: Staccato, 2019).

[20] In this view, it is not convincing to declare pacified societies to be "postheroic" societies across the board; see Herfried Münkler, "Heroische und postheroische Gesellschaften," in Spreen and von Trotha, *Krieg und Zivilgesellschaft*, 175–87. According to a study by the Social Science Institute of the German Armed Forces, German society is less "casualty-shy" than expected: see Gerhard Kümmel and Nina Leonhard, *Death, the Military and Society: Casualties and Civil-Military Relations in Germany* (Strausberg: Sozialwissenschaftliches Institut der Bundeswehr, 2005); see also Nina Leonhard, "Die postheroische Gesellschaft und ihr Militär," in *Metaphern soziologischer Zeitdiagnosen*, ed. Matthias Junge (Wiesbaden: Springer, 2016), 101–21.

[21] Ute Frevert, "Das Militär als Schule der Männlichkeiten," in *Männlichkeiten und Moderne. Geschlecht in den Wissenskulturen um 1900*, ed. Ulrike Brunotte and Rainer Herrn (Bielefeld: Transcript, 2015), 57–75.

hensive civil courage would remain lip service as long as people do not overcome their own conceit, complacency, laziness, and cowardice on the level of everyday personal feeling and thinking. For the fight against one's own arrogance requires the greatest bravery. It is true that society does not need an army to learn this. But when all other institutions reach their limits in times of greatest need, it is often the resources of the armed forces that provide solutions. The proverbial "fighting morale" of the troops is one of the resources that society as a whole can draw on, but only in a figurative sense and decidedly not in the terminological sense of the law of armed conflict.

In view of the relationship between the military and society, even more important than the cultivation of secondary virtues is the common awareness associated with the term "strategic culture." For a long time, armed conflicts within states—civil wars—have accounted for by far the largest share of warfare on earth.[22] Therefore, strategic thinking in society must focus on much more than purely military capabilities. The decisive part in overcoming and pacifying conflicts must be played by "brave" civilian actors. Hardly anyone demands this more emphatically and passionately than soldiers returning from missions. The state and civil society should listen to them and, above all, learn this insight from them.

---

[22] Heidelberg Institute for International Conflict Research, *Conflict Barometer* (Heidelberg: HIIK, 2020), 19, https://hiik.de/wp-content/uploads/2021/05/ConflictBarometer_2020_2.pdf.

The Indispensability of Virtues in the Military: Virtue Ethical Considerations Following the Guiding Concept of the *Miles Protector*[1]

Marco Hofheinz

Do We Really Need Virtues? Problematization of a Concept That Seems Antiquated

The influence of the military and defense system on late modern society cannot be denied. As in every community and social system, certain character-defining virtues have taken shape. The question arises, of course, whether these virtues are the desired ones. One need only think of soldierly excesses of violence in war and in the barracks. As a particularly extreme example, the Abu Ghraib torture scandal during the U.S. invasion of Iraq illustrates the potential danger. It involved not only soldiers but also U.S. intelligence service employees and employees of private security firms. The Haditha massacre in November 2005, when U.S. soldiers killed twenty-four Iraqi civilians, including children, in the course of a retaliatory action, is also sadly famous. Certain "steadfastness" in action was certainly evident here, as was a certain character formation that cannot be dismissed, no matter how undesirable it may be and how it must be condemned as criminal. Virtues can easily turn into their opposite and degenerate into vices, even if they are actually excellences acquired through habit: "Virtues are, as it were, the sediment that is deposited in the repeated moral behavior of man, the unintentionally forming form, or in another image: the path that is formed by being committed."[2]

It has become famous that the then German chancellor Helmut Schmidt had to accept a retort from his "party friend" Oskar Lafontaine, referring to the chancellor's political demand for "loyalty to the alliance" vis-à-vis the United States in

---

[1] For the sake of better readability, the quotations have also been translated from German into English. I would like to thank Prof. Dr. Peter D. Browning (Drury University) for translation assistance and some expert advice.

[2] Otto-Friedrich Bollnow, *Wesen und Wandel der Tugenden* (Frankfurt am Main: Ullstein, 1958), 24.

the dispute about the NATO double-track decision[3]: "Helmut Schmidt continues to speak of a sense of duty, calculability, feasibility, steadfastness... . These are secondary virtues. To put it very precisely, you can also run a concentration camp with them."[4] Secondary virtues, such as diligence, loyalty, obedience, discipline, sense of duty, punctuality, reliability, orderliness, politeness, and cleanliness comprised a "bourgeois" catalog of virtues in a Prussian-militaristic tradition.[5] In other words, they served to achieve excellence in the enforcement of certain social conventions that seem highly questionable to us today in moral terms. The concept of virtue therefore has a sound that is not only highly antiquated but also morally ambiguous.

To bring the objection against a virtue-ethical enterprise to its military-ethical point: "If virtue is fixed entirely on the aspect of felicitous fitness, it can appear useful even to wholly immoral enterprises. With courage, diligence, and loyalty, for example, even the effectiveness of raids can be increased, viewed in this light."[6] In other words, it may well be that the virtuous person does "the right thing" habitually. But what is "the right thing?"[7] What constitutes the good life? Traditional notions of the right and good have become increasingly questionable. Late modern pluralistic society, with its subjectivization of convictions as well as its relativization of authoritatively conveyed answers, does not stop at the questions of the good life and also at the military and defense system. In modern times, diverse living conditions have massively changed not only society's ethical landscape but also the entire military and defense system. Virtue ethics has to struggle with this problem, and like moral philosophy as a whole, it is experiencing great difficulties doing so.

Of course, the total and general renunciation of virtues cannot be derived from this objection, as the paradox pointed out by Jean-Pierre Wils shows: the beginning of living morally often entails just this: that someone can act "out of virtue against virtue."[8] In the military sphere, for example, it is significant that

---

[3] On one track, NATO agreed to deploy new intermediate-range U.S. missiles as a counter to Soviet missiles that could hit Europe but not the United States, while on the second track, NATO held out the prospect of negotiations with the Soviet Union to ban mid-range nuclear arms in Europe entirely.

[4] *Stern*, no. 29, Jul. 15, 1982.

[5] On the particularly controversial virtue of obedience, see Mathias Wirth, *Distanz des Gehorsams. Theorie, Ethik und Kritik einer Tugend* (Tübingen: Mohr Siebeck, 2016).

[6] Klaus Ebeling, "Tugend," in *Ethik-Kompass: 77 Leitbegriffe*, ed. Klaus Ebeling and Matthias Gillner (Freiburg: Herder, 2014), 140.

[7] See Christoph Horn, *Antike Lebenskunst. Glück und Moral von Sokrates bis zu den Neuplatonikern* (Munich: C. H. Beck, 1998), 113.

[8] Jean-Pierre Wils, "Tugend," in *Handbuch Ethik*, ed. Marcus Düwell et al., 2nd ed. (Stuttgart: J. B. Metzler, 2006), 534–38, at 536.

reports about cases of political radicalization and even violent excesses and incidents of racism are accompanied not only by the diagnosis of an "attitude problem" and a "weakness in leadership," but also by the loud call for "renewed 'attitude' and 'leadership.'" Thus, the disease and its symptoms seem to be diagnosed and prescribed for at the same time. As if caught in a spiral, we obviously cannot escape the virtue-ethical twist. One way or another, certain constants will emerge in action, which are highly significant for character formation, ethical education, and the transmission of values, but which are also in part morally highly problematic and politically highly explosive.

On the Redimensioning of Virtue Ethics

Viewed in this light, it becomes clear that virtue ethics is indispensable, because it focuses on the actor or actors of an action—in contrast to duty ethics, which asks for normative rules (laws, commandments, duties) that regulate the execution of moral action, and in contrast to goods ethics, which focuses on the effects of moral action and the goals we strive for in our actions. While duty ethics asks, "What should I/we do?" and goods ethics asks, "How do I/we want to live?" the guiding question of virtue ethics is, "How should I/we *be?*" This brings into focus the person who acts well and their characteristics, abilities, and skills. Those who ask only rule- or result-oriented questions will lose sight of the person and the force determining the person's actions.[9]

From this point of view, the "renaissance of virtue ethics" in the present is understandable. It can be explained by the rediscovery of the components of character, skill, and capacity, for example, in so-called communitarianism. Alasdair MacIntyre has lamented the loss of virtue in the face of the disorientation or moral crisis of the present.[10] Virtue ethics is also enjoying a deepened appreciation in theology. Stanley Hauerwas, for example, criticizes the focus on dilemma situations and decision-making in ethical discussions, which ignores habits and constancies that shape actions.[11] The "story" of people is thereby lost from view. Hauerwas and others can draw on a long tradition of virtue ethics that stretches from antiquity to the present and certainly includes the Reformation

---

[9] On the triad of virtue, duty, and goods doctrine, see Robin W. Lovin, *An Introduction to Christian Ethics: Goals, Duties, and Virtues* (Nashville: Abingdon Press, 2011).

[10] Alasdair MacIntyre, *After Virtue: A Study in Moral Theory*, 2nd ed. (Notre Dame, IN: University of Notre Dame Press, 1984).

[11] Stanley Hauerwas, *The Peaceable Kingdom: A Primer in Christian Ethics*, 3rd ed. (Notre Dame, IN: University of Notre Dame Press, 1986), 121–30.

(for example, Melanchthon, Calvin, and Peter Martyr Vermigli).[12] A certain renaissance can also be observed in peace and military ethics.[13]

The strength of this type of ethics lies in its plausible approach to the lifeworld of both the individual and the community, an approach that allows integration of social and individual ethical perspectives, as well as being sociologically connectable (for example, in terms of methodological induction). Due to the emphasis on learning and practicing, the approach also has high pedagogical and educational theoretical significance. A special closeness is certainly given to competence-oriented teaching and learning, for which virtue-ethical approaches to the concept and pedagogy of competences speak. Theologically, the approach can be critically questioned with regard to an underestimation of the radicality of sin and the danger of particularism. Without a correlating doctrine of goods—that is, a hierarchy of desirable goods—virtue ethics would lack standards.

For good reason, therefore, at least one critic has spoken of the "limited range of freestanding virtue ethics"[14]: "Just as they remain ethically blind without a blueprint of the good, so they fail without a complementary concept of the ought, the duty, or the law to claim the general validity of what is morally right."[15] It is therefore necessary to assume a complementary relationship between the different types of ethics, and in this sense it is also necessary to take into account the need to complement the modern ethics of norms and goods.[16] The rehabilitation of the question of virtue ethics also needs to be taken into account in the field of military ethics.[17] This has already happened in part,

---

[12] See Marco Hofheinz, "'Nicht den Pflug vor die Ochsen spannen'. Tugendethische Ansätze bei Johannes Calvin. Ein Beitrag zur ethischen Grundlagendiskussion," in Marco Hofheinz, *Ethik—reformiert! Studien zur reformierten Reformation und ihrer Rezeption im 20 Jahrhundert* (Göttingen: Vandenhoeck & Ruprecht, 2017), 64–113.

[13] See Dieter Baumann, *Militärethik. Theologische, menschenrechtliche und militärwissenschaftliche Perspektiven* (Stuttgart: Kohlhammer, 2007), 486–548; Alexander Merkl, *"Si vis pacem, para virtutes". Ein tugendethischer Beitrag zu einem Ethos der Friedfertigkeit* (Baden-Baden / Münster: Nomos / Aschendorff, 2015); and Eberhard Schockenhoff, *Kein Ende der Gewalt? Friedensethik für eine globalisierte Welt* (Freiburg: Herder, 2018), 549–77.

[14] Hans-Richard Reuter, "Tugend," in *Evangelische Ethik Kompakt. Basiswissen in Grundbegriffen*, ed. Rainer Anselm and Ulrich H. J. Körtner (Gütersloh: Gütersloher Verlagshaus, 2015), 204–11, at 211.

[15] Ibid.

[16] Ibid.: "Only as a partial aspect of an ethics integrating attitudes, goals, and norms does the question of virtues have its—then also good— meaning."

[17] With regard to an understanding of military ethics, I heuristically follow Dieter Baumann's definition (*Militärethik*, 135), which in its short form reads as follows: "Military ethics is the critical reflection on the right and good actions and behavior of soldiers as

thankfully. But before taking up newer impulses of an integrative military ethics,[18] it is first necessary to at least hint at the rich tradition in the history of ethics that can be drawn upon here.

The Doctrine of Virtue and the Soldierly Ethos

The fact that the soldierly ethos is closely connected with the doctrine of virtue becomes clear as soon as one looks at Western ethics, especially Plato's doctrine of soul and virtue, with its four so-called cardinal virtues.[19] In addition to prudence, which is assigned to the thinking faculty, and temperance (measure or moderation), which is assigned to desire, as well as justice as the epitome of the harmonious unity of the soul's faculties, Plato mentions fortitude, which corresponds to courageous feeling.

Additionally, crucial to the understanding of virtue since Aristotle is the concept of the mean or proportion (the *mesotes* doctrine).[20] According to this, courage as a virtue avoids the extremes of cowardice, on one hand, and foolhardiness or bravado on the other, both of which miss the good or happiness. With reason and a sense of proportion, the brave person stands up for his convictions even in times of danger. One can certainly speak of steadfastness here. According to Kant, bravery means "the ability and the deliberate resolution to resist a strong but unjust opponent,"[21] and is thus "lawful courage, in that which duty commands, not to shrink from even the loss of life."[22] In any case, bravery aims at overcoming fear and timidity. In this respect, it is about more than warlike behavior. Being a soldier is by no means exhausted in such behavior. And that fact brings us to the decisive virtue-ethical question of military ethics: How should soldiers *be*?[23]

---

    well as on the peace-promoting relationship between the army, the state, and the international community."

[18] See Dieter Baumann, "Integrative Militärethik. Grundzüge eines militärethischen Entwurfs," in *Friedensethik im 20. Jahrhundert*, ed. Volker Stümke and Matthias Gillner (Stuttgart: Kohlhammer, 2011), 219–46.
[19] Plato, *The Republic* (Politeia), 427c–445e.
[20] Aristotle, *Nicomachean Ethics*, 1106b 36–1107 a1.
[21] Immanuel Kant, *Metaphysik der Sitten, Tugendlehre*, A 3 (Weischedel 7, 509).
[22] Immanuel Kant, *Anthropologie in pragmatischer Hinsicht*, B 216 (Weischedel 10, 591).
[23] See Hauerwas, *The Peaceable Kingdom*, 29: "Christian Ethics, therefore, is not first of all concerned with 'Thou shalt' or 'Thou shalt not.' Its first task is to help us rightly envision the world. . . . In other words, the enterprise of Christian ethics primarily helps us to see. We can only act within the world we can envision, and we can envision the world rightly only as we are trained to see."

This is the virtue-ethical question, as distinct from the question of what soldiers should *do*. The role models that generate answers to this question have varied considerably in the course of history and have been subject to strong changes.[24] In terms of virtue ethics, it is important to note that such an ethics does not consist simply of confronting soldiers with expectations or attributes unconnected to their lives:[25] "It cannot be satisfying or morally appropriate for soldiers to have a new self-image, which would ultimately be a foreign image, imposed on them from the outside. Conversely, however, soldiers cannot simply extricate themselves from obligations they have entered into in good knowledge of what is expected of them in their role."[26]

The Ethos of the *Miles Protector*

Coming from the military, Gustav Däniker, then a division officer in the Bundeswehr (the German army), called for a new type of soldier in his reflections on the occasion of the second Gulf War,[27] the *miles protector* (Latin for soldier protector).[28] Däniker understands protection in a comprehensive sense as the protection of the national and international legal order. As he emphasizes, the military threat or use of force in today's world requires a legally impeccable and morally convincing legitimation:

> The mission of the soldier of the twenty-first century is to protect, help, save. His mission statement is to make an increasingly targeted and effective contribution to peacekeeping, peacebuilding, and securing a livable existence for the people. In line

---

[24] See Nina Leonhard, "Soldat sein. Sozialwissenschaftliche Debatten über den Wandel des Soldatenberufs," in *Aus Politik und Zeitgeschehen* (APuZ) 70, nos. 16–17 (2020): 18–24; idem, "Über den (Wesens) Kern des Soldatseins: Professionssoziologische Überlegungen zur gegenwärtigen Debatte um soldatische Berufs- und Selbstbilder im Bereich der Bundeswehr," in *Professionskulturen—Charakteristika unterschiedlicher professioneller Praxen*, ed. Silke Müller-Herrmann et al. (Wiesbaden: Springer, 2018), 7–29.

[25] See Gerhard Kümmel and Christian Leuprecht, "Selbst- und Fremdbilder des (bundes-)deutschen Soldaten," in *Handbuch Militärische Berufsethik. Bd. 2: Anwendungsfelder*, ed. Thomas Bohrmann, Karl-Heinz Lather, and Friedrich Lohmann (Wiesbaden: Springer Fachmedien, 2014), 17–40.

[26] Bernhard Koch, "Das Ethos des Nothelfers. Überlegungen zur moralischen Herausforderung von Interventionen für die Soldaten," *Militärseelsorge* 50 (2012): 137–51, at 149.

[27] On the Gulf Wars, see Charles Reed, *Just War? Changing Society and the Churches* (London: SPCK, 2004); David L. Clough and Brian Stiltner, *Faith and Force: A Christian Debate about War* (Washington, DC: Georgetown University Press, 2007), 175–219.

[28] See Gustav Däniker, *Wende Golfkrieg. Vom Wesen und Gebrauch künftiger Streitkräfte* (Frankfurt am Main: Report Verlag, 1992), 185.

with the necessary reorientation of military thinking and action, the soldier's role model is also changing. Warriors, fighters, and pure battlefield technicians are increasingly less in demand than a new type of soldier who can be called a *miles protector*, namely, one who provides protection through his efforts but is also capable of aid and rescue with the same energy and competence with which he masters combat tasks.[29]

Dieter Baumann, currently a colonel in the general staff of the Swiss army, has taken up this model and spoken of the soldier as a functionary and deputy of international law.[30] Today, he says, soldiers are no longer pure national defenders or even government agents, but cosmopolitan guardians of the law.[31] As he emphasizes, they must distinguish themselves as cosmopolitan citizens in uniform[32] through a high legal ethos and professional as well as human competence. The professional and technical training of soldiers must be complemented by ethical training.

Baumann points out that, in addition to the four cardinal virtues of justice, moderation, courage, and prudence, the *miles protector* is characterized in particular by specific "soldier virtues," namely vigilant-critical loyalty and a sense of responsibility. Vigilance means the basic attitude of carrying out to the best of one's knowledge and conscience those orders that are in the spirit of the constitution, because every member of the Swiss army, for example, has the duty to serve the Swiss Confederation and to respect its constitution and the international law of war.

If one looks at Baumann's catalog of seven soldierly virtues in its differentiation, which constitutes the ethos of the soldier, the subdivision into virtues of justice and institutional virtues is striking. In terms of virtues of justice, he mentions:

---

[29] Ibid. See also Hermann Düringer and Horst Scheffler, eds., *Internationale Polizei—Eine Alternative zur militärischen Konfliktbearbeitung* (Frankfurt am Main: Haag und Herchen, 2002), especially the preface by Horst Scheffler, 7–17.
[30] Baumann, *Militärethik*, 557.
[31] See also Wolfgang Lienemann, "The Ethics of Peace and Justice in International Order," *Studies in Christian Ethics* 20, no. 1 (2007): 77–87, at 83: "Today we are observers of a transformation of military aims, equipment and training. The result is a new type of soldier. . . . But the situation is ambivalent: There is a danger of militarization of the police and of outsourcing the political responsibility for military actions in favor of private security agencies with rather a lack of public and legal accountability. I think that it is of great importance not to blur the boundaries between soldiers and policemen, but the military functions will change following its legal embedding."
[32] So Baumann, *Militärethik*, 561.

a) Respect for human dignity: This virtue consists minimally in respect and observance of the rights due to every human being, as well as in shame for undignified behavior and actions.
b) Qualified respect for rights: Those who protect a legitimate legal system should do so with conviction and exclusively by lawful means. They must form an ethos of legal compliance. In extreme cases, however, this virtue also includes resisting corrupted law.
c) Sense of responsibility: Soldiers have a duty to exercise their responsibility in accordance with their function.
d) Moral judgment: Ethical principles and norms are not "given by nature," but can be questioned and require context-bound and situational application. For this reason, moral judgment is necessary. This corresponds to the classical virtue of prudence. In today's world, this includes a high level of cultural sensitivity and intercultural competence.[33]

The basis for the determination of these virtues of justice is the category of elementary human rights. Baumann thus emphasizes that there is no such thing as a "special soldierly ethic," but rather that the focus must be on the concretization of universal justice. In this way, he also takes up the possible objection of ignoring the divergences in the ethical conceptions of the soldier's profession, which become apparent in international comparison,[34] by not naming a common reference value. Moreover, he explicitly calls for intercultural competence.[35]

In addition to the virtues of justice, Baumann also cites institutional virtues. These, too, are not "special virtues"; rather, they, along with the justice virtues, should contribute to just peace.[36] He identifies three institutional virtues:
a) Fulfillment of duty: This virtue instructs to acquire the professional knowledge and physical and mental conditions appropriate to the function, which leads to a high and exemplary professionalism. It includes the virtue of brav-

---

[33] The list is a translation of the language in Baumann, *Militärethik*, 487.
[34] See Said AlDailami, Thomas Bohrmann, and Raphael Neth, "Ethische Konzeptionen des Soldatenberufs im internationalen Vergleich," in *Handbuch Militärische Berufsethik. Bd. 2: Anwendungsfelder*, ed. Thomas Bohrmann, Karl-Heinz Lather, and Friedrich Lohmann (Wiesbaden: Springer Fachmedien, 2014), 379–407.
[35] Today, this competence increasingly includes intercultural competence: Friedrich Lohmann, "Interkulturelle Kompetenz innerhalb- und außerhalb militärischer Strukturen," in Bohrmann, Lather, and Lohmann, *Handbuch Militärische Berufsethik. Bd. 2: Anwendungsfelder*, 93–118.
[36] On "just peace," see introduction to Marco Hofheinz, "How to Intervene? The Vision of Just Peace and Our Responsibility to Protect," in *The Present "Just Peace / Just War" Debate*, ed. Gerard C. den Hertog and Ad de Bruijne (Leipzig: Evangelische Verlagsanstalt, 2018), 94–113.

ery, that is, selfless and courageous commitment, and the acceptance of risks related to one's function.
b) Discipline and obedience: The virtues of (self-)discipline and obedience are often understood as the soldier virtues par excellence. In many armies, "absolute" command and "blind" obedience have rightly been replaced by "command in service matters" and "qualified" obedience. This means that subordinates are obligated to obey only as long as the corresponding orders do not contradict the applicable law, the international law of war, or their own conscience. These virtues are closely interrelated with comradeship and mutual trust.
c) Loyalty and integrity: A properly understood sense of duty and comradeship gives rise to vigilant and critical loyalty and integrity. This is understood to mean the basic attitude of carrying out those orders and commands to the best of one's knowledge and conscience and with integrity that are in the spirit of a legitimate, legal mission.[37]

Baumann has personally tested these virtues in various missions as part of his military service with the Swiss army, so that he cannot simply be accused of presenting a highly sophisticated list of demands from the ethicist's ivory tower.

Virtue Ethics as Community Ethics and the Military Community

Virtues cannot be commanded. Virtues must be learned. This requires a learning community, which in turn establishes a formative context of practice. For this reason, training, education, and living together in the armed forces must be designed in such a way that they serve to acquire and deepen virtues. Personal role models also play an important part. In all of this, the special affinity of the doctrine of virtue to moral education is evident, for virtues must be acquired. A "scholastic" context, as it were, is crucial in this process. The acquisition of virtues is embedded in the ethos and morality of a concrete community. Therefore, virtue ethics always means community ethics at the same time.

In *After Virtue*, Alasdair MacIntyre diagnoses our life in a pluralistic world as a fragmented culture, where we cannot find moral agreement. He pleads for the recovery of small moral communities: "What matters ... is the construction of local forms of community within which civility and intellectual and moral life can be sustained through the new dark ages which are already upon us."[38] The question is whether military communities can represent such communities. If

---

[37] The list is a translation of the language in Baumann, *Militärethik*, 487 f.
[38] MacIntyre, *After Virtue*, 263.

one thinks of certain manifestations of violent excesses and racist incidents in the military, it certainly seems as if it were part of the "new dark age" rather than that bulwark where "the tradition of the virtues was able to survive the horrors of the last dark age."[39] Should it still be possible to run military communities here and there in an exemplary sense? Iain R. Torrance, a Scottish theologian and extra chaplain to Her Majesty Queen Elizabeth II, seems to believe so when he states:

> I believe profoundly that the Army, like the Church, is a moral community. It has nurtured particular virtues and sustained a distinctive moral character. It draws upon a long and very proud history both of courage and of service. Clearly, the question is: How may the Army's nature as a moral community be kept intact? ... How do you keep the good communities good? How do you avoid having military or paramilitary groups which are racist and neo-fascist, which bestow identity on their members, but whose members then despise the civilian population in whose name they were enlisted?[40]

In historical perspective, this assessment certainly sounds somewhat idealizing, not to say naïve. Torrance does, however, make an interesting point about learning and education theory:

> The point ... has been to suggest that there are close analogies between a healthy Church and a healthy Army. The one can learn from the other. However, [I] suggest that 'communitarianism'—the thesis that values are not abstract and universal, but emerge within a moral community—is not enough. A moral community also needs transcendent references. Just as a Church, which is inward looking, tends to become a cult, so an Army, which lives largely for itself and loses answerability, may become a poisonous and oppressive place, self-justifying, defensive and bullying, no matter how much vitality it may have.[41]

Torrance also makes another important point, which is of a more fundamental nature:

> The recovery of an ethos is prior to rules (rules are simply the crystallization of an underlying substantive ethic but they become meaningless and lose power to persuade when they are detached from their underlying narrative). However, what we are addressing here is not the elaboration of a local ethic, but a series of agreements

---

[39] Ibid.
[40] Iain R. Torrance, *Ethics and the Military Community* (Camberley, Surrey: The Strategic and Combat Studies Institute, 1998), 20, 25.
[41] Ibid., 21.

which would be international and cross culture.... Such agreements would be more exploratory and have no pretensions of being a world faith.... Part of what I am suggesting here is that there is sufficient overlap between moral communities for us to retain robust local features ... and yet have agreements in common, without lapsing into a new foundationalism.[42]

Here we have to refer to the indispensable international law. It is by no means necessary to undermine it, but to make it strong. Dieter Baumann, following Wolfgang Lienemann, emphatically points this out.[43] Wherever international law seems to have lost its binding force, for whatever reason, it is necessary to ask for further possibilities of understanding in the sense of the "overlapping consensus" advocated by Torrance, following John Rawls. The diversity of coalitional possibilities should not be underestimated, especially in the pluralistic society of late modernity.

If you will, peace ethics has to operate on three levels. First, on a subjective level—though by no means purely individualistic but rather emphatically community-related—it will be necessary to ask about the subjective conditions of peace. This level concerns virtue ethics at its most elementary, insofar as it is about character formation and a peace attitude to be won. The characteristics, abilities, and skills of the peacemakers and, as *ultima ratio*, of the persons using violence are taken into consideration here. As we have seen, the model of the *miles protector* is also located at this level, although it also affects the other levels, namely, the level of the ethics of goods and the level of the ethics of rights and duties.

The goals of political and military action, which are at stake on the second level, the ethics of goods, are just as directly affected as (international) law, which the *miles protector* stands up for. The third level—that of legal or duty ethics—is concerned with rules and norms; specifically, the peace order as a (global) legal order also must be involved. On the middle level, namely, the level of the ethics of goods, is located the "overlapping consensus" (see John Rawls), which Torrance has taken into consideration. Under the ideologically pluralistic conditions of late-modern societies, it is certainly of growing importance. Cooperation on peace and the question of peace ethics can and will take place against the background of very different ideological convictions of truth-seeking commun-

---

[42] Ibid., 36.
[43] See Wolfgang Lienemann, "International Peace as Legal Order: On the Recent Debate on 'Just Wars' and Ethics of a 'Just Peace,'" in den Hertog amd de Bruijne, *The Present "Just Peace / Just War" Debate*, 35-57.

ities.[44] In any case, a sustainable peace ethic will have to be conceptually shaped in this threefold differentiation of virtue ethics, goods ethics, and duty ethics.[45]

Under the conditions of the late modern pluralistic society, it is necessary to ask not only about the community- or society-compatible standardization of social action, but also about its underlying foundations, which shape the ethos and morality of a community of people. They are also the ones that usually make an "overlapping consensus" possible.[46] What, then, do pluralistic societies, and with them of course the liberal state, actually live and feed on? Without a return to such fundamentals, it would be unpromising, indeed naïve, to carry out the task (including the political task) of maintaining and making possible functioning communities of action with the help of rules that are generally or at least widely agreeable. The former British chief rabbi Jonathan Sacks (1948–2020) once remarked: "The more plural a society we become, the more we need to reflect on what holds us together."[47]

Outlook

The question raised by Torrance about a productive-constructive (learning) relationship between church and military should be taken up again in conclusion. In doing so, I have my own church and state context in Europe and, especially, in the Federal Republic of Germany in mind. The military chaplaincy in Germany is deliberately included in this perspective. I take up the Barmen Theological Declaration, which is particularly important for the German church as a basis for confession.[48] With reference to it, the task of the church in Protestant military chaplaincy, for example, is defined as a specific function. The military chaplaincy within the German Bundeswehr sees its primary function in "keeping alive within the military organization ... the sense of the provisional and preca-

---

[44] See Hans Joachim Iwand, *Kirche und Gesellschaft. Nachgelassene Werke Bd. 1 (Neue Folge)*, ed. Ekkehard Börsch and Hans-Iwand-Stiftung (Gütersloh: Chr. Kaiser / Gütersloher Verlagshaus, 1998), 70–74.

[45] So also, emphatically, Hans-Richard Reuter, "Gerechter Frieden!—Gerechter Krieg?," *Zeitschrift für Evangelische Ethik* 52 (2007): 163–68, at 164.

[46] See John *Rawls, Political Liberalism (New York: Columbia University Press, 1993).*

[47] Jonathan Sacks, *The Persistence of Faith: Religion, Morality and Society in a Secular Age* (London: Weidenfeld and Nicolson, 1991), 67.

[48] For the historical background, see the introduction to George Hunsinger, "The Political Views of Karl Barth," in Hunsinger, *Conversational Theology: Essays on Ecumenical, Postliberal and Political Themes, with Special Reference to Karl Barth* (London: Bloomsbury, 2015), 179–204.

rious status of military force."⁴⁹ This means that the chaplaincy corresponds to the mission of the church to remind the military, in turn, of its mission, namely, to participate as a state institution in the function of the state and "to provide for law and peace under the threat and exercise of force." In the context of Nazi rule, the Barmen Theological Declaration (1934) emphasized this in its fifth thesis:

> Scripture tells us that, in the as yet unredeemed world in which the church also exists, the state has by divine appointment the task of providing for justice and peace by means of the threat and exercise of force, according to the measure of human judgment and human ability. The church acknowledges the benefit of this divine appointment in gratitude and reverence before God. It calls to mind the Kingdom of God, God's commandment and righteousness, and thereby the responsibility both of rulers and of the ruled. It trusts and obeys the power of the Word by which God upholds all things.⁵⁰

The military is undoubtedly affected by these provisions. The military "has its legitimate place within the framework of the state monopoly on the use of force, which is functionally strictly related to the preservation of human dignity, freedom, peace, and justice."⁵¹ Because the sole basis of legitimacy of the use of force, which may only take place in emergency or borderline cases as *ultima ratio*, consists in the enforcement of law for the sake of peace, any military ethics must also be developed from the ethics of peace. The legal obligation of all force must be scrupulously observed in the performance of the soldier's tasks in the service of peace. The *miles protector* knows himself committed to this obligation in his ethos and will practice this commitment in the formative context of a virtuous army (remember Alasdair MacIntyre's "community of excellence.")

Because the military as such—just like the state—is, in the words of Barth, "spiritually blind and ignorant"⁵² and, in contrast to the church, does not know

---

49 Roger Mielke, "Die Persönlichkeit zählt. Ethisches Handeln basiert auf einer umfassenden Persönlichkeitsbildung," *Zeitschrift für Innere Führung* 63, no. 4 (2019): 11–18, at 17.

50 On Barmen 5, see Marco Hofheinz, "Gewalt und Gewalten im Kontext von Barmen V. Eine friedensethische Annäherung an das 'Just Policing,'" *Kirchliche Zeitgeschichte* 29 (2016): 149–70.

51 Mielke, "Die Persönlichkeit zählt," 17.

52 Karl Barth, "Christengemeinde und Bürgergemeinde" (1946), in idem, *Rechtfertigung und Recht. Christengemeinde und Bürgergemeinde*, 4th ed. (Zürich: TVZ, 1989), 49–82, at 50. Drawing from the blindness of the state, Daniel M. Bell outlines the consequence of placing or applying the just-war tradition in the church rather than the state: *Just War as Christian Discipleship: Recentering the Tradition in the Church Rather than the State* (Grand Rapids, MI: Brazos Press, 2009). Further, see J. Daryl Charles, *Between Pac-*

about the relationship of the entire "provisional world" to the coming kingdom of God (and indeed, within the framework of a worldview-neutral constitutional state, cannot know it), the church will remind the military, like the entire state, of the coming of the kingdom of God. What is at stake here is something like a final normative embedding of the military mission. It is up to the church to keep open this—in secular terms—empty space of state and military power. In the background is a conviction that also fundamentally concerns the "military community," and which Iain R. Torrance has pointed out: "Not being self-referring and self-justifying, but having a transcendent reference is the surest guarantor of the moral health of a community."[53]

Certainly, this is not about a subtle strategy of Christianization of the army or a latent civil-religious agenda in the national interest. Rather, it is about that "skylight" that Barth once spoke of that shines as through a window in the roof. Not only theological but military work, indeed the entire military and defense system, must take place in a space that is "open from heaven, to God's word and work, and open to heaven, to God's work and word."[54] Without this skylight, there will not be the serenity that makes soldiering somehow bearable,[55] if at all, in the face of the suffering produced by killing.[56]

---

ifism and Jihad: Just War and Christian Tradition (Downers Grove, IL: InterVarsity Press, 2005).

[53] Torrance, *Ethics and the Military Community*, 26.

[54] Karl Barth, *Einführung in die evangelische Theologie*, 3rd ed. (Zürich: TVZ, 1985), 177.

[55] Michael Walzer, in *Arguing about War* (New Haven: Yale University Press, 2004), 32, noticed that "soldiering even . . . is already a hard calling. But given the suffering it often produces, it cannot be the purpose of moral philosophy to make it easier."

[56] Karl Barth, "Das Geschenk der Freiheit. Grundlegung evangelischer Freiheit" (1953), in *Freiheit im Leben mit Gott. Texte zur Tradition evangelischer Ethik*, ed. Hans G. Ulrich (Gütersloh: Chr. Kaiser / Gütersloher Verlagshaus, 1993), 336–62, at 356.

Different Missions, Different Virtues?

Keith Joseph

When I was a sergeant in the Royal Australian Army Medical Corps, I would often be attached to various units. On one occasion I was with an infantry company headquarters advancing to contact. Suddenly, shots rang out just over our heads. We all hit the deck and froze. Was this cowardice? No, it was prudence: this was a live-fire exercise on a military training range, and no one wants to be the person pointlessly killed on a training exercise.

This experience leads to the question: are the military virtues different in war as compared to peace? Does military ethics apply differently between warlike operations and peacekeeping? This is a particularly relevant question as we consider the various purposes and missions which defense forces are now engaged in. For example, the Australian Defence Force has been engaged in the following kinds of activities over the past century:
- symmetric warfare (such as the World Wars and the Korean War);
- asymmetric warfare (Vietnam, Afghanistan);
- peacekeeping between nations (Cyprus, Sinai);
- peacekeeping within a nation (Solomon Islands);
- support for the civil power (provision of military force for internal policing);
- support for civil authorities (response to natural disasters and pandemics);
- training and peacetime administration.

Further to these now-traditional operations and tasks, there are new challenges: for example drones, cyberwarfare (which may or may not be associated with conventional warfare), the impact of social media, and the increasing presence in the battle space of private contractors and nongovernmental organizations.[1] A question arises: can the traditional military virtues and frameworks for military ethics be translated from traditional forms of warfare into the various operations

---

[1] Tom Frame and Albert Palazzo, eds., *Ethics under Fire* (Sydney: University of New South Wales Press, 2017).

and tasks that confront the military in the third decade of the twenty-first century?

Military Law, Military Virtues, and Military Ethics

The body of legal instruments applying to the military is vast. There are the laws that internally govern a defense force (military law, such as the Australian Defence Force Discipline Act 1982); rules of engagement or other orders that govern the use of force; and international laws, such as the Geneva Conventions of 1949. In general, it is hoped that military law will incorporate and realize ethical precepts; however, there is always going to be a tension between law and ethics, especially on military operations and tasks.[2]

In particular, laws need to be clear and well-defined. Those subject to the laws need to know what the laws permit and what they proscribe. In contrast, ethics deals with all sorts of shades of grey. An action that is moral in one particular circumstance may not necessarily be moral in another. For example, when could a sergeant forcibly assault a recruit? The law would say never: assault on a subordinate is a serious offense. But what if you are on the rifle range of a recruit course, and a recruit turns around to ask you a question, and in so doing brings a loaded rifle around so that it starts to point away from the targets and could soon be pointing at other recruits? Physical restraint of the recruit may be the quickest and safest way to sort out the situation, even if it involves forcibly touching the recruit without consent. Legally speaking it may well be a breach of the Defence Force Discipline Act 1982, Section 34; but you would be hard put to say that it was unethical, given the need to protect the safety of others.

Consequently, we are not primarily concerned here with military law but rather with those things that make for right decision-making—that is, right character and right judgment. The military virtues are character traits considered appropriate for those who serve in the military; military ethics refers to right decision-making.

The idea of military virtue is not new: it can be traced back at least to Aristotle and the four cardinal virtues of prudence, temperance, justice, and courage. In recent decades, virtue ethics has made something of a comeback, thanks in

---

[2] "Operations" has a specific meaning in military usage, and generally refers to deployment of a force for warlike operations, peacekeeping operations, operations in support of the civil power, and humanitarian operations. In contrast, training exercises are not "operations" but may be considered a military tasking, as would a myriad of other military activities, especially in peacetime.

part to Alasdair Macintyre's *After Virtue*, published in 1981.³ This emphasis on virtue has been picked up in military ethics: for example, a rather long list of virtues is given in the recent book *Military Virtues*,⁴ which illustrates each virtue by a particular case study: justice, obedience, loyalty, courage, wisdom, honesty, integrity, perseverance, temperance, patience, humility, compassion, and professionalism.

Other versions of virtue's application to the military are a little shorter. For example, the Australian Army claims the following five values:⁵ service, courage, respect, integrity, and excellence. Aristotle's cardinal virtues appear largely incorporated in the Australian list. Certainly courage, justice (here covered by "respect" and "integrity"), and prudence (as part of "excellence") seem to be covered.

There has been a renaissance of virtue ethics in the late twentieth century as a response to the problems faced by traditional metaethical frameworks, such as deontology and consequentialism. It is supposed that having the right character would enable right decisions about moral issues. However, there are some weaknesses to such an approach, not the least being that some way of making rules and assessing consequences is still necessary for making considered ethical decisions. Accordingly, military values and military ethics can be distinguished from each other. They are both necessary for good ethical decision-making, but by themselves they are insufficient.⁶

The dominant ethical theory in the area of military ethics continues to be just-war theory. This has an ancient lineage, with elements found in early Christian theologians and philosophers, such as Augustine of Hippo and Thomas Aquinas. It is based on the idea that war is evil but sometimes permissible, and the theory attempts to set out the moral rules that apply to war and mitigate its evil. Traditionally there were two basic sets of considerations—*jus ad bellum* and *jus in bello*, with a number of applicable criteria:⁷

Jus ad bellum (justice in going to war) required (1) just cause, (2) legitimate authority (usually a state actor, but more recently nonstate actors, such as rev-

---

3   Alasdair Macintyre, *After Virtue: A Study in Moral Theology* (Notre Dame, IN: University of Notre Dame Press, 1981).
4   Michael Skerker, David Whetham, and Don Carrick, eds., *Military Virtues* (Havant, UK: Howgate Publishing, 2019).
5   Australian Army, "Our values & contract," https://www.army.gov.au/our-people/our-values-contract.
6   Peter Olsthoorn, "Virtue Ethics in the Military," *The Handbook of Virtue Ethics*, ed. Stan van Hooft and Nicole Saunders (Durham, UK: Acumen Publishing, 2013), 365–74.
7   S.v. "War," *Stanford Encyclopedia of Philosophy*, https://plato.stanford.edu/entries/war/.

olutionaries against an unjust regime),[8] (3) right intention, (4) reasonable prospects of success, (5) proportionality, and (6) last resort (necessity).

Jus in bello (justice in the conduct of war) required (1) discrimination (between legitimate military targets and noncombatants, who are not legitimate targets), (2) proportionality (the idea that in war there will be unintended but foreseeable harms, which must be proportional to the military objectives), and (3) necessity (doing the least harm possible).

More recently the idea of *jus post bellum* (justice after war) has also been posited: this is the idea that there needs to be a moral transition from war to peace. The lack of a workable exit strategy from a conflict would be an example of a breach of *jus post bellum*.

The above criteria indicate that (at least in theory) the principles of just-war theory apply to warlike operations, both symmetric and asymmetric. At the time of the preparation for the invasion of Iraq, in late 2002 and early 2003, I was peripherally engaged in some discussions in the Australian Defence Force about whether the proposed operation met the requirements of just-war theory,[9] and some possible consequences of dissent about this matter.[10] There was little doubt that some elements of *jus ad bellum* were met: Australia was a sovereign state and therefore a legitimate authority; and there were reasonable prospects of success. There was possibly right intention, in that the aim was to put in place a democratic regime rather than colonial occupation of Iraq. However, the putative cause for the war—that Saddam Hussein possessed weapons of mass destruction—seemed unlikely on the available evidence, and consequently there was not just cause.

The Iraq War is a good example of how just-war theory could, in principle, determine the morality of going to war. The other aspect of just-war theory concerns the conduct of war and what happens thereafter. In some wars (perhaps surprisingly), it appears that *jus in bello* can be put in place to the benefit of all: for example, the war between Argentina and the United Kingdom in 1982 appears to have largely been fought in accordance with all these principles:

---

[8] The Geneva Protocols of 1977 were drawn up specifically with a view to conflicts such as that going on at that time in Rhodesia and South Africa against racist regimes, with a view to protecting the opponents of such unjust regimes. This extension of the Geneva Conventions to cover nonstate actors parallels a move in just-war theory away from the traditional view that only sovereign states were legitimate authorities for the conduct of war.

[9] Tom Frame, *Living by the Sword: The Ethics of Armed Intervention* (Sydney: University of New South Wales Press, 2003), 24–25.

[10] Major Keith Joseph, "The Ethics of Selective Conscientious Objection," *Australian Defence Force Journal*, 160 (May 2003): 11–18.

1. Discrimination: by and large both sides refrained from attacking civilian targets, and the war was fought within the confines of a zone of warlike operations in the Falkland Islands and surrounding seas.
2. Proportionality: civilian casualties were very light, even in the final battle for Stanley.
3. Necessity: again, overall casualties were light, and strict observance of the Geneva Convention by both sides meant that prisoners of war were well treated and ultimately repatriated, hospitals and hospital ships were respected, and subsequently there was little loss of life apart from that necessitated by military actions.

As previously noted, the nature of warfare is continuing to evolve. Nevertheless, attempts are being made to continue to apply just-war theory to areas as diverse as cyberwarfare[11] and drones.[12]

In brief, there appears to be ready guidance about applying military virtues and military ethics to military tasks. But how does this actually work in practice, given the various roles in which military forces can now be used?

Military Ethics and Military Virtues in War

Symmetric War

Symmetric war is the paradigmatic example of military activity. It is easy to see how virtues such as loyalty, courage, and prudence feature here. A good soldier will show courage, will be loyal to his superiors and his mates, and will make a realistic assessment of the consequences of his actions. Having said that, the willingness to risk one's life—courage—is often more valued than prudence! Victoria Crosses are not won by avoiding risk.

It is possible that in modern warfare some specialties will have less need for courage—for example those operating drones or conducting cyberwarfare are not necessarily exposed to great personal danger. However, for them moral courage may be more important, and certainly they will require justice and prudence as they calculate the likely consequences of what they do.

---

[11] Klaus-Gerd Giesen, "Towards a Theory of Just Cyberwar," *Journal of Information Warfare* 12, no. 1 (2013): 22–31.

[12] Stimson Center, Ethics and Law Working Group, *Working Group Report* (Washington, DC, 2015). This report is primarily concerned with legal issues around the use of drones by the United States, but consciously invokes just-war criteria, such as proportionality and distinction (discrimination) as their ethical basis.

Just-war theory has its paradigm of application in symmetric warfare. Even more modern forms of warfare, such as cyberwarfare and the use of drones, can be assessed for their proportionality and necessity. Of course, just-war requirements are often ignored. The current war in Ukraine is an obvious example of a war that is not just in its purpose or conduct, at least with regard to Russia's actions. Nevertheless, just-war theory does give us a moral framework within which to assess the morality of both sides' actions, and to make judgments that Russia has behaved immorally.

Asymmetric War

Asymmetry refers to the type of warfare in which one side is technically more powerful than the other, and therefore the weaker side reverts to other forms of combat in which the technical prowess of the more powerful side cannot be fully brought to bear. Guerilla warfare is an example of asymmetric warfare waged against a more powerful opponent, usually when the guerillas are on home ground and can obtain support from a generally sympathetic host population.

Such warfare creates more strain on the exercise of the traditional virtues and ethical framework. For example, it is often harder to determine who combatants are, as guerillas can melt into the local population, often do not wear specific uniforms, and operate from bases that might be close to or within civilian population centers. These circumstances test the patience of opposing soldiers, who cannot easily identify the enemy and may be more tempted to commit atrocities. The recent Australian experience in Afghanistan shows how corrosive this situation can be. The high incidence of posttraumatic stress disorder and allegations of atrocities, such as those detailed in the report by the Australian Defence Force Inspector-General,[13] are due at least in part to possible unlawful killing of noncombatants in circumstances where their combatant status was unclear. In these circumstances, it might perhaps be said that the need for prudence and justice come to the fore: the ability to deal justly with civilians and to discriminate accurately between those who are combatants and those who are not becomes very important.

Likewise, there are increased difficulties in the practical application of just-war theory. Even if the cause is just (as it arguably was with the Coalition and Australian intervention in Afghanistan in late 2001), the conduct of the war can be problematic. Proportionality is difficult: when attacking a guerilla base in a

---

[13] Inspector-General of the Australian Defence Force, *Afghanistan Inquiry Report* (Canberra: Commonwealth of Australia, 2020). This report is more commonly known as the Brereton Report, after its lead author, Major General Paul Brereton, who is an Army Reserve officer and also a justice of the New South Wales Supreme Court.

village, how much "collateral damage" is acceptable? Is the destruction of infrastructure to impede the enemy acceptable, even though it will also harm civilians? Such decisions are often difficult. Nevertheless, in spite of these difficulties just-war theory continues in use, and it is argued that an appropriate response is to refine criteria such as discrimination, to enable better distinguishing between combatants and noncombatants.[14]

Military virtues and military ethics, even if stretched and challenged, appear still basically the same for symmetric and asymmetric warfare. Not every war is fought in a desert or in the almost unpopulated South Atlantic, where there are few civilians, and legitimate targets are easy to identify. In World War II, the challenges of applying just-war theory were immeasurably greater when fighting in or above populated urban areas, compared to the desert or on the oceans. Issues of urban warfare in symmetric warfare can be just as difficult as those of asymmetric warfare. Asymmetric warfare does not invalidate the framework of military ethics, but it does show how just-war criteria can be much harder to apply.

Training and Peacetime Administration

At the other end of the scale from all-out war is the peacetime military. Regarding ethics, just-war theory has little to say about peacetime activities. However, there are still ethical considerations, as there are in any large disciplined organization subject to government direction. It is just that these ethical issues do not particularly concern the use of organized force.

Activities in peacetime also evoke a very different sense of the military virtues. Physical courage is not especially required, but moral courage is an interesting quality to invoke in a bureaucratic system with all its checks and balances. Safety is encouraged, while risk-taking is not. Thus, prudence probably is more valued than it would be in warfare, while courage is not especially valued. Accordingly, while the military virtues are not absent, they are exercised with a different emphasis. That which is a virtue in war may not be a virtue in peace. But what about that which lies between peacetime and warfare?

---

[14] Isaac Taylor, "Just War Theory and the Military Response to Terrorism," *Social Theory and Practice* 43, no. 3 (Oct. 2017): 717–40.

Just-War Theory between War and Peace

Peacekeeping and Overseas Policing

Unlike peace enforcement—which is more akin to asymmetric warfare—peacekeeping and overseas policing aim to keep a desired peace rather than enforce a peace that may not be desired.

Sometimes peacekeeping is aimed at keeping the peace between two previously warring parties, such as the police peacekeeping in Cyprus, which has been present since 1974 and maintains a line between Turkish and Greek Cypriots, and the Multinational Force and Observers (MFO) in the Sinai keeping the peace between Egypt and Israel. In this task, the peacekeepers are not using force, so while their presence appears to be in accord with *jus ad bellum*—just cause, right intention, legitimate authority, etc.—the moral principles of *jus in bello* seem less applicable, though the use of arms for self-defense of the peacekeepers would require application of the principle of necessity.

Another type of peacekeeping is that of restoring and maintaining order. A good example of this is the Regional Assistance Mission to the Solomon Islands (RAMSI), an international peacekeeping force that entered the Solomon Islands in 2003 to end a five-year period of internal conflict at the request of the government of the Solomon Islands.[15] If we apply just-war theory to this situation, the test for *jus ad bellum* was met: the cause was just (restoration of internal peace); the actors were legitimate authorities; the intention to restore peace and build up democratic governance was right; and there were reasonable prospects of success. It was proportional (the forces used were sufficient to achieve the aims). However, the last condition of *jus ad bellum*—last resort—is more difficult to assess. In the case of RAMSI, it could be argued that previous attempts to establish peace (such as the Townsville Peace Agreement of 2000) had failed, and therefore calling on RAMSI was the best option. In peacekeeping, however, intervention might be appropriate before it becomes a last resort, on the grounds that a small amount of force applied early might prevent a deteriorating situation that would require a heavier use of force later.

The principles of *jus in bello* can also be applied with some sense. While I was serving with RAMSI in April 2006, there were large riots in the capital, Honiara, which burned down a considerable portion of the CBD known as Chinatown. There were approximately thirty Australian infantry soldiers, and about two hundred overseas police officers available. The soldiers were not employed in riot control; instead, they were given the task of securing vital infrastructure, especially the international airport. This was appropriate: armed soldiers con-

---

[15] The author was a member of RAMSI as an administrator with the Australian Federal Police from 2004 to 2006.

fronting rioters would have escalated the situation and caused fatalities, and would not have been proportionate.

The next decision came when the rioters forced the police back from key commercial properties, such as the Pacific Casino Hotel, which was then burned to the ground. There was some criticism of the police because of this, but I think in this the police did act proportionately. To have prevented the burning would have required the use of weapons, which would have resulted in injuries and quite likely in deaths for both the rioters and the police. Buildings can be repaired or replaced, but not lives. This again fits in nicely with just-war concepts of proportionality.

However, the issue of discrimination was a lot harder. As RAMSI was not a warlike operation, the distinction between military targets and civilian population did not exist. Rather, rioters and any militants who attacked the police force were classed as criminals, not combatants. They were then treated as potential criminal suspects under the existing law of the Solomon Islands. This mean that the concept of "discrimination" (distinguishing between legitimate military targets and the civilian population) was moot.

Peacekeeping in this kind of environment is more akin to policing. There have been attempts to extend just-war theory to the area of policing, particularly the just-war criteria for proportionality and minimization of harm.[16] Similarly, there have been attempts to extend a policing idea of just-war theory to the functions of asymmetric warfare and police enforcement that often go with policing in the war against terrorism.[17] Therefore it is not unreasonable to view the policing functions of peacekeeping as an extension of just-war theory in relation to the principles of proportionality and necessity.

Military virtues also continue to be relevant. Courage will be required from time to time, such as for police (especially those who are unarmed) who are required to carry out their duties during a riot. Prudence—for example, being able to determine that buildings should be sacrificed to save lives—was also a virtue seen in Honiara in April 2006.

---

[16] Tobias L. Winwright, "Two Rival Versions of Just War Theory and the Presumption against Harm in Policing," *The Annual of the Society of Christian Ethics* 18 (1998): 221–39.

[17] Tobias L. Winwright, "Just Cause and Preemptive Strikes in the War on Terrorism: Insights from a Just-Policing Perspective," *Journal of the Society of Christian Ethics* 26 (2006): 157–81.

Support to the Civil Power

In liberal democracies, such as Australia, the military is sometimes used for policing functions—for example, if the civilian police forces are unable to cope with a major breakdown of law and order. In Australia, the legal basis for such military support of civil power is Section 119 of the Constitution and Section 51 of the Defence Act 1903.[18] This authority has been rarely invoked in Australia. Interestingly enough, most of the principles of *jus ad bellum* still apply: there must be a good reason (a just cause) necessitating the military intervention, and it still needs to be authorized by sovereign actors—in the case of a federated nation like Australia, by both the state and federal governments. Likewise, there must be a right intention—the restoration of law and order—and the prospect of a successful intervention must also be considered as part of the decision-making process. Appropriate forces must be used under the principle of proportionality—for example, the use of artillery to suppress street rioters is unlikely to be proportional. But again, as for peacekeeping overseas, the idea of last resort is a bit malleable. Limited early intervention is likely to be preferable to later large-scale intervention.

Because there is no military target, *jus in bello* becomes rather harder to apply in this kind of situation. As in peacekeeping, those who violently oppose the military force under these circumstances are likely to be considered criminals rather than combatants. Proportionality and necessity, however, are still important moral considerations. Moreover, just as it is possible to apply just-war theory to policing, so it is possible to apply it at least in part to the use of the military for police functions.

Support for the Civil Authorities

Unlike support of the civil power, these types of operations are aimed at enhancing the abilities of the civil authorities rather than protecting them against violence. Good examples are support during emergencies, such as natural disasters, and more recently many nations have seen defense assets used during the COVID pandemic for nonmilitary ends.

In this type of operation, it is not anticipated that force will need to be used. Accordingly, just-war theory seems to have little application here; it is more akin to training and peacetime activities rather than warfare, peacekeeping, or polic-

---

[18] Elizabeth Ward, "Call out the Troops: An Examination of the Legal Basis for Australian Defence Force Involvement in 'Non-Defence' Matters," Parliament of Australia, Research Paper 8, 1997–98, https://www.aph.gov.au/About_Parliament/Parliamentary_Departments/Parliamentary_Library/pubs/rp/RP9798/98rp08.

ing operations. Likewise with the military virtues: courage may well be required (for example, in rescue missions), but prudence is likely to dominate.

Conclusion

This brief survey has considered whether there is a commonality of military virtues and military ethics across the various operations and tasks to which the military may be assigned. In recent years the ethical strains of different forms of operation have been noted. However, just-war theory seems to continue to be applicable across the various forms of operations and tasks, as are the traditional military virtues, such as courage, justice, and prudence.

The relative emphasis on aspects of just-war theory and virtues does shift, however, from operation to operation. The most obvious example is courage, which is highly regarded in war, less so in peace. In contrast, prudence becomes a significant virtue in peacetime. Likewise, just-war theory tends to be less applicable on the whole as military operations become less warlike. Discrimination becomes a significant issue in asymmetric warfare but tends to change character significantly or perhaps even disappear during policing and peacekeeping operations. Still, proportionality remains a significant consideration.

The various forms of operations and tasks involved do throw up interesting or even unique issues. However, the general framework of military virtues and military ethics, if applied with some nuances, still remains an overall framework capable of guiding thought and decision-making.

From the Playing Field to the Battlefield: Does Sport in the Military Promote the Formation of a Specific Character?

Martin Elbe

> Most of us will never know the full horrors of combat. Many servicemen and women suffer life-changing injuries, visible or otherwise, whilst serving their country. How do these men and women find the motivation to move on and not be defined by their injuries?
> —Invictus Games Foundation, 2021

Introduction

On the morning of July 1, 1916, the British Army began its attack against the German front line. Company B of the 8th East Surreys led the charge by throwing two footballs out of the trench and, rushing forward, driving them toward the enemy, running against machine-gun fire from the German positions. The company commander, who threw the first ball "into play," was Captain Neville, who did not survive the attack. On that first day of the offensive, 19,240 British soldiers died.[1] This example of British sportsmanship illustrates the basic question to be asked of military sports training: *To what extent does sport in the military help foster a particular set of character traits, values, and behaviors?*

The graphic artist Gerd Arntz got to the heart of this connection in his engraving *Sport*, from 1938. In the upper left part of the picture, a dapper young woman applauds an athlete in sports shorts who is jumping over a hurdle. In the lower right part of the picture, the same figure, now dressed in a steel helmet and uniform, jumps over a barbed-wire barrier, holding a hand grenade in his hand, and behind the wire is a cross over a grave. *So is sport a means of seducing youth—toward military docility?*

This question leads to a third narrative. In 2013, Prince Harry (the Duke of Sussex) attended the Warrior Games in the United States and was deeply im-

---

1   Iain Adams, "The Great European Cup-Tie Final, East Surreys v Bavarians, Kick Off at Zero, No Referee," *Soccer and Society* 21 (2020): 1–13.

pressed by how much "the power of sport can help physically, psychologically and socially those suffering from injuries and illness."[2] At that moment, the idea of creating an international sports movement for soldiers and veterans suffering from serious injuries or illnesses was born. It was obvious that participation in a sports event could inspire and personally contribute to the rehabilitation of those affected by such a fate and bring this group of people into the public eye. At the first Invictus Games, in 2014, more than four hundred disabled athletes from thirteen countries competed and sixty-five thousand spectators watched the games in London. Four Games later, the 2018 Invictus Games in Sydney drew 105,000 spectators. In 2023, the Invictus Games will be held in Düsseldorf under the motto "A Home for Respect." This is meant to send a message of hospitality, appreciation, and responsibility for the injured servicemen and women and veterans. Obviously, this is a success story. Sports seem to be an important aspect for injured soldiers to regain confidence in themselves and for society to show respect and appreciation. Sports have a great impact on staying healthy and getting healthy again—but also to convey values. But this seems to be exactly a new aspect in the relationship between sport and the military and leads to the third question to be addressed in this text: *To what extent is sport suitable to convey values?*

This chapter answers these three questions. To that end, the first step will be to analyze the military as an educational system, followed by an examination of the extent to which service in the military contributes to character formation. The fourth section discusses how values are conveyed in sports and the military. The final section draws a conclusion.

The Military as an Educational System

Most often, the strengthening of body and mind is associated with sports and placed under a historical connotation, often citing the Roman poet Juvenal: *mens sana in corpore sano*—a healthy mind in a healthy body. However, if Juvenal's Tenth Satire is quoted correctly, it says *orandum est ut sit mens sana in corpore sano*—pray that there be a sound mind in a sound body. This translation makes it clear that health is something to pray for, not a simple causal relationship. At the beginning of the twentieth century, Juvenal's sentence was interpreted as a call for moderate exercise. This view was countered by Pierre de Coubertin, founder of the modern Olympic Games, who proposed the motto *mens fervida in corpore lacertoso*. For Coupertin, it should be a fiery spirit in a muscular body. The fighter who overcomes resistance became the ideal, and sport was seen as the means

---

[2] Invictus Games Foundation, "The Invictus Games story," https://invictusgamesfoundation.org/foundation/story/.

to train this.[3] Schools and the military were expected to provide this training, strengthening both character and body. In the United States, a manual for the military prepared by Edward Frank Allen[4] was circulated, propagating a broad "sports program"—quite in the original sense of the word—as a comprehensive approach to recreation, with physical training as only one component of all-round care, alongside the provision of consumer goods in the post exchange, but also singing, reading, and other diversions together.

In the German Empire, as Maria Derenda makes clear,[5] the declaration of the military as the "school of the [male] nation" at the end of the nineteenth century became part of an educational program to militarize society. Accordingly, the question "Have you served?" served to clarify social claims to participation. The answer made clear whether men had undergone training in discipline, bearing, and socially demanded value education and were thus reliable—finally, whether they could expect appropriate respect within the framework of their respective social class.

However, Derenda's article also makes clear that this expectation continues to have repercussions today—at least to the extent that addressing the topic is still a recommended aspect of teaching history in schools today. Reflective engagement with the topic, however, takes a different direction than it did at the height of societal militarization. Ernst Jünger's 1930 call for total mobilization, which was to begin in the nursery,[6] had its precursor a century earlier in a widespread children's Christmas carol by Hoffmann von Fallersleben:

> Tomorrow Santa comes,
> Comes with his gifts.
> Drum, pipe, and gun
> Flag and saber and a lot more,
> Yes, a whole war's army
> I'd like to have!

---

[3] Arndt Krüger, "Mens fervida in corpore lacertoso oder Coubertins Ablehnung der schwedischen Gymnastik," Proceedings of the HISPA 8th International Congress, Uppsala, 1979, 145–53.

[4] Edward Frank Allen, *Keeping Our Fighters Fit for War and After* (New York: Century, 1918).

[5] Maria Derenda, "'Ham'se jedient?' Das Militär als 'Schule der (männlichen) Nation,'" *Praxis Geschichte* 1 (2019): 18–26.

[6] Frank Reichherzer, *"Alles ist Front!": Wehrwissenschaften in Deutschland und die Bellifizierung der Gesellschaft vom Ersten Weltkrieg bis in den Kalten Krieg* (Paderborn: Schöningh, 2012).

Disciplining through sports in schools and sports clubs, however, cannot be reduced to early military education through toys, clothing, and songs, but was part of the comprehensive educational program in the wake of the Enlightenment. It is different with the scout movement, which simulated already for children a life in the field and military scouting. The foundation of the Pathfinder movement by the British general Robert Baden Powell, in 1907, combined the childlike urge for movement with the desire for adventure and military structures. This program was further reinforced in totalitarian regimes by the duplication of the scout movement in the Hitler Youth of National Socialist Germany, and later in the German Democratic Republic (GDR, East Germany) with the Pioneer Organization Ernst Thälmann and the Free German Youth (FDJ).[7] In summary, it is not sport but a comprehensively militaristic socialization that brings youth to the military.

From a historical perspective, one can say that sport was an important part of training in the German armies before and during the First World War.[8] It was assumed that sport helped to train character and body, and thus sport became an instrument of both broad military training and special training. Military sports were supposed to educate to a higher level of independence on the battlefield and thus to reflect the increased demands of modern war with performance incentives and free-play elements. The previous training system had been based on discipline, instruction, and supervision, but was now to be supplemented by techniques of military self-direction, which also changed the image of the soldier. He was now granted the aspect of self-initiative, which was to be integrated into military training through sports. The ideal was a soldier who was basically obedient and willing to perform, who could at the same time act independently, and who accepted the military order as a guiding principle and framework for action.[9]

In the military, character building is the subject of soldierly education. For the Bundeswehr, this is made clear by the military disciplinary code in its section on educational measures:

> Educational measures serve the purpose of soldierly education.... Soldierly education promotes the development of the personality with the aim of maintaining discipline and obedience out of insight, to strengthen the will to serve and to put aside one's own interests in favor of the community.... Soldierly education strengthens

---

[7] Jakob Benecke, *Außerschulische Jugendorganisationen. Eine sozialisationstheoretische und bildungshistorische Analyse* (Weinheim: Beltz, 2020).

[8] Christoph Nübel, "'Die Waffe Mensch'. Sport, Ausbildung und soldatische Selbstständigkeit in der Zeit des Ersten Weltkrieges," *MGZ–Militärgeschichtliche Zeitschrift* 80, no. 2 (2021): 261–87.

[9] Ibid.

soldierly order, discipline, and comradely cohesion... . Soldierly education shapes the self-image of soldiers and enables them to fulfill their mission with conviction—even under the special stresses of deployment... . Educational deficiencies are basically caused by the insufficient will of the soldiers.[10]

Character Formation in the Context of Sport and the Military

Character is a multilayered term that can take on different meanings in everyday language as well as in science. Basically, character refers to a sum of qualities inherent to a specific entity. With regard to people, the concept of character often has a normative aspect, which aims at moral, socially expected behavior—whereby the perspective of social expectation is tied to the social positions of the participants in an interaction. For example, greeting behavior in the German military is regulated as a function of the ranks of the participants, and the concrete fulfillment of these requirements is interpreted as an expression of a respective disposition of character. Character thus has a socializing aspect and appears malleable.

The idea of the connection between character formation and education is also effective in the sports concept of the Bundeswehr:

> The overall effect of sport in the military service on the whole person is to improve and maintain performance. It promotes the development of the individual's abilities and compensates for his or her weaknesses. In addition, it strengthens the sense of community and provides valuable contributions to health maintenance and leisure activities... . Sport in the Bundeswehr is an important component of the education, personality development and training of soldiers and civilian personnel of the Bundeswehr.[11]

These two quotations from Bundeswehr manuals refer to personality development, not to character formation. Here a further development of earlier language use can be seen, when the character forces to be formed were explicitly addressed. The idea of adult education as a task of the military, however, remains unchanged and is to be promoted, particularly through service sport.

Against this background, it becomes clear that the purpose and understanding of sport in the military are subject to a functional-instrumental conception

---

[10] Bundesministerium der Verteidigung (BMVg -), *A-2160/6, Zentrale Dienstvorschrift. Wehrdisziplinarordnung und Wehrbeschwerdeordnung*, Version 4.1 (Berlin: BMVg, 2021).
[11] Kdo SKB—Kommando Streitkräftebasis, *A1-224/0-1. Zentralvorschrift. Sport und Körperliche Leistungsfähigkeit* (Bonn: Kdo SKB, 2017), 8.

and practice, which have an effect from the everyday sports activities of average service members to top-class sport as the life of internationally competitive soldier athletes.[12] The goal remains character building, which is also of central importance for the officer corps. This aim not only tested the previous educational practice in the selection of officer candidates through an extensive sports test but also sought to deepen the common sports practice in general sports training and in officer sports. Compared to character traits, more quantifiable criteria such as knowledge, ability, and performance only slowly gained importance, as Peter Donaldson noted for the British Army at the beginning of the twentieth century,[13] but this was also true for the Bundeswehr and for other armies well into the twentieth century and—as the quotes from the relevant regulations have shown—continues to have an impact today.

In Germany, too, an extensive discussion had developed in the military and in print media in the 1920 s that emphasized the importance of sports for the military, and as a result, sports training occupied an increasingly larger space in military training.[14] In addition to physical preparation for combat, it was character strengths that were specifically required of officers. This was also reflected in corresponding regulations on troop leadership, which was described as an activity based on character and skill, as art and creative design, which, despite a systematic approach, did not tolerate rigid specifications and could not be presented in an exhaustive manner—according to the divisional regulation on troop leadership of 1917.[15] The general need for a stronger emphasis on sport in military training was derived from the experiences of the First World War: "War has taught us the necessity of sport. War demands from the soldier a body accustomed to exertion and privation, nerves of steel, determination and independent action, courage and joy in danger and victory; whole men, men of action, fighters. Sport gives us all this."[16]

---

[12] Frank Reichherzer and Martin Elbe, "Verteidigung oder Angriff über die Flanke? Perspektiven auf Militär und Sport," in *Der Sport des Militärs. Perspektiven aus Forschung, Lehre und Praxis*, ed. Martin Elbe and Frank Reichherzer (Potsdam: ZMSBw, 2022, forthcoming).

[13] Peter Donaldson, "'We Are Having a Very Enjoyable Game': Britain, Sport and the South African War, 1899–1902," *War in History* 25, no. 1 (2018): 4–25.

[14] Herkules Reimann, "Sport in der Bundeswehr. Zur Geschichte, Struktur und Funktion des Militärsports in der Bundesrepublik Deutschland" (Diss., Münster: Westfälische Wilhelms-Universität, 2015).

[15] Martin Rink, "Krieg, Spiel, Kriegsspiel—und die Frage nach dem spielerischen (Un)Ernst," in Elbe and Reichherzer, *Der Sport des Militärs*.

[16] Johannes Runge, "Die Leibesübungen in der Reichswehr," in *Stadion. Das Buch von Sport und Turnen/Gymnastik und Spiel*, ed. Carl Diem, Hans Sippel, and Franz Breithaupt (Berlin: Neufeld & Henius, 1928), 432–37, at 435.

Shortly after the First World War, sport was seen as a *means of advertising and communication* for the Reichswehr, and military sports clubs were founded in order to circumvent the personnel restrictions of the Treaty of Versailles. However, another reason for the emphasis on sport was the poor performance of soldiers of the German Army in comparative competitions with civilian athletes.[17] As Peter Tauber points out,[18] specialization in certain sports can be seen in this context, which should be avoided for military sports—after all, these were meant to strengthen a basic physical and character disposition rather than expertise in individual sports. However, until the end of World War II, athletes in the military in the German armed forces always found opportunities to practice their sport (for example, soccer) outside of service sports, and even to compete within the military and in competitions with civilian teams.[19]

After World War II, different developments took effect in the two German states until 1991. In the East German National People's Army, sport was cultivated as military physical training (MKE), with particular importance and effectiveness attributed to early morning sport—immediately after waking. Although there were concerns about health-damaging influences of the immediate change of stress between rest and athletic exertion, these were ignored, especially since early-morning sport was thought to have a character-forming and personality-building effect.[20] As Rüdiger Wenzke has shown,[21] even in Schwedt military prison, early morning exercise had to be performed by the prisoners—this did not exist in any other prison in the GDR.

On the other hand, as Tauber has shown, "In the Bundeswehr, sport was part of training from the very beginning. Sports scientists and educators turned their attention to the question of which sports were suitable and how soldiers could be encouraged to engage in 'off-duty sports.' Here, too, the claim was not to train the body alone."[22] According to Lutz Bresser,[23] soldiers in the West German Bun-

---

[17] Reimann, "Sport in der Bundeswehr."
[18] Peter Tauber, *Vom Schützengraben auf den grünen Rasen. Der Erste Weltkrieg und die Entwicklung des Sports in Deutschland* (Berlin: Lit, 2008), 87.
[19] Markwart Herzog, "'Sportliche Soldatenkämpfer im großen Kriege' 1939–1945. Fußball im Militär–Kameradschaftsentwürfe repräsentativer Männlichkeit," in *Fußball zur Zeit des Nationalsozialismus. Alltag–Medien–Künste–Stars*, ed. Markwart Herzog (Stuttgart: Kohlhammer, 2008), 67–148.
[20] Joachim Tappert and Herbert Jodl, *Körperertüchtigung und Sport für die sozialistische Landesverteidigung* (Berlin: Militärverlag, 1973).
[21] Rüdiger Wenzke, *Ab nach Schwedt! Die Geschichte des DDR-Militärstrafvollzuges*, 3rd ed. (Berlin: Christoph Links, 2016).
[22] Peter Tauber, "'Schon das Spiel ist Kampf, Krieg im kleinen ...' Sport und Militär von der Antike bis heute," *Militärgeschichte. Zeitschrift für historische Bildung* 3 (2019): 4–9, at 8.

deswehr should be educated as physical, mental, and spiritual personalities who fit into the military community with a clean character. Bresser's 1959 *Sportbuch für die Bundeswehr* (Sports book for the German armed forces) was intended to support instructors in finding an appropriate tone for sports training in the Bundeswehr and in taking leave of the usual barracks tone in character building and physical training. Young soldiers were now no longer seen as compliant recruits who had surrendered their individuality and civic rights by joining the Bundeswehr, but as citizens in uniform. Accordingly, sports training also had to see itself as part of the education of adults to become mature soldiers, who were to develop their character and personality in the context of political education and life-skills classes as well as in sports training. As Tauber points out,[24] the objectives at that time were hardly different from the requirements for today's sports education. Healthy performance, the experience of personal-best performance, and the individual physical and character development to a mature personality were the goal then[25] and still are today.

We should note that the concept of character in the social sciences and psychology lost considerable popularity in the second half of the twentieth century and was increasingly displaced by concepts of personality (with respect to individuals) and cultural attributions (with respect to groups, organizations, and societies). This is also true for the discussion in sports science.[26] However, character is experiencing a renaissance, specifically in the U.S. approach to *character education*—now as a competence to act morally.[27] This approach also applies to sport, which, on one hand, conveys the experience of competence through the performance of the body and, on the other hand, addresses the cognitive disposition with regard to one's own effectiveness in the context of action with others. This connection points to another important link between sport and war: the aspects of mimetics, simulation, or emulation.[28] Sporting competition is meant to prepare for martial combat in terms of physical ability and strength of character,[29] with sport representing that which cannot be concretely represented, and

---

[23] Lutz Besser, *Sportbuch für die Bundeswehr* (Darmstadt: Wehr und Wissen, 1959).
[24] Tauber, "'Schon das Spiel ist Kampf, Krieg im kleinen.'"
[25] Bresser, *Sportbuch für die Bundeswehr*.
[26] Brenda Bredemeier and David Shield, *Sports and Character Development*, Research Digest, series 7, no. 1. (Washington, DC: President's Council on Physical Fitness and Sport, 2006).
[27] William Damon, *Bringing in a New Era in Character Education* (Stanford, CA: Hoover Institution Press, 2022).
[28] Frank Reichherzer, "Offiziere. Zwei essayistische Erkundungen in die Grenzregionen von Arbeit und freier Zeit um 1900," *Werkstatt Geschichte* 78 (2018/19): 9–27.
[29] Norbert Elias and Eric Dunning, *Sport im Zivilisationsprozess. Studien zur Figurationssoziologie* (Münster: Lit Verlag, 1983).

thus creating a space of experience that not only provides concepts of action for uncertainty (the "fog of war") but also trains assertiveness.[30]

Sport should thus help train competencies that strengthen the military through the disposition of soldiers to act. However, as the first of our examples at the beginning of the chapter has shown (the "soccer game of Surreys"), this concept transports us back to the battlefields of the twentieth century and makes military action seem playful and sporty, which has also been reflected in war reportage and (another volte-face) feeds back to the coverage of sporting events when talking about attack or defense in team sports.[31] The intertwining of the military and sport via the direct instrumentality of military sport is clearly evident in the practice of the armed forces' involvement in elite sport. This expansion of the military field of action beyond its core tasks, such as national and alliance defense, can be interpreted as a form of militarization and—in the case of the Bundeswehr—as a measure to increase its acceptance among the population.[32] However, the extent to which sport is actually important for the character formation of soldiers, or whether it positively influences socialization in the respective groups, has not been empirically proven.[33]

Sport psychology pursues less a long-term socialization approach and more an immediate effect with its approaches to mental training, which focus directly on the cognitive components of physical practices and on the will component. In this context, Sebastian Brückner describes the programs that the U.S. military has set up to promote mental strength in soldiers.[34] Especially with the help of the Master Resilience Training, mental techniques are instilled in the troops but also taught to leaders, who are then supposed to act as multipliers.

As described by Karen Reivich and Martin Seligman,[35] the Master Resilience Training provides for a multiday program divided into modules that also reflect on the usefulness of resilience techniques for everyday military life. The modules include a psycho-educational approach to resilience that taps into self-

---

[30] Reichherzer and Elbe, "Verteidigung oder Angriff über die Flanke? Perspektiven auf Militär und Sport."

[31] Ibid.

[32] Mia Fischer, "Aktiv. Attraktiv. Anders? The Bundeswehr's Deployment of Sport Soldiers," in *Sport and Militarism: Contemporary Global Perspective*, ed. Michael Butterworth (New York: Routledge, 2017), 65-78.

[33] Michael Krüger et al., "Bewegung, Spiel und Sport in Kultur und Gesellschaft—Sozialwissenschaften des Sports," in *Sport. Das Lehrbuch für das Sportstudium*, ed. Arne Güllich and Michael Krüger (Berlin: Springer, 2013) 337-93, at 374.

[34] Sebastian Brückner, "Spitzenleistung unter Druck. Sport und Militär aus sportpsychologischer Sicht," in Elbe and Reichherzer, *Der Sport des Militärs*.

[35] Karen Reivich and Martin Seligmann, "Master Resilience Training in the U.S. Army," *American Psychologist* 66, no. 1 (2011): 25-34.

awareness, self-regulation, and optimism, as well as individual character strengths and resources. The training goes beyond cognitive-behavioral training and draws on ideas from positive psychology to cognitively reassess, avoid thought traps, tap into energy management and problem-solving strategies, and access mindfulness-based approaches. This training opens the approaches of a resource-oriented perspective and corresponding self-training, which enable the participants to use their character strengths and to develop them further, as well as to find and help develop strengths in other persons.[36] In each case, the mental training of sports psychology complements the physical training and, through its cognitive and reflective orientation, contributes in a special way to developing a "strong character."

The importance that sports psychology has gained for sport in the military but also for military performance itself can be seen, for example, in a special issue of the journal *Military Psychology*,[37] which examined the influences of sport psychology on military psychology research in general and on military research in the behavioral sciences. Particular opportunities for collaboration are seen in the areas of skill development, simulation and training, and team effectiveness. The extent to which this has already found its way into everyday training practice is shown by the example of "combat tactical breathing," as it is taught in the U.S. Navy:

This technique, known as combat or tactical breathing, is an excellent way to reduce your stress and calm down. This breathing strategy has been used by first responders, the military and athletes to focus, gain control and manage stress. In addition, it appears to help control worry and nervousness.

> Relax yourself by taking 3 to 5 breaths as described below.
> Visualize each number as you count.
>
> Breathe in counting 1, 2, 3, 4
> Stop and hold your breath counting 1, 2, 3, 4
> Exhale counting 1, 2, 3, 4
>
> Repeat the breathing Breath in counting 1, 2, 3, 4
> Pause and hold your breath counting 1, 2, 3, 4
> Exhale counting 1, 2, 3, 4.[38]

---

[36] Brückner, "Spitzenleistung unter Druck."

[37] Gerald Goodwin, "Psychology in Sports and the Military: Building Understanding and Collaboration across Disciplines," *Military Psychology* 20, no. 1 (2020): 147–53.

[38] General Navy Medical Inquiries, "Combat Tactical Breathing," 2020, https://www.med.navy.mil/Portals/62/Documents/NMFA/NMCPHC/root/Documents/health-promotion-wellness/psychological-emotional-wellbeing/Combat-Tactical-Breathing.pdf.

The adoption of sports psychology techniques in general character education in the armed forces continues a tradition that has long existed in the U.S. military. For example, football as a sports program in the military academies dates back to 1879, as this sport appeared to be particularly suitable for promoting physical and character strength in equal measure.[39] General Douglas MacArthur was credited as early as the 1950 s with saying that football was a symbol of the best qualities of the United States: bravery, perseverance, and efficient coordination—moreover, it was football players that MacArthur considered most trustworthy during his long service.[40] The U.S. armed forces have football teams in their military academies that not only produce many professional players but also compete in the highest division of college football and generate national excitement with the annual Army-Navy Game. The simultaneous development of physical and character strength through military sports—especially in the rough-and-tumble form of the game of football—is thus considered an important component in the training of soldiers in the U.S. armed forces.

In this context, it is worth referring once again to the personality perspective, as a psychological construct which—unlike character—has undergone quantification and can thus be measured in concrete terms. In particular, the construct of the "Big Five," with five central personality areas, has become established here.[41] This construct measures extroversion (activity, sociability, enthusiasm), agreeableness (trust, cooperation, compassion), conscientiousness (self-control, accuracy, goal orientation), neuroticism (emotional lability, insecurity, worry), and openness to new things (open-mindedness, curiosity, independence). Martin Elbe measured the Big Five of former Bundeswehr officers (n=1,028) as a self-assessment and employers' assessment of officers' personality structure with the same instrument (n=1,054).[42] The *personality profile* of former officers based on the self-assessment can be outlined as follows. They are on average extroverted, knowledgeable, and unstable, but less open and agreeable than the population average. Employers, on the other hand, rate former officers as less agreeable and open, but more conscientious and neurotic. There are hardly any differences with regard to extroversion. Thus, former officers have a more

---

[39] Dieter Kollmer, "'Both in War and Peace—It Is the Football Men, That I Found My Greatest Reliance'. Beobachtungen zum American Football und den US-Streitkräften," in Elbe and Reichherzer, *Der Sport des Militärs*.

[40] Ibid.

[41] Beatrice Rammstedt et al., "Big Five Inventory 10 (BFI-10)," *Zusammenstellung sozialwissenschaftlicher Items und Skalen*, 2014 (doi:10.6102/zis76).

[42] Martin Elbe, "Der Offizier und die Anderen: Persönlichkeit im sozioökonomischen Kontext," in *Charakter—Haltung—Habitus. Persönlichkeit und Verantwortung in der Bundeswehr*, ed. Angelika Dörferl-Dierken and Christian Göbel (Berlin: Springer, 2022, forthcoming).

positive perception of their own personality than company representatives. This also corresponds with attributions regarding the former officers' competencies, which were also measured. In almost all aspects, the employers assess the former officers as significantly more competent than the officers assess themselves. The greatest differences are found in the area of officer-typical secondary virtues: reliability, readiness to make decisions, self-discipline, assertiveness, resilience, loyalty, organizational ability, and sense of responsibility. It is these aspects that are often attributed to a strong character. Here, employers expect officers to possess competencies due to military socialization, but these competencies do not correspond to the self-image of former officers. However, respondents know that these competencies are attributed to them.

Overall, this study shows that the former officers of the German armed forces orient themselves less toward the secondary virtues typical of officers and more toward competencies that have a positive connotation in civil society today, such as flexibility, economic thinking, and creativity, while civilian employers rate them less highly in these areas. All officers are required to participate in official sports, are expected to demonstrate a high level of athletic performance, which is also tested annually, and are trained as sports leaders. But all of this has not changed the self-image described above, which does not support the assumption of specific character development based on (official) sports activities.

However, if one assumes that character is a complex, multifaceted concept and not a synonym for personality, and if one rather attaches a moral or ethical connotation to the term "character,"[43] then the concept becomes accessible to both sporting and military socialization effects and approaches value-oriented ethical education with the goal of reducing socially undesirable behavior and promoting prosocial behavior.

Values in Sport and in the Military

With the question of the importance of *values in sport*, ethics and, thus, the philosophy of sport comes to the forefront of consideration.[44] James Keating applies this question to sport itself and examines the moral standards associated with the concept of sport and the spirit of sport.[45] In doing so, he distinguishes between recreational sports and competitive sports and finds that the ethical standards in the two areas differ considerably. While recreational sports are in-

---

[43] Bredemeier and Shield, *Sports and Character Development.*
[44] John Willilam Devine and Francisco Javier Lopez Frias, "Philosophy of Sport," in *The Stanford Encyclopedia of Philosophy*, ed. Edward Zalta, Fall 2020, https://plato.stanford.edu/archives/fall2020/entries/sport/.
[45] James Keating, "Sportsmanship as a Moral Category," *Ethics* 75, no. 1 (1964): 25–35.

deed about leisure time and, thus, pleasant diversion as well as playful ease—which also includes a certain generosity in dealing with rules—competitive sports are entirely designed for competition, victory, and performance enhancement—formal fairness and adherence to rules are unalterable here.[46] The moral requirements in the two areas thus differ to a considerable degree, and the concept of sportsmanship can take on virtually opposite meanings. While in recreational sports, stubborn adherence to rules does not correspond to the spirit of sport, rule-breaking in competitive sports is not tolerable. In relation to sport and the military, this difference results in tension, since both areas of sport have an effect here. In the attitude of chivalry, one's own fairness should unite with generosity toward the weaknesses of others; at the same time, the efficiency orientation of martial combat teaches that only success counts here, not the "sporting attitude." Eliza Riedi illustrates this tension in a particularly vivid way and shows how polo—the sport of great estates—with the corresponding pride of rank in the British Army at the beginning of the twentieth century, had a dysfunctional effect on the modernization of the armed forces and what role the game of polo played as a mechanism of distinction. Here the sporting attitude counted only toward those who were part of the game.[47] This downward demarcation was supplemented in World War I to the extent that the army itself was now called "the best football team, the best platoon,"[48] which was intended to describe a tendency toward proletarianization in the British armed forces.

Military principles and concepts have helped shape the development of sport, and terms such as assault, attack, and defense are everyday concepts of coordinated action in team sports.[49] Beyond that, however, there are numerous sports that simulate military action and demand the corresponding skills in civilian competition instead of in deadly battle:

> Exemplary for the competitions is the Modern Pentathlon, which first appeared on the Olympic program in 1912. It includes essential elements of military training from shooting, fencing, swimming and riding to cross-country running. ... The values of modern sports corresponded to military needs: The measurement of performance, the improvement of performance, but also the practice of rules and norms including

---

[46] Devine and Frias, "Philosophy of Sport."
[47] Eliza Riedi, "Brains or Polo? Equestrian Sport, Army Reform and the Gentlemanly Officer Tradition, 1900-1914," *Journal of the Society for Army Historical Research* 84 (2006): 236-53.
[48] James Roberts, "'The Best Football Team, the Best Platoon': The Role of Football in the Proletarianization of the British Expeditionary Force, 1914-1918," *Sport in History* 26, no. 1 (2006): 26-46.
[49] Tauber, "'Schon das Spiel ist Kampf, Krieg im kleinen . . .'. Sport und Militär von der Antike bis heute."

fair play were not only images of modern industrial society, but also of the modern military, which therefore gradually adapted sport. The aforementioned Modern Pentathlon, for example, was practiced by officers. The origin of this sport reflects the national mood of the time and the high status of the military in all European societies.[50]

In the Scandinavian countries, the UK, the United States, France, and Germany, especially in the nineteenth century, forms of physical self-training developed and were soon integrated into military training and premilitary education in schools. While team sports oriented to fairness and rules took on a special significance in England, gymnastics with a liberal and national character established itself in Germany at the time of the Napoleonic wars, and was directly linked to the idea of military education. "Physical education for discipline, for harmony of movement, for self-control—of the body, but also of the mind—corresponded to the requirements for the soldiers of the emerging popular armies."[51]

Here, however, we can assume an interrelationship in the influence of sport and the military. While sport initially gained reputation from its association with the military, the military contributed to the *establishment of sport* through this appropriation and helped to establish the influences of sport and gymnastics—with their different value concepts—as a comprehensive concept of physical culture in Germany.[52] This development can be seen in a similar way for all modern states. It is generally true that with regard to an emphasis on values of duty and acceptance in the military as well as in (competitive) sports, toughness above all —toward oneself and against others—becomes a central basis for action.[53]

Basically, sport and military are social subsystems that can be represented in ideal types.[54] With this typification, it becomes possible to assess specific educational measures and social practices in terms of their orientation to one of the two systems and thus in terms of specific attributions of meaning and value that underlie the contexts of action. The following criteria are to be applied:

- Institutional orientation: Social rules, structures, and processes result from institutionalization in the respective subsystem.
- Carrying out of competition: Social competition is carried out differently in the subsystems.
- Success: The assessment of success is based on a better position within the system over time.

---

[50] Ibid., 6.
[51] Ibid., 5.
[52] Tauber, *Vom Schützengraben auf den grünen Rasen*.
[53] Brückner, "Spitzenleistung unter Druck."
[54] Martin Elbe, "Sport und Bewegung im Militär: Soziologische Bezüge," in Elbe and Reichherzer, *Der Sport des Militärs*.

- Social reference: The central reference groups are derived from the competitive and community orientation in the social subsystems.
- Communicability: Attributes, competencies, and action orientation are responsive within the social subsystem.

Based on these criteria, the two subsystems that constitute the relationship between sport and the military can be differentiated:

Table 1: Sport and military as social subsystems.

	Sport	Military
Institution	sports system (e.g., sports club)	military system (e.g., German armed forces)
Competition	competition	fight
Success	relative best (gold)	absolute best (winner)
Social reference	team membership	part of a military unit
Marketability	perfect athlete	perfect soldier

Applying the ideal type, one can say that a *sports soldier* of the Bundeswehr meets certain criteria. These sports solders are uniform wearers who have committed themselves to be soldiers for a certain period of time, but primarily pursue their own competitive sport—this is the main object of their service. These soldiers can move independently in both institutions, adapting their own actions to the respective rationality. The starting point is the top athlete's will to win. Despite a fundamental team orientation, the sports soldier is aware that, in terms of performance assessment, everyone is ultimately on their own. In sports, it is generally true that those who perform the best are nominated for competitions; this also applies to the nomination for a match in a team sport. And in the military, the bitter truth is, "Together we stand, divided we fall." In terms of success, the ideal type of sports soldier is performance-oriented, but adaptive; the respective criteria for success are taken as the basis for one's actions, which also applies to the communicability of the self: the perfect soldier and the perfect athlete combine physicality, striving for perfection, and discipline. With regard to the competitive performance, the combat orientation dominates in the sports soldier; it is adapted to the respective arenas of performance (competition or war) precisely with regard to the choice of means.[55]

In general, military sports are intended to promote physical fitness. Associated with this, the socialization goals in the military are the ability and the will to fight, as well as the discipline necessary to realize success within the framework of the military as an organization. This socialization is imparted primarily through practices of general education, but also through sports training. From a socialization point of view, one function of sport is to make it possible to experience structures of inclusion and exclusion through the sport system, whereby inclusion and exclusion mechanisms are mutually dependent. Sport remains competition and performance on a physical basis; it requires opposition, on one hand (in order to be able to measure oneself against others), and camaraderie on the other (in order to be able to compete as a team and maintain the training infrastructure). Both aspects are generated in the military through the special kind of solidarity that forms the social closure of organizational membership and makes a soldier into a comrade.[56]

The *socialization potential* of sport is thus limited with regard to the reinforcement of solidarity, since solidarity with others is limited by the opposition in the competition and the competition for nomination. This is especially true when the probability of success decreases and in crises—that is, especially when solidarity should prove itself.[57] It is precisely this bondage to success that the sports system and the military system have in common. From the point of view of socialization theory, one can say that long-term value transmission takes place in early phases of development (especially in the family and school) and leads to the permanent shaping of behavior.[58] Later modifications of behavior are highly dependent on success and no longer have an effect when the pressure to succeed decreases. Physical practice, as taught in military sports training, does not have a value-building effect in this sense.

An example of this is football quarterback Roger Staubach (born 1942), who won the Super Bowl twice in the National Football League (NFL) in the 1970 s with the Dallas Cowboys. His nickname, "Captain America," was not accidental; he was a graduate of one of the military academies and was seen as a personification of American values (including hard work, sincerity, fighting strength, determination, integrity, religiosity, national pride, and family orientation).[59]

---

[55] Ibid.
[56] Ibid.
[57] Klaus Heinemann, *Einführung in die Soziologie des Sports*, 3rd ed. (Schorndorf: Hofmann, 1990).
[58] Elbe, "Sport und Bewegung im Militär."
[59] Kollmer, "'Both in War and Peace—It Is the Football Men, That I Found My Greatest Reliance.'"

While at the U.S. Naval Academy, he had already led the Navy Midshipmen to the final game of the college championship in 1963 as quarterback, but had then gone to Vietnam as a supply officer and finished his military service before joining the Dallas Cowboys in the NFL in 1969. Clearly, Staubach had already brought these qualities with him, rather than having trained them through sports.

> Sport in the Bundeswehr takes many forms and is more deeply interwoven with the core tasks of the armed forces than one might think at first glance. As a task shared by the Bundeswehr, sport is centralized at key points in the armed forces base. Its many facets range from top-class sport as a means of communicating with society, through its function as a bridge linking the armed forces with other nations, to its task of keeping people in the Bundeswehr healthy or restoring them to health. Through it, it succeeds in transporting values and expressing appreciation.[60]

The fact that sport fundamentally implies *value-based action* lies in the dual orientation to success and rules and the limitation of interaction to the sporting arena. Military sport is thus also suitable for contributing to understanding in an international setting, such as the international military sport competitions of the CISM (Conseil International du Sport Militaire). Similarly, the Invictus Games are an international military sports event for injured soldiers. Here, the health perspective still comes into play, as sport—an important aspect of rehabilitation and thus also of social participation—offers recognition to people who have suffered impairments in military service.

Summary

As the example of the Invictus Games suggests, teaching values through sport may have a different focus than is often assumed. Perhaps sport is less about individual character building and the socializing effect, and more about creating opportunities to experience community. This value orientation, which was already inherent in the Olympic idea, is also noticeable in international military sports, whereby the integrating function, as assumed by the Invictus Games, works in numerous social subsystems and thus becomes one of the basic functions of sport.[61] As has been shown, sport and the military are two of these subsystems, and in the connection of these two systems it is quite possible to trans-

---

[60] Georg Klein and Christian Lützkendorf, "Zur Bedeutung des Sports für die Bundeswehr," in Elbe and Reichherzer, *Der Sport des Militärs*.

[61] Timo Schädler, *Integration im Sportverein. Entwicklung eines sozialwissenschaftlich begründeten Qualitätsmanagementmodells* (Saarbrücken: SVH, 2016).

port values. However, this happens rather *en passant*, for example, by the fact that the quarterback and officer Staubach is perceived as exemplary and virtuous—a true Captain America—or that the will of the injured athletes of the Invictus Games to get back to performance and social participation is perceived as inspiring and conveying values. Thus, sport not only influences staying healthy and getting healthy again, but also conveys values. Thus, the third question that was posed in this text—to what extent is sport suitable to conveying values?—can be answered: Sport is indeed suitable. In relation to sport and the military, however, this suitability lies less in the individual-socialization sense and more in the collective-model sense.

This answer leads to another basic question: *To what extent does sport in the military help to promote a certain set of character traits, values, and behaviors.* The answer to this question must first of all be based on the conviction that the military can have an educational effect on adults. If this is the case, then sports training is of course also suitable for building the character of soldiers. However, there is much to be said for the fact that sports training primarily achieves physical effects. There is no doubt that targeted sports psychology training can also improve cognitive performance and promote mental strength—but there is hardly any talk of character building here. The analysis of the personality of former officers also indicates that it is not so much a specific character that is imparted as competencies that the former officers want to match with general social expectations and do not want to be seen as character stereotypes of officer-typical secondary virtues.

This also helps to clarify the second question: *Is sport, then, a means of seducing youth?* Although soldiers—and especially officers—are attributed with certain character traits (order, discipline, assertiveness, perseverance, organizational talent, etc.), it seems to be rather the case that the primary socializing imprints lie in the primary and secondary socialization phase—that is, in childhood and adolescence—and are not made up for in adulthood. Here it is not sport that brings youth to the military, but rather military-related educational opportunities. Of course, even as an adult, when one enters the military, one can still develop physical skills and play sports, but the character disposition is already there. What remains is simple adaptive behavior, not character building. A more profound effect, however, can be assumed from the exemplary impact of top athletes. Numerous top athletes who compete as soldiers in national and international competitions and win medals, as well as the special military competitions such as CISM (International Military Sports Council) or Invictus, convey an image of strength and will that is rewarded by social recognition. This can certainly lead to emulation of these role models, although the evaluation of this effect as seduction is just as value-laden as the rule-bound sporting activity itself.

After Chivalry

Torsten Meireis

Introduction

When reflecting on his role in the German resistance movement against the Nazi rule in Germany, Dietrich Bonhoeffer coined the term "acceptance of guilt"[1] to describe what he understood as an aspect central to responsible behavior. To him, deciding between two possible wrongs was an aspect that couldn't be taken lightly. Bonhoeffer's plight may well shed a valuable light on the values and identity formation of agents of force in late modern society, to whom the prestigious social imaginary of the chivalrous knight in shining armor is no longer an easily accessible option—if it ever was.[2]

Despite the industrialization and the ongoing robotization of warfare in the late modern nation-state, there is a need for a value-based self-image of agents of force, who include not only military personnel but also the police. Official catalogues of army values, but also popular depictions of the late modern soldier, enumerate loyalty, duty, respect, selfless service, honor, integrity, and personal courage among the soldierly virtues.[3] The heroic veteran, wounded in body and soul, but prepared to forcefully stand up to the "bad guys" and sacrificing his life in the process, is still an eminent figure in popular movies, such as Clint Eastwood's *Gran Torino*. The equally heroic imagery of the *Die Hard* policeman, ruthlessly enforcing what he understands as the law, is present not only in the famous Bruce Willis action movie series by that name, but also in the iconic *Dirty Harry* films starring Clint Eastwood.

However, reality tends to differ from that image. The image of the agent of force in society has become strangely ambivalent. On duty, soldiers tend to be

---

[1] Dietrich Bonhoeffer, *Ethik*, ed. Ilse Tödt et al., vol. 6 of *Dietrich Bonhoeffer Werke* (Munich: Christian Kaiser, 1992), 275–85.
[2] Bernhard Koch, ed., *Chivalrous Combatants? The Meaning of Military Virtue Past and Present* (Baden-Baden: Nomos, 2019).
[3] United States Army, "The Army Values," https://www.army.mil/values/index.html.

cherished as chivalrous heroes, or at least as "our boys" (and girls), whereas the returning personnel of warfare are often considered as a liability—suffering from PTSD,[4] suspected of indecent behavior while fighting, and asked by the general public to keep their wartime experience to themselves, especially when military intervention meets with societal and political criticism.[5] For that reason, the image of the good soldier defending loved ones and putting paid to the bad guy in a just war has suffered—but not his image alone: as the "Black Lives Matter" rallies and comparable protests against racial or xenophobic profiling have shown, the image of the police officer has also lost in reputation.

Increasingly, the moral status of agents of force has become problematic, or so I argue in this chapter. Even if both institutions—the military and the police—are usually understood as necessary, and thus their existence meets with general public approval,[6] they are seen as morally ambiguous at best. Rightly put, the question is not in which way the values of organizations of force influence society, but rather how society deals with the normative insecurity in its armed forces, whether military or police. Rather than opting for a legitimization of violence, Bonhoeffer's concept of responsibility and the acceptance of guilt may pave a viable track here.

To argue this point, I first briefly sketch some developments in the military and police and explain why I treat both in parallel as organizations of force. In a second step, I look into some empirical findings regarding the ethos of military and police personnel. A third step expounds the ethical dilemmas that agents of force face from a theological and philosophical point of view. Finally, I try to draw some conclusions.

Ethos and the Future of Agencies of Force

Germany might be a good point to start looking, as it has been a place of extreme binaries in regard to agencies of force. While for almost a century the military

---

[4] Karl Heinz Biesold and Klaus Barre, "Militär," in *Posttraumatische Belastungsstörungen*, ed. Andreas Maercker, 4th ed. (Berlin: Springer, 2013), 487–507.

[5] See, for instance, Charles A. Figley and Seymour Leventman, eds., *Strangers at Home: Vietnam Veterans Since the War* (New York: Praeger, 1980). For Germany, see the controversial public debate about a memorial for Bundeswehr members killed during active service: Nina Leonhardt and Heiko Biehl, "Militär und Tradition," in *Militärsoziologie—Eine Einführung*, ed. Nina Leonhard and Ines Jacqueline Werkner (Wiesbaden: Springer, 2021), 314–41, esp. 330–33.

[6] Marjan Malešic and Maja Garb, "Public Trust in the Military from Global, Regional and National Perspectives," in *Handbook of the Sociology of the Military*, ed. Guiseppe Caforio and Mariana Nuciari, 2nd ed. (Cham: Springer, 2018), 145–60.

and police were held in highest esteem as educational and nation-building institutions, the post-World War II period understandably saw equally strong reservations in that regard. When German chancellor Willy Brandt publicly argued in 1969 that "The school of the nation is the school,"[7] everybody in Germany understood this as a quip against the notorious idea of the military as the school of the nation. From the beginnings of the modern German nation-state after the Franco-German War of 1870, the military had a crucial role in cultural formation, especially regarding masculinity.[8] After World War I, when tens of thousands of traumatized soldiers returned from the carnage of the trenches—often to a grim social reality of poverty and unemployment—many were vulnerable to political propaganda that blamed politicians, social democrats, the Jews, or all of the above for the lost war and their economic plight. The glorious army, so the notorious "backstabbing" narrative went, could have won, but greedy and cowardly civilians blundered its victories away. This nefarious legend was consumed eagerly, as it gave meaning to the terrible trauma—as did the aesthetic glorification of the war experience propagated by artists like Ernst Juenger and books like *Storm of Steel* (German: *In Stahlgewittern*).[9] And it led the way to a modern reactivation of dreams of chivalry by Nazi ideologists like Alfred Rosenberg[10] or Heinrich Himmler, who, in his notorious Posen speech to generals of the SS, claimed decency and chivalry for his men in the midst of genocide: "Most of you will know what it means when there are a hundred corpses lying together, five hundred or a thousand. Having endured this and remained decent—except for some cases of human weakness—has made us tough. This is a glorious chapter of our history which has never been written and will never be written."[11]

---

[7] Quoted in Heinz-Elmar Tenorth, "'Die Schule der Nation ist die Schule'—Bildung im Konflikt zwischen Staat und 'Nation,'" in *Bürger bilden*, ed. Otfried Höffe and Oliver Primavesi (Berlin: de Gruyter, 2019), 179–210, at 179.

[8] Ute Frevert, "Das Militär als Schule der Männlichkeiten" in *Männlichkeiten und Moderne in den Wissenskulturen um 1900*, ed. Ulrike Brunotte and Rainer Herrn (Bielefeld: Transcript, 2008), 57–75.

[9] Ulrich Baron and Hans-Harald Müller, "Weltkriege und Kriegsromane. Die literarische Bewältigung des Krieges nach 1918 und 1945–eine Skizze," *Zeitschrift für Literaturwissenschaft und Linguistik* 75 (1989): 14–38.

[10] Dina Gusejnova, *European Elites and Ideas of Empire, 1917–1957* (Cambridge: Cambridge University Press, 2016), 177–207.

[11] Excerpt from Himmler's Posen Speech (1943) in *Der Prozess gegen die Hauptkriegsverbrecher vor dem Internationalen Militärgerichtshof.* Nürnberg 14. November – 1. Oktober 1946. Amtlicher Text, deutsche Ausgabe. Bd. 29: Urkunden und anderes Beweismaterial Nr. 1850 – Nr. 2233. Nürnberg 1948, pp. 110–73, BSB Munich, https://1000dok.digitale-sammlungen.de/dok_0008_pos.pdf (English translation by the author).

It is not hard to understand why the first Social Democrat German chancellor remained skeptical regarding military virtues in education. His attitude mirrored the feeling of many, especially young, Germans, who saw the military as a deeply problematic institution, even though especially the newly founded agencies of force in East and West Germany tried to connect to traditions differing from the German warrior ideology. Thus, the Bundeswehr of the Bonn republic tried to replace the authoritarian spirit of the Prussian era with the image of the "citizen in uniform," strengthening the idea of civic responsibility—at least at the level of official policy,[12] and in accordance with republican political theory, which normatively proclaims a strong link between the military and the state mediated by the citizen soldier.[13]

As organizations of force wield considerable weaponry, trained agents, and relatively tightly knit, hierarchical organization with a strong stress on obedience and loyalty, they always pose a considerable threat to governments and societies at large. Late modern societies therefore largely strive to contain those organizations rather than allowing for their strong impact on society.[14]

But even in societies with a less militaristic history and a different military tradition, such as the United States of America, a certain type skepticism toward the virtues of military organizations has grown in recent decades. As an example, we may turn to Michael Walzer, the philosopher who has written the most influential book on just-war theory in the second half of the twentieth century. Walzer, himself by no means a pacifist, takes great pains to mark the difference between just and unjust wars. World War II, for him, is largely an example of a just war on the side of the Allies in their fight against the genocides and atrocities committed by Nazi Germany and Japan. The Vietnam War, however, signifies to him just the opposite,[15] and he explores the moral problems of military organizations in great depth.[16] Social marginalization and attitudes of indifference and apathy toward the military—which may paradoxically correspond to a high level of general trust toward the institution[17]—can be empirically backed

---

[12] See Wolf Graf von Baudissin, *Nie wieder Sieg! Programmatische Schriften 1951-1981*, ed. Cornelia Bührle and Claus von Rosen (Munich: Piper, 1982). Regarding the social reality of that concept, see Ulrich vom Hagen, *Homo Militaris. Perspektiven einer kritischen Militärsoziologie* (Bielefeld: Transcript, 2012), 142-54.

[13] See Ulrich vom Hagen, "Zivil-militärische Beziehungen," in Leonhard and Werkner, *Militärsoziologie*, 88-116.

[14] See Aurel Croissant and David Kühn, *Militär und zivile Politik* (Munich: Oldenbourg, 2011), 61-122.

[15] Michael Walzer, *Just and Unjust Wars: A Moral Argument with Historical Illustrations*, 4th ed. (New York: Basic Books, 2006), xix-xx, 96-101, 186-96, 299.

[16] Ibid., 304-27.

[17] See Malešic and Garb, "Public Trust in the Military," 145, 155-57.

not only by surveys but also by looking at recruiting successes. Sociological evidence suggests that the structure and type of military organization and its culture develop a social bias in attracting especially the lower strata of society in late modern times, while this organization and culture are shunned by the middle and upper classes, who in former times used to staff the officers' ranks.[18] But if the general attitude toward the military in society may be paraphrased along the lines of "it is probably good to have it, but we don't like it and won't join if we have a choice," then the question of social recognition of agents of this force has to be considered.

The military is not the only organization of force that has an ambiguous reputation. The police also need to be considered. Even though modern police forces in democratic states are subject to a number of checks and controls, charges of racial profiling, undue violence, and corruption are far from unusual, not only in U.S. police departments but elsewhere as well,[19] and the popularity of derogatory labels for police, especially in youth cultures, speaks to the feelings of anguish that minority groups in particular may experience regarding the police.[20]

A short clarification of the parallelization of military and police as agencies of force might be in order here, as both organizations are usually treated as distinct in conventional debate. Three arguments are crucial here. The first pertains to the obvious parallels in authorization, means, and ends of both institutions: both have developed in relation to the modern nation-state and are connected to its governance structure, and both rely ultimately on the skilled use of force to provide security from attacks on life, limb, property of citizens, and territorial

---

[18] See Nina Leohnhardt and Heiko Biehl, "Beruf: Soldat," in Leonhard and Werkner, *Militärsoziologie*, 393–427, at 409–11; and Patricia Danette Light, *Marching Upward: The Role of the Military in Social Stratification and Mobility in American Society* (Blacksburg: Virginia Tech, 1998), 127–30.

[19] See the President's Task Force on 21st Century Policing, "Final Report of the President's Task Force on 21st Century Policing" (Washington, DC: Office of Community Oriented Policing Services, 2015); Hendrik Cremer, *"Racial Profiling"–Menschenrechtswidrige Personenkontrollen nach § 22 Abs. 1a Bundespolizeigesetz. Empfehlungen an den Gesetzgeber, Gerichte und Polizei* (Berlin: Deutsches Institut für Menschenrechte, 2013); Rafael Behr, "Verdacht und Vorurteil. Die polizeiliche Konstruktion der 'gefährlichen Fremden,'" in *Polizei und Gesellschaft. Transdisziplinäre Perspektiven zu Methoden, Theorie und Empirie reflexiver Polizeiforschung*, ed. Christiane Howe and Lars Ostermeier (Wiesbaden: Springer, 2019), 17–45; and Elena Isabel Zum-Bruch, *Polizeiliche pro-organisationale Devianz. Eine Typologie* (Wiesbaden: Springer, 2019), 19–48.

[20] Ronald Weitzer and Rod K. Brunson, "Strategic Responses to the Police among Inner-City Youth," *The Sociological Quarterly* 50 (2009): 235–56; and Rafael Behr, "Diskriminierung durch Polizeibehörden," in *Handbuch Diskriminierung*, ed. Albert Scherr, Aladin El-Mafaalani, and Gökçen Yüksel (Wiesbaden: Springer, 2017), 301–20.

sovereignty. Second, as I've argued here, both share an ambiguous reputation. Third, the boundaries between the two institutions are blurring. Traditionally, the military was characterized by providing security from threats external to the nation-state, while the police provided internal security by enforcing the law. However, while military defense used to be directed at the threat of foreign enemies, and policing used to provide security from deviant citizens, these areas of agency are merging—a phenomenon usually known as the constabularization of the military and the militarization of the police. As conventional warfare between nation-states increasingly gives way to hybrid or guerilla warfare, to civil wars, or to self-sustaining wars in failed states, and as military agents are charged with complex peace missions abroad rather than the defense of national territory—even though desperate autocrats may try to bring aggressive nationalist warfare back, as the late Russian invasions of Crimea and Ukraine show—military personnel increasingly have to fulfill police duties, while police forces are charged with countering terrorist attacks from supposedly foreign perpetrators. Whether soldiers are sent out on peace-keeping missions internationally, or are charged with treading the slippery ground of containing civil strife at home—which might or might not turn out to be hybrid warfare—as they are charged with law enforcement duties they are obliged to adhere to a framing of possible adversaries as deviant citizens rather than as enemies or hostile combatants. On the other hand, a militarization of the police is visible as police forces are facing criminal organizations armed with military-grade weaponry or are charged with combatting terrorist attacks that do not easily allow for de-escalation strategies.[21] The gist of the argument presented here is not the suggestion that police and military are simply the same or will ultimately merge again, as in premodern times, but that there are enough similarities to treat the members of both as agents of force that increasingly face similar problems of morality and societal recognition.

We currently seem a long way from the heroic image of the chivalrous agent of force, valiant against the aggressive, shielding the vulnerable, merciful against the defeated—and the lack of recognition is set off against ever increasing demands on the agents of force. Thus, the adequate question may not be how military or police values impact society, but, rather, in which way a given society values its organizations of force and deals with their marginalization.

---

[21] See Donald J. Campbell and Kathleen M. Campbell, "Soldiers as Police Officers/ Police Officers as Soldiers: Role Evolution and Revolution in the United States," *Armed Forces & Society* 36, no. 2 (2010): 327–50; Gerhard Kümmel, "Die Hybridisierung der Streitkräfte: Militärische Aufgaben im Wandel," in Leonhard and Werkner, *Militärsoziologie*, 117–38; and Delphine Resteigne and Philippe Manigar, "Boots on the Streets: A 'Policization' of the Armed Forces as the New Normal?," *Journal of Military Studies* 8 (2019): 16–27.

Marginalized Agents of Force

The increasing marginalization of the organizations of force in general society is mirrored by the attitudes of those organizations' members. Charles Moskos's famous distinction of an occupational versus an institutional orientation of agents of force alongside newer studies shows a complex picture. Moskos's distinction rested on the difference between an occupational attitude, which was comparable to that of participants in the regular labor market, and an institutional one, which focused on the special character of the military. Modern soldiers don't envisage themselves as chivalrous heroes or dashing figures but rather as skilled military workers[22] who are challenged by the multitude of roles and tasks they need to be familiar with.[23]

As occupational and career-oriented attitudes play an increasingly stronger role in inducing persons to join the military as well as the police, the exceptional character of organizations of force in dealing with violence actively as well as passively becomes a challenge that agents need to face. Especially if taken up as a job like any other, the constant risk of trauma through the use of violence or exposure to it sets the agents of force apart from the "normal" citizen and widens the experienced gap between society and the organizations of force, especially as threats of life give rise to a particularly strong social cohesion in the force.[24] In the military, this gap is partly due to the missions of international intervention, during which soldiers experience the exceptional strain of combat and then return to a society that never felt "at war," and to which the soldiers' experiences remain alien. In the police, similar experiences may arise from confrontation with terrorism or organized and highly weaponized perpetrators. The gap between regular social existence and being a member of the force—usually conceptualized as the "civil-military gap"[25] but extendable to the police as well—may then appear in various forms. It may show itself in an insecurity of police personnel who feel disrespected,[26] or in identity crises of veterans leaving the serv-

---

[22] This relates to the distinction of institutional vs. occupational perspectives developed by Charles C. Moskos: see Leonhard and Biehl, "Beruf: Soldat"; also Heiko Biehl, "Einsatzmotivation und Kampfmoral," in Leonhard and Werkner, *Mitliärsoziologie*, 447–74.

[23] Gerhard Kümmel, "Military Identity and Identity within the Military," in Caforio and Nuciari, *Handbook of the Sociology of the Military*, 477–93, esp. 489.

[24] In military sociology, this is discussed in the binary of "task cohesion" and "social cohesion"; see Biehl, "Einsatzmotivation und Kampfmoral."

[25] Malešic and Garb, "Public Trust in the Military," 156.

[26] Rafael Behr, "Rechtserhaltende Gewalt als Zentrum polizeilicher Organisationskultur?," in *Gewalt und Gewalten. Zur Ausübung, Legitimität und Ambivalenz rechtserhaltender Gewalt*, ed. Torsten Meireis (Tübingen: Mohr Siebeck, 2012), 69–89, esp. 77–81.

ice and having a difficult time adapting to the daily workings of nonmilitary society.[27]

But it is not only the concrete experiences of military and police personnel that set them apart from society at large. So do the official and (even more) unofficial set of values connected to military and police organizations,[28] including courage and a certain type of heroism, especially as these values are often entangled with a certain image of masculinity.[29] Empirical findings show that the relation of the ethos of agents of force to the values of society at large is a troubled one.

This is especially true as warlike or even forceful behavior is widely shunned in late modern postheroic societies.[30] The binary of "'civil perspectives of the post-heroic majority' and 'bellicose perspectives of a heroic minority,'"[31] problematized by military sociologist Maren Tomforde, points to the normative problems addressed in this chapter. The obvious contradiction of needing and keeping institutions and organizations of force, on one hand, while marginalizing their agents, on the other, not only may prove dangerous regarding the role of such organizations in democratic societies, but also seems morally problematic in regard to the military and police persons involved. The question of values must be addressed, however. Societies that—at least in theory—shun violence yet support agencies that are expert in violence will run into problems if they just "outsource" violence and give no thought to bridging the gap, especially as the agents of force deserve not to be left alone with that issue. This then leads to the question of how we normatively understand security, force, and war, and which ethical theory might be best equipped to deal with the problem of the gap between general societal values and agencies of force.

---

[27] Alexandria M. Hammond, *Coming Home: Veterans Leaving Service Face a Deadly Identity Crisis* (New York: CUNY Academic Works, 2019), https://academicworks.cuny.edu/gj_etds/387.

[28] See Rafael Behr, *Cop Culture—Der Alltag des Gewaltmonopols: Männlichkeit, Handlungsmuster und Kultur in der Polizei*, 2nd ed. (Wiesbaden: Verlag für Sozialwissenschaften, 2008).

[29] Behr, *Cop Culture*; David G. Barrie and Susan Broomhall, eds., *A History of Police and Masculinities, 1700–2010* (London: Routledge, 2012); Frevert, "Das Militär als Schule der Männlichkeiten"; and Louise Pears, "Military Masculinities on Television: Who Dares Wins," *NORMA* 17, no. 1 (2022): 67–82.

[30] Herfried Münkler, *Kriegssplitter. Die Evolution der Gewalt im 20. und 21. Jahrhundert* (Reinbek: Rowohlt, 2015),143–87.

[31] Maren Tomforde, "Combat Soldiers and Their Experiences of Violence: Returning to Post-Heroic Societies?," in Caforio and Nuciari, *Handbook of the Sociology of the Military*, 203–19, at 216.

Agencies in a Normative Context: After Chivalry

Of course, a simple solution for the problem of the marginalization of organizations of force might be the reversion to a societal warrior ethos, brandishing an aggressive nationalism in external relations and a punitive law-and-order regime internally. In fact, such a perspective is not unheard of, as it was not uncommon in pre–World War I Europe, especially Germany of notorious memory,[32] and it is sported by authoritarian populists all over the world, notably Russia. However, the ethical viability of such a position seems dubious at the very least, no matter which perspective is consulted. To elucidate the problems that agents of force face in late modern societies averse to violence, it is worth consulting three ethical positions: just-war theory, revisionist just-war theory, and conditional pacifism in the form of just-peace theory. As absolute pacifism eschews any agency of force, this position is not directly addressed in this paper.

In a renewed just-war tradition usually linked to Michael Walzer's seminal work,[33] war is seen as justifiable by a set of criteria developed by, among others, Augustine and seminally put by Thomas Aquinas. Among these criteria are the questions of authority, just cause, rightful end, and adequate means. A just war cannot be waged by just anyone or for just any reason; it needs to aim for peace and to employ means that don't forestall that end. In contrast to Thomas's thinking, which presupposed an *orbis christianus* governed by an emperor and by an accessible natural law, the presupposition changed after the Peace of Westphalia brought an end to the Thirty Years' War. In a post-Westphalian world, it was assumed that there is no authority above the nation-state, so that the right to conduct war—*jus ad bellum*—couldn't be denied to any state, as its proponents would always see their cause as just, and there is no authority above them to appeal to. Thus, modern just-war theory focused on moral rules in war—*jus in bello*—which were codified in humanitarian laws like the Geneva Convention. As Michael Walzer argues, however, war is a moral condition, and thus not only the *jus in bello* but also the *jus ad bellum* criteria need to be discussed.[34] To Walzer, then, wars are justified in so far as they are defensive wars of states protecting their political sovereignty or territorial integrity.[35] To his mind, allowances have to be made for preemptive strikes in cases of imminent threats of war;[36] for foreign interventions in cases of majority-based political secessions; in situations

---

[32] Münkler, *Kriegssplitter*, 167–86.
[33] Walzer, *Just and Unjust Wars*.
[34] Ibid., 41.
[35] Ibid., 61–73.
[36] Ibid., 85.

where prior interventions of other powers need counter-balancing; and "to rescue people threatened with massacre."[37]

Regarding *jus in bello*, the central assumption is the equal right to kill.[38] As modern wars between nation-states are characterized by the conscription of large numbers of citizens who have little influence individually on the decision to go to war, they are to be held responsible only in the limits of a *jus in bello*, not the *jus ad bellum*. As soldiers from different sides meet each other as armed combatants on the battlefield under threat of death, the mutual possibility of being killed allows for the killing of others—as long as they are combatants. For that reason, the rule of discrimination is key: as soon as people cease to be combatants, they are entitled to maximum protection from violence. For a late modern situation characterized by the militarization of the police and the constabularization of the military, however, the situation may be less clear. Civil and hybrid wars, international interventions, terrorism, and professional rather than conscripted forces on the side of nation-states all complicate matters, as does the multitude of different types of agents whose categorization is often difficult—national troops on UN missions, private military firms employing mercenaries and contracted also by nation-states, different types of guerilla fighters, informal armies claiming legitimate national representation under leaders often labelled as warlords, different groups in civil wars, outright criminal groups or religious fanatics trying to establish dominion. In the face of a dissolving possibility of discriminating between combatants and noncombatants, and in view of the politically as well as morally highly ambiguous situations characteristic of the late modern situation—for example, the invasions of Iraq and Afghanistan—clinging to the idea of a just war usually deepens the gap rather than healing it, especially as professional armies take over from conscripted ones. And, of course, this is not to consider questions of police at all. As clear defensive conditions of well-defined national-states become the exception rather than the rule, the danger increases that the idea of a just war becomes a blind for geopolitical power play, for neocolonial attempts of domination, or for the shielding of naked economic interest. Veterans of professional national armies then have to live under the general suspicion of having killed as well as having suffered without a plausible cause.

In an attempt to mediate the gap between civil and military morality (albeit keeping the police out of the equation), revisionist just-war theory, proposed by authors such as Jeff McMahan, Cécile Fabre, and David Rodin, has undertaken to tackle the problem by concentrating on the moral responsibility of individual

---

[37] Ibid., 108.
[38] Ibid., 41.

agents of force.³⁹ The core ethical questions raised by this liberal individualist position concern the distinction of *jus ad bellum* and *jus in bello* and the principle of discrimination. The critique of those distinctions rests on four main arguments. First, war is not seen as a separate moral reality: what is wrong in general must also be wrong in war.⁴⁰ Second, a suspension of the moral obligation of the individual is understood as faulty: a wrong act may be excused if it has been committed under duress, but that does not make the act legitimate; thus, fighting in an unjust war is always morally wrong.⁴¹ Third, and most important, a moral equality between combatants is denied: if a war is unjust, the combatants are, too. Epistemic or institutional arguments intended to ground moral equality in the impossibility to hold combatants individually responsible are refuted by reference to a number of descriptive and prescriptive arguments reaching from the significance of political decision-making in democratic societies to the difference of subjective and objective legitimation.⁴² Finally, the discrimination between combatants and noncombatants is challenged. While such a supposition might be based on phenomena like guerilla or hybrid wars or terrorist attacks, where a distinction *in situ* is difficult the revisionist just-war theory aims at civilian participants in an unjust war effort—for instance, chemists whose research contributes to weapons development. Even though such persons usually do not participate in armed combat and may not even be part of the organized military, the protection afforded by the discrimination principle should not be extended to them, or so the argument runs.

Considering the new challenges of hybrid or guerilla warfare, terrorist threats, the constabularization of the military, and the militarization of police, the revisionist position appears better equipped than classic just-war theory to address the moral situation that agents of force face today, because it refuses to see armed conflict as a separate moral reality—no matter whether in police or in military organizations. Additionally, the presupposition of unchanging moral standards may help to bridge the gap that soldiers, especially, encounter when leaving the force or coming back from engagements abroad: if actions in situations of armed conflict are judged by the same principles as they are in civilian life, there is no different moral reality to face. Even if critics like Nigel Biggar cling to the idea of a clearly discernible natural law,⁴³ it is the situated individual

---

³⁹ Jeff McMahan, *Killing in War* (Oxford: Clarendon Press, 2009); Cécile Fabre, *Cosmopolitan War* (Oxford: Oxford University Press, 2012); David Rodin, *War and Self-Defense* (New York: Oxford University Press, 2003).
⁴⁰ McMahan, *Killing in War*, 35–37, 156.
⁴¹ Ibid., 115–18, 131–37, 150–54, 214–31.
⁴² Ibid., 66–84.
⁴³ Nigel Biggar, "In Defence of War: What Is It All About?," *Soundings: An Interdisciplinary Journal*, 97, no. 2 (2014): 169–74.

who assumes responsibility and the right of judgment in late modern times. That is exactly why revisionists, who opt for a moral realism that is in some aspects quite close to a natural-law theory, refuse to cede to a moral collectivism.

However, the liberal individualist position of the revisionists does have grave shortcomings. Protagonists like McMahan understand the law as a convention strictly distinct from morals and concede that legal and military realities are a far cry from the revisionist way of thinking. He thus recommends that we understand the moral argument he makes as strictly theoretical, especially as an immediate application of that kind of thinking might erode existing legal and habitual protection in situations of armed conflict. This of course strips the theory of any practical use regarding the moral load of agents of force.[44] Moreover, the assumption of the possibility of a just war and the thematic limitation to war and the military in general—rather than a broader take on conflict and issues of force—remain unquestioned. Thus, the overall benefit for the problem of the gap between the personnel of the armed forces and civil society remains limited.

A third position of contingent pacifism was developed in Christian churches under the threat of weapons of mass destruction in the age of nuclear deterrence. Especially in a German-speaking context, historical analysis of individual Christians' and churches' contribution to a warlike nationalism and the attempt to come to terms with the role of churches in Nazi Germany led to a controversial debate within churches and resulted in a position of legal pacifism, labeled as the doctrine of just peace and expounded, for instance, in an influential 2007 memorandum.[45] The main theoretical interest of this position is a reframing of the issues of conflict. Its theological rationale consists of a reconciliation of love and justice and God's promise of shalom (see Psalm 85:11). In spite of the awareness that this shalom cannot be achieved by human effort, as shalom belongs to God's ultimate reality, it is understood to inspire human initiative in the penultimate, the world we live in.[46] Thus, the doctrine aims at a mediation of Christian doctrinal abhorrence of violence and the necessity of resisting evil in a world not yet redeemed, while taking into account the necessity of responsible action involving guilt.

Such a concept needs to come to terms with political and legal realities, so the doctrine of just peace is designed as a normative political model that may be the object of an overlapping consensus. One of the basic insights is that war can never be fully justified, even in cases where a just cause and a rightful intention are given, because collateral damage, atrocity through traumatized or brutalized soldiers, innocent loss of life and sanity on a genocidal scale, and terrible con-

---

[44] McMahan, *Killing in War*, 109–10.
[45] Evangelische Kirche in Deutschland (EKD), *Aus Gottes Frieden leben—für gerechten Frieden sorgen. Eine Denkschrift des Rates der EKD* (Gütersloh: Gütersloher, 2007).
[46] Bonhoeffer, *Ethik*, 148–57.

sequences for generations to come may never be avoided, especially in an age of weapons of mass destruction, smart bombs, and robotized weaponry. The doctrine of just peace is by definition not confined to questions of armed military conflict or other types of war, but attempts a broad approach to the resolution of conflict. As a normative political model, it is centered on the idea of human dignity implying human rights to equal recognition, the protection of life and limb, and the opportunity to attain basic subsistence. "Just peace" then normatively describes a process of reducing violence and increasing social and political justice by the establishment of fair and participatory legal regimes considered necessary to enable equitable conflict resolution without resorting to violence. Ideally, just peace involves a participatory rule of law based on civil reciprocal recognition and a monopoly of force on the national level as well as a nonviolent regime of conflict resolution on the international level.

Human relations are often far from ideal, however, and in a Christian perspective the toleration of evil is evil in itself. But as violence breeds violence, the just-peace doctrine views the use of force only as a last resort to hinder atrocity and thus to prepare a space for nonviolent conflict resolution through a fair legal regime. The classical criteria of the just-war tradition—just cause, rightful intention, legitimate authority, adequate means—are then reframed to fit a concept of law-sustaining force.[47] The threat or use of force may then be seen as a last resort in cases where fair legal conflict resolution systematically fails and basic human rights are grossly violated. On an international level, examples would include cases of genocide or unprovoked and unilateral violent aggression, such as the Russian invasion of case in Ukraine. On a national level, examples would include cases of imminent lethal threat to victims of crime or terrorism; legitimate self-defense; and legitimate political resistance in cases where a legal system is captured by a dictatorial and murderous regime. However, as the use of force is always ambiguous and usually creates new injury, violation, and trauma —not only in its sufferer but also in its agent—it needs to be severely restricted.

Even though the concept of just peace condones organizations of force—the police and the military—it understands force and violence as a means of last resort that can never be fully justified. Treating another person violently signifies in itself a breach of that reciprocal recognition that is basic for the upholding of human rights as an implication of human dignity. If force needs to be applied, societal prevention of conflict has failed, and the agents of force have to take the brunt of that failure. For that reason, they need to be invested and equipped to undertake a task that is psychologically and morally taxing, as it involves the acceptance of societal guilt.[48] To prioritize peace means to put crime or armed conflict into context and to focus on prevention regarding the reasons for con-

---

[47] EKD, *Aus Gottes Frieden leben*, 65–79.
[48] Bonhoeffer, *Ethik*, 275.

flict.⁴⁹ However, the realism inherent in the concept takes into account that prevention may fail and does so quite often, and that the use of force usually does not bring about a conflict resolution. For that reason, force is accepted only as a last resort to put an end to violence and to enable other forms of conflict resolution. This is why the police may use force, for instance, against the enraged violent husband only after they have tried to call him to reason by speaking to him, and why concepts like community policing become more and more important. This is why the classical military war paradigm treating opponents as enemies that need to be neutralized at all cost is often replaced by a law paradigm that considers even hostiles as perpetrators with human rights rather than simply as legitimate targets that need to be eliminated.⁵⁰ Peacemaking is then instrumental to be able to concentrate on peace-building.

In the wake of this kind of concept, the normative images of the agents of force are also changing. The soldier becomes a *miles protector*,⁵¹ the police person the neighborhood mediator in community policing.⁵² Thus, this kind of integrated approach may pave a way for the solution of a number of problems sketched above. It provides an overarching set of criteria that takes into account the constabularization of the military and the militarization of the police. In the broad approach to conflict solution, different types of conflicts and their reasons are taken into consideration long before the use of force has to be considered. Conflicts of participation and freedom, of fair distribution, of recognition are approached with a broad analysis that considers first of all nonviolent legal and political instruments of conflict mediation and solution. In this approach, the gap between a civil society that cherishes nonviolence, on one hand, and the organizations of force, on the other, is mediated in at least two ways. First, the task and image of agents of force are adapted accordingly. Second, the organizations of force are integrated in a concept of nonviolent conflict resolution that provides robust criteria for the use of force as a means of last resort.

As a matter of course, the implementation of such a visionary, albeit deeply realistic, concept does not come cheap. Mediation of different roles in the agencies of force—the conflict mediator also skilled in the use of force—is demanding

---

[49] See Torsten Meireis, "Der gerechte Frieden und die Ambivalenz rechtswahrender Gewalt—eine Synthese," in *Rechtserhaltende Gewalt—eine ethische Verortung, Fragen zur Gewalt*, vol. 2, ed. Ines-Jacqueline Werkner and Torsten Meireis (Wiesbaden: Springer, 2019), 149–60.

[50] See Nils Melzer, *Targeted Killing under the International Normative Paradigms of Law Enforcement and Hostilities* (Zurich: Schulthess Juristische Medien, 2007), 125, 524.

[51] Dieter Baumann, *Militärethik. Theologische, menschenrechtliche und militärwissenschaftliche Perspektiven* (Stuttgart: Kohlhammer, 2008), 436–548.

[52] See Wesley G. Skogan, *Police and Community in Chicago: A Tale of Three Cities* (Oxford: Oxford University Press, 2009), 3–17.

and requires large institutional and educational support. Additionally, society needs to accept its responsibility toward those who professionally deal with its failures at prevention. This acceptance includes reconstituting the imagery of those professionals.

Part Three:
Moral Injury and Character

Moral Injury, Moral Character, and Military Combatants

Seumas Miller

Introduction

The traumatic effect of war on military combatants is well established. In particular, posttraumatic stress disorder (PTSD) among veterans is now a matter of common knowledge and is widely reported on. More recently, the phenomenon referred to as moral injury has come to the fore.[1] Military combatants are held to be especially vulnerable to moral injury. The standard view of the relationship between PTSD and moral injury is that moral injury is a species of PTSD; roughly speaking, moral injury is held to be PTSD in which the moral values of the sufferer have been violated by himself or by others. For instance, combatants who perpetrate or are the victims of war crimes can suffer moral injury. It is agreed on all hands that PTSD and moral injury are closely related, in that both are very serious forms of psychological injury and have similar causes and symptoms (of which more below). Moreover, since moral injury and PTSD are forms of psychological *injury*, both are analogous to physical injury, in that both PTSD and moral injury consist in damage, albeit psychological damage, that is in need of repair. So, if one is morally injured, one has not merely been morally wronged (or done wrong to another) or suffered a relatively transient harm.

As is the case with PTSD, serious moral injury is a consequence of highly stressful, traumatic events. Among combatants, notable relevant stressors are a traumatic event or series of events that generate fear, grief, helplessness, shame, and other strong negative emotions—especially events that threaten one's life or cause one serious injury or death, or serious harms to others that one witnesses at first hand, for example, lethal shootings or bombings.

---

[1] Jonathan Shay, *Achilles in Vietnam: Combat Trauma and the Undoing of Character* (New York: Simon and Schuster, 1995); and Nancy Sherman, *Afterwar: Healing the Moral Wounds of Our Soldiers* (Oxford: Oxford University Press, 2015).

The above set of stressors are characteristic of PTSD.[2] The traumatic event(s) in question cause: (1) extreme mental distress, such as fear, horror, anger, shame, and depression; and (2) physical/cognitive impairments, such as memory loss and insomnia. As will become clear below, the mental distress and cognitive impairments in question are morally loaded. The symptoms of PTSD include intrusion symptoms, such as recurrent memories, dreams, and flashbacks; avoidance of memories, thoughts, or other reminders of traumatic events; negative changes in cognitions and mood; negative emotions or beliefs about oneself or others; feelings of detachment; and marked alteration in arousal and reactivity, such as aggression, excessive vigilance, and insomnia.

As noted, PTSD is usually distinguished from moral injury, albeit they are typically held to be closely related. From the above description of PTSD, we can extract the following short definition of PTSD: (1) severe distress and functional impairments (2) resulting from traumatic events. Moral injury is typically defined in part in terms of the same stressors and effects; however, as defined, it has an additional property of involving a violation of an individual's moral values.[3] Thus, moral injury is: (1) severe distress and functional impairments (2) resulting from traumatic events that (3) violate an individual's moral values. Accordingly, the supposed difference between PTSD and moral injury is that moral injury involves traumatic events that violate an individual's moral values—that is, moral injury is, in effect, a species of PTSD. The violations of one's moral values might include moral transgressions by oneself, such as killing an innocent person, or by others, such as one's felt betrayal by a superior officer in a combat zone. Moreover, according to Jonathan Shay, "Moral injury is an essential part of any combat trauma that leads to lifelong psychological injury. Veterans can usually recover from horror, fear and grief so long as 'what's right' has also not been violated."[4] Thus, according to Shay, if a veteran suffers from PTSD and, additionally, feels that he has been wronged, then he is frequently possessed by an ongoing "indignant rage" that militates against his recovery.

In this chapter I argue that, contrary to the standard view, moral injury is not a species of PTSD. Rather, on the most coherent conception of moral injury, PTSD is (in effect) a species of moral injury. Importantly, on this view the constitutive moral features of PTSD come into view. These constitutive moral features are obscured or even denied on the standard view in favor of what might be referred to as an implicit medicalized conception. In proffering this view of PTSD as a species of moral injury, I make use of the notion of caring deeply about something or someone worthy of being cared deeply about. In short, I am

---

[2] Shay, *Achilles in Vietnam*; Jonathan Glover, *Alien Landscapes: Interpreting Disordered Minds* (Cambridge, MA: Belknap Press of Harvard University Press, 2014), 321.
[3] Shay, *Achilles in Vietnam*.
[4] Ibid., 20.

framing both PTSD and moral injury in terms of a moral-psychological conception.

Caring Deeply and Moral Identity

For my purposes here, I invoke the notion of caring deeply about something or someone—a notion that seems to me and many others[5] to have a heavy moral loading. Thus, most people care deeply about their relatives and close friends and, perhaps, the communities, institutions, and nation-states to which they belong, but they also care about compliance with moral principles, such as the prohibitions mentioned above, and the possession of virtues, such as prudence, courage, and honesty.

Of course, many people care deeply about clearly morally undesirable things, such as the establishment of the Third Reich or the Caliphate of the Islamic State. I wish to exclude such morally undesirable things that might, nevertheless, be deeply cared about. Accordingly, I qualify the notion of caring deeply. This notion should not be confused with, though it has affinities to, so-called care ethics.[6] The more specific notion I wish to invoke is the somewhat objective notion of caring deeply about something which, or someone who, is *worthy of being cared deeply about.* According to the principle derivable from this notion, a moral agent ought to care deeply about something or someone worthy of being cared deeply about and, conversely, ought not to care deeply about something or someone unworthy of being cared deeply about.

This notion and the derived principle are subject to various interpretations and theoretical renderings. For instance, on some theoretical accounts what is ultimately worth caring about is what is good, but on others it is what is right. In my view, both the good and the right can be worth caring about. That is, I adopt a limited and objectivist pluralist position. That said, I accept that there is bound to be disagreement about what is worthy of being cared deeply about or, perhaps more likely, disagreement about how to resolve dilemmas in which one has to choose between two things that are both cared deeply about (and worthy of being cared deeply about). Nevertheless, there is the possibility in many instances of resolving this disagreement by recourse to reflection and argument, and on the basis of moral considerations such as moral rights (for example, to personal security), emotional needs, (for example, friendship, love, and recognition), and a range of other human goods (for example, social recognition). After all, what is cared about and what is worthy of being cared about potentially stand in some tension, the relief of which calls for reflection.

---

[5] Virginia Held, *Ethics of Care* (Oxford: Oxford University Press, 2006).
[6] Carol Gilligan, *In a Different Voice* (Cambridge, MA: Harvard University Press, 1982).

Further, I cannot in this short chapter provide a detailed elaboration and defense of the notion of caring deeply about persons or things worth caring about. However, it is a common-sense notion that has considerable intuitive force and, given some additional specification and elaboration, is serviceable for my purposes here. Indeed, I hope to show that it is a particularly useful notion for understanding PTSD, moral injury, and the relation between them.

The notion of care that I am invoking is of an emotion constituted in part by cognitive states, as well as by feelings and desires. So it is not a simple feeling, such as a bodily sensation of pain or pleasure, or a simple desire that might attach to such feelings, such as a desire that the pain desist or the pleasure continue, or a mere combination of such feelings and desires. Moreover, being an emotion worth having, it is subject to evaluative rationality. Further, evaluative rationality is internal to the emotion of caring in question. Accordingly, if the caring person comes to believe that the object of caring is not worthy of being cared deeply about, then this caring attitude is likely to wane, and all the more so if the caring person is highly sensitive to rational considerations and if their belief in the unworthiness of the object of their initial caring attitude is well founded.

What of the content of the emotion of caring deeply? Most human beings care deeply about their own life and well-being, and thus will take extreme measures to avert death, in particular. Most human beings also care deeply about the lives and well-being of their children, parents, spouses, close friends, and, in the case of combatants, the lives and well-being of their comrades-in-arms. Most human beings care deeply about their own autonomy and the autonomy of significant others (at least), and care deeply about extremely unjust treatment of themselves and extremely unjust treatment of significant others (at least). Hence, the general abhorrence of slavery and other extreme forms of injustice. Indeed, one's autonomy and receipt of just treatment are in part constitutive of one's well-being.

Again, most human beings care deeply about the approval of at least some others—for example, family, friends, and fellow citizens. Moreover, life, autonomy, and justice are things worthy of being cared deeply about. Doubtless, some disagree that life, autonomy, or justice are worthy of being cared deeply about. However, most do not disagree, and there is a vast philosophical literature explaining why they are worth being cared about—for example, life is a precondition for all other human goods, and so on. Moreover, if a person cares deeply about something that is worthless or evil, such as Hitler's Nazi regime in Germany, then they might be distressed if what they care about ceases to exist. However, this would not, on my account, be a *moral* injury, even if it is a psychological injury. A person's psychological injuries that result from the failure of his or her evil (or worthless) enterprise are not, on my account, per se moral injuries. On the other hand, if a person cares deeply about something that is in fact evil (or worthless), then they are, to that extent, morally defective. Psychopaths are an extreme case of this: morally defective to the point of being amoral. However, to be morally defective is not necessarily to be morally injured.

What of the approval of others? Here I note that most people want the approval of others but want also to be worthy of that approval. The consequence of their being worthy of the approval of others or, at least, of believing that they are worthy of the approval of others, is that they are also worthy of their own approval (or, at least, believe themselves to be worthy of their own approval); that is, they approve of themselves, and this approval is justified (or so they believe). Indeed, those who do not believe themselves to be worthy of the approval of others are unlikely to have self-approval.

> So a caring self (in my sense) typically cares deeply about his or her life, well-being, autonomy, just treatment, and approval from others, but also about the life, well-being, autonomy, just treatment, and approval of (at least) significant others. Moreover, these things and persons that the caring self cares deeply about—things and persons worthy of being cared about—are in large part constitutive of the identity of the caring self. Accordingly, if one or more of these things or persons are taken away, the identity of the caring self is to some extent damaged, or at least there is a serious risk of damage.
>
> Consider a parent who loses a child, or a person who is unjustly incarcerated for a lengthy period, or whose reputation is unjustifiably destroyed. Let us refer to the identity of the caring self as that person's moral identity, where the term "moral" connotes, in effect, something or someone deeply cared about and worthy of being deeply cared about. This use of the term "moral" might strike some as idiosyncratic because they want to reserve it for a much narrower set of considerations—especially prohibitions against serious wrongdoing. However, this restriction has, potentially at least, a distorting effect, in that it can tend to restrict the range of considerations of the highest importance to these prohibitions—which is not to say that these prohibitions are not among the most important considerations. By contrast, the wider connotation of the term "moral" reflects my view that an important dimension of morality is in fact what is deeply cared about and is worth being deeply cared about, including self-regarding things, such as one's own life.
>
> Notice that the term "moral" in use here refers in part to self-regarding features of a person—notably, the person's own life, well-being, or self-approval. Moreover, the loss of, or threat to, these self-regarding features might not involve any wrongdoing on the part of oneself or others. For instance, a painter whose life revolved around his work as a painter might lose his sight, and hence his ability to paint, in a car accident, and, as a consequence, his moral identity (as I am using the term) might be damaged. Again, a woman whose children are killed in an earthquake that struck her home might be so traumatized and grief-stricken that her moral identity (again, as I am using the term) is severely damaged. Notice that this damage to her moral identity might manifest itself in ongoing severe distress and functional im-

pairments, such as memory loss. In short, the traumatic event of the death of the woman's children in the earthquake might cause PTSD, as has in fact occurred on many occasions.[7]

Evidently, then, there is a three-way relationship between the caring self, the moral identity of the caring self, and PTSD-inducing traumatic events, such that: (1) traumatic events cause PTSD (an established psychological fact); (2) such traumatic events are traumatic in large part because they strike at what a caring self most deeply cares about and knows is worth caring about (for example, they cause the loss of loved ones or threaten the caring self's own life; and (3) the trauma in question consists in damage to the moral identity of a caring self (my quasi-theoretical claim) (for example, a mother's loss of her child), and manifests itself in ongoing severe distress and functional impairments. Bearing in mind this three-way relationship, let us now focus the discussion on military combatants, in particular.

Moral Injury and Moral Identity: Military Combatants

Many combatants who have *justifiably* killed enemy combatants[8] have, nevertheless, experienced flashbacks, suffered from insomnia, constantly been in an unnecessary hyper-alert state, and, more generally, suffered ongoing stress and distress many years after the cessation of hostilities; the war is over, but their stress and distress continue. Evidently, the fact that a combatant engages in morally justifiable killing does not necessarily provide peace of mind (so to speak). Perhaps in such cases there is an unresolved tension in the former combatant between, on one hand, his natural—and, typically, morally reinforced—aversion to killing another human being and putting his own life at risk, and, on the other hand, his occupancy of a role as a combatant not only trained to kill and to suppress his own fear of death, but institutionally required, indeed morally obliged, to have the courage under fire to kill in defense of himself, his comrades in arms, and (let us assume) a greater moral good, such as the nation in self-defense against unjustified military aggression. In short, perhaps there is an inherent sociopsychological tension at the heart of the occupational role of combatant. Moreover, this tension is reflected in, rather than necessarily resolved by, prevailing sociomoral norms and associated moral beliefs (even if it can be resolved by objective morality). For the norms and beliefs that prevail among ordinary

---

[7] Wenjie Dai et al., "The Incidence of Post-Traumatic Stress Disorder among Survivors after Earthquakes," *BMC Psychiatry* 16 (2016): 188.

[8] Seumas Miller, *Shooting to Kill: The Ethics of Police and Military Use of Lethal Force* (New York: Oxford University Press, 2016).

citizens of contemporary liberal democracies, and outside war zones, emphasize the prohibition against killing and contribute to a culture of nonviolence, yet those norms and beliefs prevalent in the military promote the martial virtues and contribute to the institutionalization of the ability and disposition to kill and to risk one's life for a higher purpose. However, those who are or were combatants are also ordinary citizens. Naturally, as Shay points out, this tension is exacerbated if the combatant comes to doubt that the war he fought in was in fact morally justified or if the community he was fighting for (that is, killing others and risking his life for) comes to doubt this, as in the case of the wars in Iraq and Vietnam.[9]

The upshot of this discussion of combatants is that while they obviously deeply care about many things that most human beings deeply care about, including their own life and well-being, as well as the lives and well-being of significant others (at least) and the approval of self and others, important differences exist by virtue of their institutional role, notably their willingness to put themselves in harm's way and their disposition to use harmful methods for a higher purpose. Moreover, these differences generate not only high levels of stress but also sociopsychological (and moral) tensions conducive to psychological injury and, in extreme cases, PTSD—that is, by the lights of the care-based account, conducive to moral injury. What are the implications of these differences and consequences in terms of PTSD for our notions of the caring self and of moral identity?

At this point it might be helpful to reflect on a good that combatants care deeply about, but which ordinary civilians, at least in contemporary liberal democracies, often care much less about, namely, honor. The failure of combatants to live up to their code of honor is regarded by combatants as shameful, so much so that it is likely to destroy an offender's reputation and lead to social ostracism. But what is this notion of honor,[10] and what function does it have in warfighting?

Combatants are evidently regarded as worthy of honor if they possess the set of virtues in large part definitive of their institutional roles. These virtues include loyalty to comrades in arms or fellow police officers; physical courage; physical and mental resilience; self-discipline in the face of danger; strength and skill in a fight (with or without a weapon); internalized, automatic responses to specific threats; and, more generally, competence and reliability with respect to the performance of the key individual tasks constitutive of the joint activity definitive of the respective roles. These virtues are developed (for example, in training programs), mutually reinforced (for example, in war stories and displays of respect), and exercised in large part in joint activity (notably in fighting

---

[9] Shay, *Achilles in Vietnam*.
[10] Peter Olsthoorn, *Honor in Political and Moral Philosophy* (New York: SUNY Press, 2015).

a war). Moreover, it is clear that these virtues are derived from, first, the institutional purposes of the role of combatants (notably to win wars) and, second, the demandingness of the individual and joint activity (for example, warfighting) required to realize those purposes.

These and other virtues are constitutive of honor and, as such, are both deeply cared about by combatants and believed to be worthy of being deeply cared about. Moreover, being constitutive of honor, these (and other) virtues are ones upon which depends the reputation of a combatant among peers, and without which self-worth and worth in the eyes of others in the group is severely damaged, if not destroyed. Further, these virtues—being deeply cared about, definitive in part of self-worth, and internalized—are constitutive elements of the moral identity of combatants. Accordingly, cowardice, lack of physical and mental resilience, and other forms of weakness are regarded as unacceptable vices and, as such, both a matter of acute shame and undermining of the moral identity of combatants. Moreover, these collectively held attitudes to cowardice and other forms of weakness are institutionally reinforced by the discipline system. It is no accident that, for instance, military law provides for severe punishments for acts of cowardice: historically, the death sentence for desertion in the face of the enemy or surrendering to the enemy against orders.

PTSD and Moral Injury

As we have seen, traumatic events either remove or threaten what the traumatized person deeply cares about (the person's own life, the life of the person's significant others, the person's autonomy, or that of the person's significant others) or make the traumatized person a witness, often on an ongoing basis, to the removal of what other persons, often strangers, care most deeply about (for example, a war correspondent who frequently witnesses the victims of aerial bombing raids). I also note that the objects of care are often in part constitutive of one another and are also, for that matter, components of a unified self[11] (the core of which is one's moral identity, in my parlance), and, therefore, damage to one is not easily compartmentalized and contained, at either the individual or the group level.

At the level of an individual combatant, for instance, an ongoing threat of being killed in a war zone can generate in this person, including after the war, not simply occasional moments of fear but a sustained condition of fearfulness, which in turn can undermine the person's morally informed rational judgment and further undermine his or her autonomy and (relatedly) self-worth, thereby exacerbating the prior condition of fearfulness—and so on in a vicious circle of

---

[11] Charles Taylor, *Sources of the Self* (Cambridge: Cambridge University Press, 1989).

psychological decline and damage. At the group level, objects of care are often held in common; therefore, the traumatic effects of the event of, for instance, a parent's loss of a son in a war or a combatant's loss of a number of close comrades in a firefight can ramify through the group (the family or the army unit). Thus, in the case of the son, it is not simply the mother's or the father's own direct loss that is felt by each, since, in addition, the mother's trauma is felt by the father and, likewise, the father's trauma by the mother. Similarly, in the case of the fallen comrades in arms, each warfighter's own presence at the traumatic event and direct loss of comrades might have been witnessed by the others in the unit (who themselves also suffered a direct loss).

Let us now turn to the relationship between PTSD and moral injury. As we saw above, both PTSD and moral injury are defined in terms of severe distress and functional impairments caused by traumatic events. However, on the standard account there is an important distinction between them: moral injury (but not necessarily PTSD) involves either: (1) the traumatized person's own wrongdoing or complicity in wrongdoing (for example, a combatant who deliberately kills civilians) or (2) a real or imagined wrong done to the traumatized person (for example, a combatant who is betrayed by his or her superior).

On the care-based account, the moral injury might or might not involve the traumatized person's own wrongdoing (or complicity, real or imagined)) or wrong done to him or her (for example, the traumatic event might be experiencing an earthquake or simply being a bystander, as in the case of the war correspondent). However, the point is that on the care-based account, the traumatic event, whether it involves moral wrongdoing or not, does consist in removing or threatening to remove someone or something deeply cared about and worthy of being deeply cared about. In doing so, the traumatic event damages the person's moral identity by undermining core elements of that identity, such as the person's ability to care deeply (for example, emotional emptiness caused by extreme grief over loss of loved ones), the person's autonomy (for example, an ongoing condition of fear and feelings of helplessness), or the person's moral sense (for example, moral confusion resulting from an unjustified killing of a civilian in war). A further point here is that the loss of the ability to care deeply appears to be connected to the distancing from the traumatic events suffered. Distancing is, of course, a natural and often necessary process. However, if the traumatized person never comes to terms with the traumatic event, then distancing may become part of the problem.

On the care-based account, what is deeply cared about and worthy of being deeply cared about provides much of the content of actions regarded as morally wrong; for example, murder is morally wrong precisely because we care deeply about life, and life is worth caring deeply about. The point here is not that what makes murder wrong is simply that we care about life, *but also that life is, objectively speaking, worth caring deeply about,* that is, life is important because, for instance, it underpins all other things worth doing. Of course, and notwithstanding my claim above that a restrictive use of the term "moral" can have a distorting effect, it might be insisted that the term "moral" be used exclusively to refer to moral wrongdoing (and perhaps doing what is morally right). If so, this would not vitiate my argument in favor of the care-based view, but would simply render the dispute a purely semantic one and lead to the need to come up with a different term with a wider use—for example, "moral*." At the very least, in terms of our focus here, what is *most* traumatizing about murder is not that it is a morally wrong action but, rather, that human life (whether terminated in a morally permissible way or not) is cared deeply about (and is worthy of being cared deeply about). Hence, to do what is morally wrong or to be morally wronged is not necessarily, or even typically, traumatizing. It is generally only traumatizing if the wrong involves the removal or threatened removal of what is deeply cared about, including, of course, avowedly moral conditions such as autonomy, as in the case of torture. Torture inflicts extreme physical and psychological suffering, but it is also, importantly, an attack on autonomy.[12]

Notice that on the care-base account, moral injury is not a species of PTSD; rather, in effect, PTSD is a species of moral injury. For PTSD typically results from traumatic events that bring about the removal or threatened removal of what one cares deeply about, for example, one's own life or the lives of significant others. However, if PTSD consists in severe distress and functional impairments, then, strictly speaking, perhaps PTSD is a manifestation of very serious moral injury rather than a species of it.

While, on the care-based view, PTSD is (speaking roughly) a species of moral injury, nevertheless, the moral injury manifest in PTSD is of two types. The two types in question mirror the types referred to on the standard view as (respectively) PTSD and moral injury. The first type involves moral responsibility for the moral injury—the moral responsibility of the injured person or of someone else for his or her injury.The second type does not involve moral responsibility of the injured person or of some other person for the moral injury in question. I suggest that it is the lack of moral responsibility in play in the second type that leads to the tendency to exclude it from the sphere of morality and, indeed, medicalize it as PTSD conceived in nonmoral terms. This is, as I have suggested, a mistake. Let me explain further.

Given the existence of the second type, on the care-based account one's moral identity—that is, what one most deeply cares about, including one's autonomy—can be undermined or substantially diminished by traumatic events beyond one's own control—for example, aerial bombardments by the enemy in a war zone. Indeed, one's moral identity can be undermined by traumatic events be-

---

[12] Seumas Miller, "Is Torture Ever Morally Justifiable?," *International Journal of Applied Philosophy* 19, no. 2 (2005): 179–92.

yond *anyone's* control, such as natural disasters. Moreover, the traumatic events in question might be such that no human being could avoid being substantially psychologically damaged by them; as is often said, *everyone* has a breaking point. It seems to follow from this that on the care-based account, traumatized persons are not necessarily fully morally responsible for their moral identity, that is, what they deeply care about, including those elements of their moral identity that consist of such other-regarding virtues as honesty and fairness. After all, it is entirely possible that traumatic events have unavoidably undermined a person's autonomy. Of course, it does not follow from this that those who suffer from serious moral injuries manifest in PTSD are in principle unable to undergo moral-psychological repair (so to speak).

Conclusion

It is now well established that military combatants are vulnerable to moral injury. According to the standard view of moral injury, it is a species of PTSD; roughly speaking, moral injury is held to be PTSD in which the moral values of the sufferer have been violated by himself or by others. By contrast, I have argued that moral injury is not a species of PTSD; rather, PTSD is (in effect) a species of moral injury. Importantly, on this view the constitutively moral features of PTSD are displayed, rather than denied or obscured as they are on the standard view which tends to medicalize PTSD. Moreover, my moral-psychological conception makes use of the notion of caring deeply about something or someone worthy of being cared deeply about. Accordingly, I proffer a care-based account of moral injury (and, therefore, of PTSD). On the care-based account, one's moral identity—that is, what one most deeply cares about, including one's autonomy and, in the case of military combatants, one's honor—can be undermined or substantially diminished by traumatic events beyond one's own control. Thus, combatants can suffer moral injury, and their moral character, indeed their moral identity, can be undermined if they engage in war crimes, but also if they suffer aerial bombardments by the enemy in a war zone in which combatants on both sides are compliant with the generally accepted moral principles applicable to waging war.

In the Shadow of the Operation: Moral and Spiritual Injuries as New Challenges for Pastoral Care in the German Armed Forces

Isolde Karle and Niklas Peuckmann

Entry

Over the past twenty-five years, the Bundeswehr (German Armed Forces) has transformed itself into an operational army. The consequences of this fundamental reorientation have been borne first and foremost by the servicemen and women and their families. They report on their deployment experiences, worries, and hardships in field letters. These unvarnished snapshots impressively show the dark side of the Bundeswehr's new operational reality. In a field post letter, a German soldier in Afghanistan writes:

> April 29 is a beautiful, almost midsummer day, no special incidents for days. When we are all still standing together in front of the MEDEVC container [Medical Evacuation Container] after dinner, IRF [Immediate Reaction Force] is alerted. Off we go in the tank and forward to the grove of honor. On the radio, I hear already on the way that the Quebec platoon is in trouble. Next, I hear that the Juliet platoon, which was supposed to patrol the river loop tonight, is already coming to Quebec's aid. I suddenly feel different. We've had a few patrols fired on at night, but this sounds intense. Also, there is a BAT [mobile medical team] of us with them. Maria, the doctor, is on her first mission. Hopefully, nothing happened to them. Then we also get information from the deputy IRF platoon leader. Quebec has been ambushed. I hear on the radio that the JOC [command center] is discussing with Quebec to open the camp gate on radio call to drive the BAT straight through to the rescue center. This does not bode well.... Now there is nothing left but to wait. Alone, I stand in the rear of our tank in the open hatch and experience the most intense wait of my life under an incongruously beautiful starry sky. Thoughts circle around Quebec, the wounded man, and my upcoming mission. Then, over Tetrapol, comes the JOC situation briefing: "JOC to all, situation briefing: at approximately 7 p.m., the Quebec platoon was ambushed northwest of Kunduz. Parts of the platoon were able to evade into the PRT [temporary field camp]. One soldier was seriously injured and succumbed to his in-

juries at the rescue center." Dead. The unexpected happened, yet so far everything always went well. In my stomach, and certainly not only in my stomach, a paralyzing emptiness spreads.[1]

In his letter home, the soldier describes how he witnessed over the radio the attack on the Quebec patrol platoon on April 29, 2009. On that day, the first German Bundeswehr soldier lost his life in Afghanistan as a result of an attack or, as it is called in the official language of the Bundeswehr, through foreign influence. By the time the troops leave in the summer of 2021, thirty-four more soldiers will have lost their lives due to "external causes" in this mission (ISAF) and the follow-on mission (RS); twenty-four more soldiers will have died as a result of accidents or unexplained causes of death in Afghanistan. Since the beginning of the Bundeswehr's operational reality, that is, since 1992, a total of 114 soldiers have died in various missions—most of them in Afghanistan (fifty-nine). Moreover, the hasty withdrawal of troops after the Taliban regained power in the summer of 2021 called the entire mission into question. This means that the soldiers not only risked a great deal and, in some cases, had traumatic experiences, but in retrospect also have to come to terms with the fact that their actions may have been in vain, that the mission, in any case, did not achieve the goals it was supposed to.

Death and wounding are part of the reality of being a soldier. They are *visible signs* that the Bundeswehr is an operational army, that it uses military force to achieve its goals, but that at the same time it can itself become the target of military force. These visible signs of the new operational practice were the subject of much discussion in society as a whole in the 2000 s. The "fallen" and the "wounded returning from war" were certainly present in the public sphere. Funeral services for soldiers who died in action were broadcast live on television.[2] In Berlin, the cornerstone was laid in 2008 for the Bundeswehr Memorial, which was ceremonially inaugurated in 2009 by then President Horst Köhler.[3]

The operational reality of the Bundeswehr confronts soldiers with death and wounding. But it is not only visible injuries but also invisible ones that leave their mark on the soldiers. They return from deployment changed; there they

---

[1] Translated from Marc Baumann et al., eds., *Feldpost. Briefe deutscher Soldaten aus Afghanistan* (Hamburg: Bundeszentrale für Politische Bildung, 2011), 147–49 (explanatory inserts by authors).

[2] Gertrud Schäfer, "Sie haben ihr Leben riskiert. Zentrale Trauerfeiern für in Afghanistan getötete deutsche Soldaten (2007/2010)," in *Riskante Liturgien. Gottesdienste in der gesellschaftlichen Öffentlichkeit*, ed. Kristian Fechtner and Thomas Klie (Stuttgart: Kohlhammer, 2011), 43–66, at 45–49 and 54–56.

[3] Gerald Kretzschmar, "Das Ehrenmal der Bundeswehr. Ein zivilreligiöser Weg in die neue Bundesrepublik," in Fechtner and Klie, *Riskante Liturgien*, 67–78.

have seen images that traumatize them and call their value orientation into question. Soldiers of the Bundeswehr suffer psychological wounds because of foreign missions, wounds that are not visible and are therefore hardly noticed by society or the military.

Such "hidden wounds of war"[4] are usually associated with the clinical picture of posttraumatic stress disorder (PTSD). A 2012 study by the Technical University of Dresden in cooperation with the Center for Psychiatry and Psychotraumatology at the Bundeswehr Hospital in Berlin estimates that, on average, 3 percent of soldiers with deployment experience develop clinically significant posttraumatic stress disorder.[5] This figure may sound low; comparable studies of the U.S. military, for example, assume 9 to 20 percent. But even 3 percent represents a major problem in absolute terms. The authors of the study assume that the total number of soldiers suffering from PTSD is in the thousands, probably even exceeding ten thousand, which is plausible given the more than four hundred thousand soldiers who have been sent on Bundeswehr missions abroad in the past twenty-five years. The problem is that about half of these *invisible signs* of the reality of deployment, the "hidden wounds of war," remain undiscovered and are accordingly not treated. Posttraumatic stress disorders are not infrequently accompanied by other deployment-related stress reactions. A special variant of such a reaction will be discussed in the following section: *moral injuries* or *spiritual injuries*. In particular, the question arises as to what extent these mission-related stress reactions represent a topic for military pastoral care,[6] and how pastors in the Bundeswehr can make room for these experiences in pastoral care.

Moral and Spiritual Injuries

Periods of deployment place very special demands on soldiers. The men and women of the Bundeswehr who are deployed on missions today experience a daily routine that can hardly be compared with life at home. They are immersed in a world dominated by technology, military equipment, and clear rules. There

---

[4] Rita Nakashima Brock and Gabriella Lettini, *Soul Repair: Recovering from Moral Injury after War* (Boston: Beacon Press, 2012), 93.

[5] See Hans-Ulrich Wittchen et al., "Traumatische Ereignisse und posttraumatische Belastungsstörungen bei im Ausland eingesetzten Soldaten. Wie hoch ist die Dunkelziffer?," *Deutsches Ärzteblatt* 109, nos. 35–36 (2012): 559–68.

[6] On the subject of pastoral care in the Bundeswehr, see in detail Niklas Peuckmann, *In kritischer Solidarität. Eine Theorie der Militärseelsorge* (Leipzig, 2022 forthcoming).

is hardly any privacy,[7] and they are separated from their own families for several months. The workweek is tightly structured with little variety. In soldier jargon, every day is Wednesday during deployment.[8] Soldiers perceive the deployment period as an incredibly intense time. This is especially true of those moments when the order of the operational world is turned upside down. The field letter quoted at the beginning of this article suggests this. These moments are felt to be particularly intense because they suddenly confront the soldiers with a state of emergency that defies control, despite all the security standards, equipment, and preparation. In these moments, however, it is not only the external measures of military protection that reach their limits; the psychological resilience of the soldiers is also put to the test. Not infrequently, these experiences cast a long shadow.

It has long been known that periods of deployment have a psychological impact on soldiers. However, scientific research into these stress reactions has been conducted only since the second half of the twentieth century. The focus has mostly been on posttraumatic stress disorders. Against this background, the "war tremblers of the past [have become the] traumatized of today."[9]

Comparatively new within the research field is the concept of *moral injury*. It was first described and defined as a distinct symptom complex by Jonathan Shay and James Munroe in 1998.[10] Since then, the term has been intensively discussed, especially in the Anglo-American world.[11] On one hand, there was interest in a precise definition of the term, and on the other hand, there was the question to what extent moral injuries differ from posttraumatic stress disorder (PTSD), or whether they rather represent a specific variant of this symptom com-

---

[7] Jonathan Schnitt, *Foxtrott 4. Sechs Monate mit deutschen Soldaten in Afghanistan*, 2nd ed. (Munich: Bertelsmann, 2012), 64.

[8] Gotthold Patberg, "Nicht jeder Tag ist Mittwoch—Der Sonntagsgottesdienst im Auslandseinsatz," in *Für Ruhe in der Seele sorgen. Evangelische Militärpfarrer im Auslandseinsatz der Bundeswehr*, ed. Peter Michaelis and Evangelisches Kirchenamt für die Bundeswehr (Leipzig: Evangelische Verlagsanstalt, 2003), 81–85.

[9] Translated from Marcel Bohnert and Björn Schreiber, "Die Neuen Veteranen," *Die unsichtbaren Veteranen. Kriegsheimkehrer in der deutschen Gesellschaft*, ed. Marcel Bohnert et al. (Berlin: Carola Hartmann, 2016), 33–42, at 33.

[10] Jonathan Shay and James Munroe, "Group and Milieu Therapy for Veterans with Complex Posttraumatic Stress Disorder," in *Posttraumatic Stress Disorder: A Comprehensive Text*, ed. Philip A. Saigh and J. Douglas Bremner (Boston: Allyn and Baker, 1998), 391–413.

[11] A systematic compilation of the literature published to date on the subject of "moral injury" is provided by: Lindsay B. Carey et al., "Moral Injury, Spiritual Care and the Role of Chaplains: An Exploratory Scoping Review of Literature and Resources," *Journal of Religion and Health* 55, no. 4 (2016): 1218–45.

plex.¹² Meanwhile, there are many indications that it is useful to distinguish moral injuries from PTSD,¹³ although there are parallels and, in individual cases, interdependencies between the two syndromes. Moral injuries can be traced back to a lasting shaking of the moral-value orientation, whereas posttraumatic stress disorder is a physiological reaction to an extreme situation.¹⁴ Accordingly, the symptoms of the two clinical pictures differ. Posttraumatic stress disorders are often accompanied by flashbacks, intrusions, and anxiety attacks. Comparable somatic reactions are not detectable in moral injuries. Rather, they influence the emotional experience and feelings of those affected. Thus, it can be said that in PTSD, *anxiety states* are in the foreground, whereas in moral injuries, *feelings of shame* and *guilt* dominate.¹⁵

Feelings of shame and guilt play an important role in Christian anthropology. The complex of themes is reflected in many narratives of biblical prehistory (Genesis 3:7; 4:14; 9:22–25).¹⁶ Against this background, it is not surprising that moral violations are also reflected upon in terms of their religious implications. In this context, the concept of *spiritual injury* was developed. With the concept of spiritual injury, the value orientation that is disrupted in moral injuries is interpreted in religious terms. Such an injury is then interpreted in terms of damage to the relationship between human and creation or between human and God.¹⁷ The anchor point for this relationship is provided by *soul*. Thus, theologian Jan Grimell writes, "Spiritual injury also closely relates to terms such as 'soul wound,' 'soul injury' and 'soul repair.'"¹⁸

The ongoing discussions of spiritual injury help to sharpen the concept of moral injury. At the same time, they lead to new imprecisions, since the terms used can hardly be defined concretely. For example, the question arises as to

---

12 Ibid., 1220.
13 Craig J. Bryan et al., "Moral Injury, Posttraumatic Stress Disorder, and Suicidal Behavior among National Guard Personnel," *Psychological Trauma* 10, no. 1 (2018): 36–45.
14 Brock and Lettini, *Soul Repair*, xiii.
15 *Thomas Thiel*, "Geteiltes Leben. Seelsorgliche Begleitung traumatisierter Soldaten," *Wege zum Menschen* 70, no. 6 (2018): 497–509, at 503–06.
16 Michael Klessmann, "Ich armer, elender, sündiger Mensch . . .'. Das Christentum, die Schuld und die Scham—im Kontext der Gefängnisseelsorge," in *Nachdenkliche Seelsorge –seelsorgliches Nachdenken. Festschrift für Christoph Morgenthaler zum 65*, ed. Isabelle Noth and Ralph Kunz (Göttingen: Vandenhoeck & Ruprecht, 2012), 152–69, at 154–60.
17 Jan Grimell elaborates this definition: "From a theological point of view, a spiritual injury can be understood as a violation of a sacred nexus within a person, which can damage a person's sense of strong connectedness with the whole of creation, God and/or a transcendent dimension." Jan Grimell, "Veterans, the Hidden Wounds of War, and Soul Repair," *Spiritual Care* 7, no. 4 (2018): 353–63, at 356.
18 Ibid., 355.

how the terms "spirituality" or "soul" are to be understood.[19] Particularly in the U.S. context, thought is being given to the extent to which religion can be used as a coping strategy to deal with the particular stresses and strains of servicemen and women.[20] With the concept of spiritual injury, it becomes clear that the shaking of value orientation results in a disruption of the ability to relate. Moral injuries put a strain on the relationships of the soldiers, including the relationships with oneself, with the social environment, and with God—especially when it comes to the questions of how to live with guilt, what forgiveness means, and how one can live with a deep moral-spiritual injury.

Deployment as a Test of Endurance for the Soldiers' Families

Foreign deployments are a stress test for soldiers' relationships. For several months, they live apart from their usual social environment, especially their families. They experience a daily routine that differs in many ways from life at home. "The family situation at home evolves just like normal everyday life back home. The children grow, the partner's hair turns grayer, things in everyday life break and are replaced—and the soldier is not there, cannot support or does not experience it."[21] Soldiers also sometimes miss biographically important events, such as the birth or enrollment of a child, a milestone birthday of a good friend, or the death and funeral of a close relative.[22] Deployment is like a time bubble into which the soldiers are taken. They become part of a parallel world that has little in common with their other everyday world. As a result, experiences of distance come between the families and the soldiers. During a telephone call,

---

[19] On the term "soul," see Elis Eichener, "Seele und Seelsorge. Eine emergenztheoretische Reformulierung des Seelenbegriffs," *Evangelische Theologie* 79, no. 6 (2019): 437-49; on the term "spirituality," see Isolde Karle, *Praktische Theologie* (Leipzig: Evangelische Verlagsanstalt, 2020), 79-87.

[20] For example, Ron Hassner, a scholar of religion, sees religion as having the potential as a coping strategy that can help deal with posttraumatic stress disorder. See Ron Hassner, "Hypotheses on Religion in the Military," *International Studies Review* 18, no. 2 (2016): 312-32, at 323.

[21] Translated from Christoph Sommer, "Seelsorge an Bord einer seegehenden Einheit der Deutschen Marine. Perspektiven aus der Praxis," in *Seelsorge in der Bundeswehr. Perspektiven aus Theorie und Praxis*, ed. Isolde Karle and Niklas Peuckmann (Leipzig: Evangelische Verlagsanstalt, 2020), 99-114, at 111.

[22] Katrin Schwarz, ed. *Ich kämpf' mich zu dir durch, mein Schatz. Briefe von der Heimatfront (2000-2010)* ([n.p.]: Sankt Augustin, 2011), 186.

conflict can arise because it is difficult to understand each other. The telephone is considered a "medium of misunderstanding" during deployment anyway.[23]

The partner[24] in the home country also experiences a state of emergency during the deployment period. During this time, she or he has to take sole responsibility for everyday life, for organizing the family, raising the children, and managing the household. In addition, there are constant worries about the partner in the distant crisis or war zone. Soldiers' families also perceive this state of emergency as a deployment experience—they speak of *life on the home front*.[25] Sometimes the stresses are so great that the relationship breaks up during deployment. The separation rate for the Bundeswehr is significantly higher than the average for Germany as a whole.

When the deployment is over, the stresses on relationships do not automatically disappear. Usually, the "greatest challenge for the relationship ... comes to those involved [only] after the deployment."[26] Here, the motto "'after the deployment is before the deployment'"[27] applies. This means that after the end of the temporary separation during the deployment, it is important to reconcile the parallel everyday worlds and, ideally, to reconnect them with each other. However, "only" reintegration of the soldier into his original environment takes place. The parallel worlds of experience do not meet at eye level, the soldier must draw a line under the last four to six months and fit into the familiar structures of family life. The neuralgic phase of reintegration into the old environment carries the risk that deployment-related stress reactions will develop. If soldiers have suffered moral-spiritual injuries during deployment, have seen images that make them doubt their previous value orientation, or have had experiences that can hardly be put into words, then they cannot simply reintegrate into their old life. Having faced suffering, violence, and death, they will experience many things in their homeland as trivial and foreign to them. This expe-

---

[23] Peter Wendl, *Soldat im Einsatz—Partnerschaft im Einsatz. Praxis- und Arbeitsbuch für Paare und Familien in Auslandseinsatz und Wochenendbeziehung*, Freiburg i. Br.: Herder, 2011), 13.

[24] The following applies to the Bundeswehr: in general, there are still vastly more male soldiers on deployment while their female spouses are at home. The percentage of female soldiers on deployment has been less than 5 percent for the past twenty-five years, although women have had access to all branches of the Bundeswehr—including the fighting branches—only since 2001. On the subject of the dominance of male soldiers, see Gerhard Kümmel, "Das Militär, die Frauen und die Militärseelsorge," in Karle and Peuckmann, *Seelsorge in der Bundeswehr*, 55–66.

[25] Schwarz, *Ich kämpf' mich zu dir durch*.

[26] Translated from Luise Hautmann, "Sechs Monate sind eine lange Zeit—Erfahrungen von Soldatenfrauen," in Michaelis, *Für Ruhe in der Seele sorgen*, 137–41, at 141.

[27] Ibid.

rience triggers a creeping process of marginalization or alienation. The partner will initially leave the returning soldier alone in the hope that, with time, the usual normality will return. Children may react to the change in their returning parent's behavior with distance, partly because they find it difficult to cope with the discontinuity caused by the deployment. They then often turn more to the parent who took care of them during the deployment period, and who thus stands for continuity.[28] The returning soldier will also withdraw—becoming uncommunicative because lacking the words to express what he has experienced.

The initial distance can turn into deep rifts that put a strain on family togetherness. For example, even weeks after returning home, a soldier may not communicate that he or she is seeking refuge in seclusion or alcohol.[29] These situations are extremely stressful for all involved. At the same time, there are deceptive hopes that everything will soon change, that everything will return to the way it used to be. The soldier is left alone with the best of intentions, but in fact, she feels left alone because she receives no help and is offered no space in which to at least attempt to articulate feelings and experiences.

This negative dynamic is reinforced institutionally. Soldiers rarely turn to the Bundeswehr's troop psychological service of their own accord—partly because they fear that a psychiatric diagnosis could jeopardize their career in the armed forces. Moreover, as a result of the reality of deployment, soldiers' families have been pushed out of the immediate vicinity of the military.[30] There are hardly any contact points within the armed forces to support them in the event of a deployment-related stress reaction on the part of their partner. Moreover, soldiers' families report that they receive no help from civilian therapists.[31] The support services and therapy programs offered by the German armed forces, on the other hand, have the shortcoming that they generally focus only on the individual soldier, neglecting the stresses and strains on the social system.

---

[28] Peter Wendl, *Gelingende Fern-Beziehung: entfernt–zusammen–wachsen*, 8th ed. (Freiburg i. Br.: Herder, 2017), 76.

[29] Peter Zimmermann, "Einsatz, Werte und psychische Gesundheit bei Bundeswehrsoldaten," in *Kollateralopfer. Die Tötung von Unschuldigen als rechtliches und moralisches Problem*, ed. Matthias Gillner and Volker Stümke (Münster: Aschendorff, 2014), 173–94, at 173.

[30] Michael Gmelch and Richard Hartmann, eds., *Soldatenfamilien im Stress. Kriegseinsätze als Herausforderung für die Militärseelsorge mit den Familien* (Würzburg: Echter, 2014).

[31] Kerstin Lammer, *Wie Seelsorge wirkt* (Stuttgart: Kohlhammer, 2020), 198.

Military Chaplaincy—ASEM Project

The military chaplaincy has recognized this gap and is now working to fill it. In 2012, the chaplaincy launched a corresponding pastoral care project, which became an independent field of work in 2017.[32] The field of *pastoral care for people suffering from the consequences of deployment and service* (*Arbeitsfeld Seelsorge für unter Einsatz- und Dienstfolgen leidende*)—ASEM for short—pursues the goal of opening *inclusive spaces* in which not only the soldiers but also their families have a permanent place. The response this field of work has generated among military families has been remarkable. Since 2012, over four hundred seminars and events have been held. Currently, up to sixty events can be offered annually. In total, 2,897 people, including 856 children, have participated in the programs of this special work to date.[33] However, the need on the part of military families is much greater.[34]

Pastoral care for people suffering from the consequences of deployment and service is appreciated not only by soldiers and their families. It also has a remarkable impact on the Bundeswehr, the church, and the management of the military chaplaincy.[35] Because of this broad impact, the pastoral care project was solidified in 2017 as an independent field of work, with structural assurances and financial support. The state established three permanent service positions for management and administration,[36] while the church included this field of work in the regular budget of the military chaplaincy. Between 2014 and 2017, an empirical evaluation of the field was part of an examination of selected pastoral care models. A major finding of the study, which was published in 2020, was that the "satisfaction with pastoral care is extraordinarily high among all participants."[37]

---

[32] This pastoral care project is an ecumenical field of work for which the Catholic military chaplaincy is jointly responsible. The management and administrative responsibility, however, lie on the side of the Protestant military chaplaincy. See Christian Fischer, "Bericht ASEM zur 65. Gesamtkonferenz 2020 in Wittenberg," Berlin, 2020, https://www.bundeswehr.de/resource/blob/252260/42ead811b91d437d1dd0270b791af624/bericht-asem-zur-gesamtkonferenz-2020-data.pdf, 1.

[33] Ibid., 4.

[34] Ibid., 2.

[35] Matthias Heimer, "'Heilsame Irritationen'. Leitsätze für die Seelsorge in der Bundeswehr und was es braucht, um sie mit Leben zu füllen," in Karle and Peuckmann, *Seelsorge in der Bundeswehr*, 187–204, at 194.

[36] Fischer, "Bericht ASEM zur 65," 1.

[37] Translated from Lammer, *Wie Seelsorge wirkt*, 321 (emphasis removed). The study, directed by Lammer, was undertaken by the Institute for Interdisciplinary Theology and Counseling Research at the Protestant University of Applied Sciences in Freiburg.

The positive feedback shows that ASEM offers an important and, above all, professional service of care and support. This is very welcome from the point of view of pastoral theology. One of the great strengths of ASEM is that it opens up spaces that enable new encounters within the military family. ASEM follows a multiprofessional approach, offering programs and events in cooperation with psychologists, doctors, therapists, pedagogues, and others. Management of the program falls to the military chaplaincy. Despite the multiprofessional cooperation, professional boundaries are not blurred or abandoned. Thus, in the ASEM seminars, no medical appropriation of religion takes place. This is ensured above all by the fact that the religious offerings are ritual in nature and structure the events: each morning and evening, a spiritual moment frames the event in a pastoral way. This framing in turn opens up free spaces within which the other professions can work independently. At the same time, these short devotions provide an orienting daily structure that is perceived and appreciated as a resource that gives strength and comfort. Participants in the seminars report on this: "Even these very, very short devotions, ... these short few words, they bring SO much strength. It's just insane because they always get the point."[38]

This multiprofessional approach also gives ASEM great potential for innovation. This is particularly evident in the work with children. In close cooperation with the Psychotrauma Center of the German Armed Forces Hospital in Berlin, for example, a didactically high-quality comic book was developed that explains in a circumspect and illustrative way what posttraumatic stress disorders are and how they can change family life together. Titled "Shady Places. My Dad Has PTSD!,"[39] it presents and explains even bulky topics such as apathy, alcoholism, emotional alienation, and flashbacks in a child-friendly way. This approach can also be applied to work with children whose parents have suffered moral injuries. For these children, too, it is important to be able to understand that there is a reason for the change in their father or mother, but that at the same time they can be helped to deal with the stressful deployment experiences.

In terms of methods, ASEM also shows a great willingness to try out new concepts and integrate them into its work. For example, animal-assisted services have been available for several years.[40] Animals can facilitate low-threshold relationships and thus also offer a resonance space that can become a new meeting place for a stressed soldier's family through communal caring. At the same time, when dealing with an animal, soldiers learn to take responsibility again for a foreign counterpart. For children, the encounter with animals and the relationship that builds with them is also enriching. They create a positive and generally

---

[38] Translated from Lammer, *Wie Seelsorge wirkt*, 315.
[39] Translated from Kathrin Schrocke and Lilli L'Arronge, *Schattige Plätzchen. Mein Papa hat PTBS!*, 3rd ed. (Berlin, 2018).
[40] Fischer, "Bericht ASEM zur 65," 2.

calming atmosphere. These opportunities are not pastoral care in the sense of religious communication; they are rather to be understood as a form of animal-assisted therapy.[41] The Bundeswehr has remarkably taken up this initiative of the ASEM project and commissioned scientific studies in Koblenz and Berlin, which are to survey the therapeutic added value of animal-assisted offerings in the care of soldiers who have been injured in action.[42] In this respect, the field of pastoral care for people suffering from the consequences of deployment and service has an exploratory character that is significant for the entire Bundeswehr.

At ASEM, pastoral care takes place not least by people's sharing life with each other.[43] The aim is to open up spaces that stimulate a new self-awareness, offer the opportunity to communicate, and take into account the associations of the soldiers' families with one another to uncover distances and promote mutual understanding. By sharing life, families develop a new understanding of each other, so that overall relationships are strengthened. This in particular is immensely relieving for servicemen and women who have suffered moral-spiritual injuries, as they can develop a sense that their entire value orientation has not been called into question by the deployment experience. They can have the healing experience of still being able to live securely within a social system that wants to support and help them. On this basis, the moral and spiritual injuries can be sensitively discussed and dealt with by the respective professions.

With all appreciation for this field of work, it is nevertheless necessary to point out a critical point. ASEM deals with the dark sides of the reality of deployment of the Bundeswehr. The pastors in this field of work become secondary witnesses to the stresses and abysses of deployment practice. The field of pastoral care for people suffering from the consequences of deployment and service therefore also has a *seismograph function* for the German armed forces. This is reflected in the fact that the number of seminars offered each year and the probable need for such offerings is now precisely recorded. However, the military chaplaincy has not yet derived any consequences from this seismograph function. It praises the existence of ASEM, but does not criticize the fact that such a program is needed at all, and that the consequences of war for soldiers and their families are often serious.

Since the 1960 s, pastoral care in the German armed forces has repeatedly been described with the guiding concept of *critical solidarity*. That it is immense-

---

[41] Niklas Peuckmann, "Tiere im Wahrnehmungsfokus von Seelsorge. Überlegungen anhand aktueller Vollzüge von gelebter Religion," *Evangelische Theologie* 78, no. 3 (2018): 219–29.

[42] Peter Zimmermann, "Psychische Erkrankungen in der Bundeswehr," *WMM* 59, no. 2 (2015): 34–37.

[43] Fischer, "Bericht ASEM zur 65," 1.

ly challenging for pastors in practice to deal constructively with the tension between criticism and solidarity is evident not least in the ASEM project. As important and good as this work is, it remains indispensable for the military chaplaincy to critically point out the problematic overall development, which is evident in the increase in the number of soldiers who have been injured in action. So far, the chaplaincy has not lived up to this mandate.

A New Culture of the Heroic

The military chaplaincy should strive for a public discussion regarding soldiers' psychological and emotional injuries from deployment—the moral and spiritual injuries—not least because the deployment practice of the Bundeswehr is carried out "in the name" of German society or parliament. Former defense minister Peter Struck (2002–05) summed up this connection with a now much-cited statement: "The security of the Federal Republic of Germany will also be defended in the Hindu Kush." Almost twenty years later—after the withdrawal of NATO troops and the explosive resurgence of the Taliban—this notion is being severely challenged. The Bundeswehr is a parliamentary army; its foreign deployments are mandated by the German Bundestag with specific durations and troop quotas. The missions do not serve a genuine military purpose, nor are they carried out in the name of economic, power, or geopolitical interests. They are intended to serve the political goals of freedom, security, and peace. Because of these noble goals, the question arises as to how to deal socially with the consequences of deployment practice, especially when the goals have been so poorly achieved as in the Afghanistan mission. On one hand, soldiers were damaged by the particular stresses they suffered as a result of the violent conflicts during the mission, and they were wounded both morally and spiritually. On the other hand, they—and not least the relatives of fallen soldiers—are now also being psychologically frustrated by the questioning of the meaning of their deployment, the outcome of which is far from the desired success. These questions must be discussed publicly—and the military chaplaincy would do well to initiate such a discussion and to enrich it with the differentiated experiences of critically reflective and, at the same time, supportive chaplains.

German society is commonly described as a *postheroic society*.[44] This means that it is not constituted by heroic deeds and does not derive its community identity from heroic narratives about past wars. The heroic plays no role in social, cultural, and public togetherness in a postheroic society. Nevertheless, German society also seems to remain dependent on a residuum of the heroic. Thus, for

---

[44] Herfried Münkler, *Kriegssplitter. Die Evolution der Gewalt im 20. und 21. Jahrhundert* (Berlin: Rowohlt, 2015).

the military and the police, heroic deeds and narratives are still significant, especially for their own identity formation.⁴⁵ The question is whether this heroic nature does not also rub off on military chaplains, some of whom are particularly proud to be present in the field, and what problems arise from this. Werner Schiewek pleads for military chaplains to learn to cultivate a kind of "second-order heroism" that maintains an appreciative-critical distance not only from the heroism of the soldiers but also from their own "heroic parts."⁴⁶

For the Bundeswehr, at any rate, the phenomenon of the heroic plays a conspicuously important role in the context of operational practice. Heroic deeds in action are honored with medals and decorations. At the same time, the Bundeswehr Memorial in Berlin has become a central place of remembrance for soldiers who have lost their lives in the line of duty. The reality of deployment has prompted the Bundeswehr to train a new culture of heroism. The visible consequences of the reality of deployment are recognizably in the foreground. However, the darker side of this new culture of heroism is hardly noticed. This is also reflected in the self-image of returning soldiers: they describe themselves as *invisible veterans*.⁴⁷

For soldiers who have been injured in action or who have been exposed to action, the one-sided focus on the "heroic" poses a problem. They perform their service in the Bundeswehr, mandated by parliament, in a foreign mission and are understood as specialists for international crisis areas.⁴⁸ At the same time, the phenomenon of the heroic is associated in the public sphere almost exclusively with the soldierly virtues of sacrifice and bravery.⁴⁹ As a result, soldiers who return from a mission area emotionally wounded do not feel understood, because they cannot or do not want to conform to the publicly staged image of a brave or sacrificial fighter.

In a postheroic society, soldiers usually appear only as marginal figures. This is especially true for soldiers who do not correspond to the heroic image of a brave or sacrificial fighter. The new culture of the heroic, which has inten-

---

[45] Werner Schiewek, "Heroismus in der Seelsorge. Über Chancen, Risiken und Nebenwirkungen einer seelsorglichen Ressource in Militär und Polizei," in Karle and Peuckmann, *Seelsorge in der Bundeswehr*, 85–98, at 86.

[46] Ibid., 95 f.

[47] Bohnert and Schreiber, *Die unsichtbaren Veteranen*.

[48] Niklas Peuckmann, "Kirche(n) unter Soldaten—Zur Ökumene in der Militärseelsorge," *Lebendige Seelsorge* 69, no. 4 (2018), 288–93, at 289.

[49] This is particularly evident from the public addresses given about servicemen and women who have lost their lives in action. See Stefanie Hammer, "Die Rede des Verteidigungsministers im zivilreligiösen Ritual der Trauerfeier für die 'gefallenen' Soldaten," Pastoraltheologie 103, no. 1 (2014), 36–46; and Stefanie Hammer, *Wie der Staat trauert. Zivilreligionspolitik in der Bundesrepublik Deutschland* (Wiesbaden: Springer, 2015).

sified in the German armed forces since the beginning of the Bundeswehr's deployment practice, is in this respect a problem for deployed soldiers who are hardly or not at all perceived in the social and military sphere.

Conclusion: Pastoral Care in the Shadow of Deployment

The operational practice of the Bundeswehr casts a long shadow. It confronts soldiers with situations that stress them, traumatize them, or call their value orientation into question. It imposes on the families of returning soldiers profoundly hurtful experiences. At the same time, it challenges society, which in the course of deployment practice has increasingly retreated to an attitude of "friendly disinterest" (Horst Köhler), to adopt a new approach to the "invisible veterans." In this respect, the Bundeswehr's deployment practice casts a long shadow, which is accompanied by specific challenges at different levels.

Military chaplaincy has the potential to deal with these challenges in a multidimensional way. In its companionship, it addresses both the soldiers and their families.[50] As a church in the Bundeswehr, it also plays a public role. On one hand, it creates its own public sphere in the armed forces; on the other, it facilitates public discourse in society about general developments and processes in the Bundeswehr. So far, the dark sides of operational practice have been addressed too little. Projects such as pastoral care for people suffering from the consequences of deployment and service are a first step toward reaching out to traumatized and morally and spiritually wounded soldiers and their families and making their problems public.

For the public sphere, it remains a challenge to perceive and acknowledge the invisible signs of the reality of deployment—the hidden wounds of war—and to address them with sensitivity. The fact that the phrase "the fallen" has now become commonplace in public news broadcasts is evidence of increased sensitivity. This is important in easing the way back into society and everyday life for those soldiers who return from a crisis area burdened by deployment or traumatized. At the same time, the mental and spiritual wounds challenge us to reflect publicly and with the courage to criticize the sense or nonsense of foreign missions and their dark sides.

---

[50] Isolde Karle and Niklas Peuckmann, "Seelsorge in der Lebenswelt Bundeswehr. Poimenische Leitlinien der Militärseelsorge," in Karle and Peuckmann, *Seelsorge in der Bundeswehr*, 17–37.

Communal Responses to the Business of War[1]

Justin Bronson Barringer

Introduction

It seems that most popular and scholarly discussions about war focus on the violence done by militaries and on the appropriateness of governments putting these militaries into battle, but fewer discussions address the social and economic conditions that might instigate or necessitate war in the first place. It is important to recall, however, that the business of war is just that—a business. And that business ought to be considered through the same lenses through which we assess the moral and ethical aspects of other businesses. However, warmaking is also a unique sort of business because of the way it relies on destruction of lives and property; social infrastructures and economic systems; morality and decency. Thus, for Christians this aspect of the business of war ought to raise questions about how the church can offer a response to both the economic, violent, and moral aspects of war, preferably at the same time. What might be appropriate and distinctly Christian responses to the business of war?

A few biblical texts come to mind with regard to the focus on business and war. Each biblical text showcases a community with practice and ways of being in the world that relate to the business of war in opposing ways. The first is exemplified in Sodom, about which Ezekiel wrote, "'Now this was the sin of your sister Sodom: She and her daughters were arrogant, overfed and unconcerned; they did not help the poor and needy" (16:49).[2] The second and third texts are a pair that together provide an alternative to the arrogance, apathy, greed, and

---

[1] This essay first appeared as "Communal Responses to the Business of War," in *The Business of War: Theological and Ethical Reflections on the Military-Industrial Complex*, ed. James McCarty, Matthew Tapie, and Justin Bronson Barringer (Eugene, OR: Cascade Books, 2020), 161–78. The essay is reprinted here with slight stylistic modification. Used with permission of Wipf and Stock Publishers, www.wipfandstock.com.

[2] Unless indicated otherwise, all scriptural quotations are from the New International Version.

gluttony of Sodom. Acts chapters 2 and 4 delineate four practices in which the earliest Christians participated together: simplicity, community, charity, and spirituality. These first Christians shared everything in common and even sold extra possessions for the good of the group and its mission, thus embodying a form of simplicity that values others over excess possessions. In this way, along with their shared meals and common purse, they practiced community. Their community not only shared money and possessions but also made sure that everyone's needs were met, thus practicing charity. And finally, they prayed, shared in the Eucharist, preached, and performed miracles, all constituent parts of the practice of Christian spirituality. In this essay, I argue that the practices in the book of Acts offer an antidote to the malady known as the military-industrial complex (MIC), which deadens us to the cry of the poor like those content to turn deaf ears to them in Sodom.

In this essay, I argue for specific practices that seek to serve as both prophetic witness and practical social strategy, shaping disciples to refuse, as much as possible, to participate in the systems—economic, political, and philosophical—that perpetuate war and its requisite moral deformation, oppression, and isolation. In what follows, I examine the work and witness of Andrew Bacevich, Bayard Rustin, James William McClendon, the Berrigan brothers, and others with attention to what seems to me to be deep resonance in their work with the practices from the Acts texts above. I hope to show that these practices—simplicity, community, charity, spirituality— are deeply relevant for Christians who seek to resist, subvert, or provide prophetic critiques of the MIC.

Daniel Berrigan sets up the complex interconnectedness of the problem of neoliberal capitalist business and war, on one hand, and the grounds for the practices that form a Christian response to this death-dealing duo, on the other, when he writes,

> Suppose the implications of the Death game stink in one's nostrils, with all their assorted smells and whiffs of duplicity, of political corruption, or promises broken, and life destroyed, and property misused, and racism encouraged, the poor benignly neglected, and the rich seated unassailably in places of power. And religion in the midst of this game ambiguous in its own voice, and the spiritual goods of the people diminished beyond recognition.
>
> Supposing all this to be true, what is the tactic of the believer? Quite simply, I think, reading the New Testament, one says NO. Quite simply, one puts his life where the Gospel tells him it should be, if indeed the Gospel has something to say at all. One submits in a very true way to Death, in order to destroy the power of Death from within.
>
> There are, of course, ... many ways of doing this... . But as

The Savior reminds us, with a certain vigor, based upon a certain unkillable vision of his own, our reaction had better be something—something of this sort.³

This powerful poetic description of problem and response leads to questions about what the "something of this sort" might look like in the face of the business of war in particular. To begin suggesting what such a "something" might be, I turn to Bayard Rustin, activist and mentor of Martin Luther King Jr., who asserts, "For eight years I have believed war to be impractical and a denial of our Hebrew-Christian tradition. The social teachings of Jesus are: (1) respect for personality; (2) service to the 'summum bonum'; (3) overcoming evil with good; and (4) the brotherhood of man."⁴ Rustin further claims that each of those principles is broken by Christian participation in war and capitulation to current unjust economic arrangements.

It was this sort of thinking that caused Rustin to set his life against war and often make declarations like the following, which he said during the beginning of World War II: "I came to the firm and immovable conviction that war was wrong and opposed directly to the Christian ideal."⁵ Rustin's summation of Jesus's social teaching and his suggestion that the business of war violates that teaching provides the basis for my argument that the four aforementioned practices—simplicity, community, charity, and spirituality—are both a faithful and a potentially effective response offered by Christians to the economics and violence of war. I will attempt to show the connection of respect for personality to the practice of simplicity, service as the *summum bonum* to the practice of charity, overcoming evil with good to the practice of spirituality, and the "brotherhood of man" (that is, the fellowship of humanity) with the practice of community.

It may be too simple to state it as such, but the economic and social problem that undergirds American warmaking the most could be summed up in one word—consumption. Philip Berrigan recognizes this unfortunate truth, noting the two-way stream of consumption: "Indeed, few Americans understand how both the capitalistic and Soviet technocracies make people as mass-produced as assembly-line productions, with about as few options. In effect, people begin to resemble the products they consume: The system digests them, they digest its

---

[3] Daniel Berrigan, quoted in William Stringfellow and Anthony Towne. *Suspect Tenderness: The Ethics of the Berrigan Witness* (New York: Holt, Rinehart & Winston, 1971), 6.

[4] Michael G. Long, ed. *I Must Resist: Bayard Rustin's Life in Letters* (San Francisco: City Lights, 2012), 10.

[5] John D'Emilio, *Lost Prophet: The Life and Times of Bayard Rustin* (Chicago: University of Chicago Press, 2003), 72.

products."⁶ Other theologians and ethicists have demonstrated how the neoliberal, global economic system demands warmaking,⁷ but it is also worth suggesting that the system desensitizes people to its supposed necessity by producing people that are little more than consumers, whose hearts and minds are replaced by digestive tracts that care more about more than about what that more is costing others. Distinctly Christian practices remind us of our unique yet shared identity in Christ. We do not need to be slaves to consumption, anonymous to the rest of the world, willfully ignorant of the way our choices perpetuate injustice, and lulled into hopeless spiritual ennui as we capitulate to the system and abdicate our responsibilities to an only ostensibly trustworthy establishment. Simplicity frees us from consumption, community elevates us above anonymity, charity (in its more classical meaning) liberates us from willful ignorance, and spirituality unshackles us from hopelessness—or, more precisely put, it is friendship with Jesus, demonstrated in obedient praxis, that frees us from all these death-dealing powers.

Andrew Bacevich suggests that Americans in particular dress up war by pointing to a supposed tradition of being a liberating force in the world.

> Many Americans find such sentiments compelling. Yet to credit the United States with possessing a "liberating tradition" is equivalent to saying that Hollywood has a "a tradition of artistic excellence." The movie business is just that—a business. Its purpose is to make money. If once in a while a studio produces a film of aesthetic value, that may be cause for celebration, but profit, not revealing truth and beauty, defines the purpose of the enterprise. Something of the same can be said of the enterprise launched on July 4, 1776. Their purpose was not to save mankind. It was to ensure that people like themselves enjoyed unencumbered access to the Jeffersonian trinity.⁸

That Jeffersonian trinity—life, liberty, and the pursuit of happiness—has grown to mean freedom to consume, or perhaps it always meant that, at least for those to whom such a luxury was available. Now, however, what was once a rare luxury has become the norm for many Americans, which, with whatever good that has afforded the masses in this country, has exacerbated the arrogance, apathy, and gluttony that Ezekiel condemned, perhaps making America the new Sodom and certainly the epicenter of warmaking as an economic necessity. Bacevich points to Reinhold Niebuhr:

---

⁶ Philip Berrigan, *Prison Journals of a Priest Revolutionary* (New York: Holt, Rinehart & Winston, 1970), 23.

⁷ See the collected essays in McCarty, Tapie, and Barringer, *The Business of War.*

⁸ Andrew J. Bacevich, *The Limits of Power: The End of American Exceptionalism* (New York: Metropolitan, 2008), 18-19.

Niebuhr once wrote disapprovingly of Americans, their "culture soft and vulgar, equating joy with happiness and happiness with comfort." Were he alive today, Niebuhr might amend that judgment, with Americans increasingly equating comfort with self-indulgence.

The collective capacity of our domestic political economy to satisfy those appetites has not kept pace with demand. As a result, sustaining our pursuit of life, liberty, and happiness at home requires increasingly that Americans look beyond our borders. Whether the issue at hand be oil, credit, or the availability of cheap consumer goods, we expect the world to accommodate the American way of life.

The resulting sense of entitlement has great implications for foreign policy. Simply put, as the American appetite for freedom has grown, so too has our penchant for empire."[9]

In other words, "for Americans, [William Appleman Williams] observed, 'abundance' [is] freedom, and freedom [is] abundance."[10]

Christians ought to know better and to live better. We believe that freedom is slavery to Christ and that slavery to Christ is actually friendship with Christ, life, and life abundant. But how do we make the case that freedom is in consuming Christ's body and blood rather than consuming goods paid for with countless other lives? James William McClendon argues that the virtue and practice of presence is fundamental to Christian embodiment of such an ethic because it is aligned with and flowing from the presence of God with us as the basis for lives of simplicity, community, charity, and spirituality. He writes, "We remember that God's presence with us is one of the great gifts of the gospel, associated with the incarnation of the Word, the giving of the Spirit, and the return of the Lord; we recall that in Christian history his presence is celebrated at every eucharistic meal, invoked at every baptism, and claimed anew at every gathering of disciples."[11] That being the case, Christians live in such a way that rather than focusing on our own consumption, we instead focus on making our very selves, not just some excess resources, available for others, a way of living inconsonant with the notion of the plentitude of goods and the leisure to consume them unendingly as freedom. This way of living is costly, yet in it, abundance has no end because it does not depend on models of economic scarcity but on the everlasting graciousness of God, which guarantees that we hunger and thirst no more. One might rightly ask what such a life of presence looks like. McClendon writes, "Presence is being one's self for someone else; it is refusing the temptation to withdraw mentally and emotionally; but it is also on occasion putting our own

---

[9] Ibid., 9.
[10] Ibid., 23.
[11] James William McClendon Jr., *Systematic Theology*, vol. 1, *Ethics* (Nashville: Abingdon, 1986), 106.

body's weight and shape alongside the neighbor, the friend, the lover in need."[12] This, perhaps more than any other act, testifies to the truth of Christian convictions and our hope for a world in which relationships of presence, such as friendship, are the order of the day instead of neoliberal capitalism and the scourge of war, both of which keep people apart, alienating one from another and creating jealousy, enmity, and estrangement.

We are to live in such a way that the ends we seek for the world are embodied now in the life of the church. If our ends are a just society where warmaking is no more and where economic justice prevails, then we are implored by the Christian faith to use means befitting those ends. But we cannot, must not, settle for simply less war or less rabid consumption, because we are called beyond that to the ministry of reconciliation, of presence with others, of friendship with those who are now our enemies or economic competitors. This sort of world would be one where community, simplicity, charity, and spirituality were more common than radical individualism, self-indulgence, greed, and shallow religion, and therefore ought to be the sort of society Christians embody now.

Simplicity: Respect for Personality

In the immediate aftermath of 9/11, President George W. Bush's response was to encourage the American people to go shopping, to buy, to spend—to consume. Soon after, of course, he declared that the United States would deploy "shock and awe" as the military invaded Iraq. The two—shopping and invading—are not unrelated. The MIC trades on such greed and violence, often under the guises of liberty and safety. In short, the message, at least implicitly, is that Americans' right to convenient consumerism is more important than the lives of Iraqi people. The multifaceted connection between greed and violence was evident both in the terrorist attacks of 9/11 and in the American response. It was, after all, the centers of commerce and the military that were hit by those airliners.

Recognition of the connection between greed and violence is very old. In fact, church fathers like Chrysostom and Basil essentially called greed itself violence. Chrysostom wrote, for instance, "You should think the same way about those who are rich and greedy. They are a kind of robbers lying in wait on the roads, stealing from passers-by, and burying others' goods in their own houses as if in caves and holes."[13] Basil even takes it a step further in his homily "In Time of Famine and Drought," saying, "For whoever has the ability to remedy the suffering of others, but chooses rather to withhold aid out of selfish motives,

---

[12] Ibid., 106.
[13] Saint John Chrysostom, *On Wealth and Poverty*, trans. Catharine P. Roth (Crestwood, NY: St. Vladimir's Seminary Press, 1984), 36.

may properly be judged the equivalent of a murderer."[14] It is often the case that in the name of remedying the suffering of others, the MIC swings into action around the globe, but what if, in fact, it was for more selfish reasons that its major players typically bang the drums of war?

Bacevich seems to think that these less altruistic motives drive the American economy and its warmaking, as he notes the confusion of freedom with consumerism, the simple meeting of needs with the drive for having it all and then some. For example, he writes, "If one were to choose a single word to characterize [American] identity, it would have to be more. For the majority of contemporary Americans, the essence of life, liberty, and the pursuit of happiness centers on a relentless personal quest to acquire, to consume, to indulge, and to shed whatever constraints might interfere with those endeavors."[15] Christians, however, are to be a people defined by less (Philippians 2). We ought to be on a relentless quest to give, to create, to show restraint, and to throw off whatever hinders these good works (Hebrews 12:1). Each of these requires both a desire for and a persistent pursuit of simplicity. Simplicity, as I am using the word here, is intended to be about both disentanglement from an abundance of material goods and an undivided will. The witness of the Berrigan brothers is particularly compelling on both these points. Daniel and Philip lived their lives willing that the world be a peaceful and just place, and to that end they embraced the freedom of letting go of excess possessions and the desire to please others. A friend of Daniel's wrote, "Daniel Berrigan was a saintly man. He was tremendously difficult to deal with, very uncompromising. Saintliness does not bespeak of politesse. It makes life both difficult and simple. When you follow your own moral compass, you're not pushed and pulled by everyday pressures of life. You don't have the same complexity in your decisions."[16] Daniel's simplicity is poignantly depicted in an episode that took place after he was arrested and tried for one of his many acts of civil disobedience. "When he walked out of the courtroom, Dan, grinning, pulled out a toothbrush from his shirt pocket, telling reporters he had come ready for 'anything, including jail.'"[17] Who knew that dental hygiene could serve as Christian witness? Dan Berrigan argued that it was precisely this sort of simplicity that was itself a real threat to violent and unjust

---

[14] Saint Basil of Caesarea, "In Time of Famine and Drought," in *On Social Justice*, trans. C. Paul Schroeder (Crestwood, NY: St. Vladimir's Seminary Press, 2009), 73–88, at 85.
[15] Bacevich, *Limits of Power*, 16.
[16] Murray Polner and Jim O'Grady, *Disarmed and Dangerous: The Radical Life and Times of Daniel and Philip Berrigan, Brothers in Religious Faith and Civil Disobedience* (Boulder, CO: Westview, 1998), 8.
[17] Ibid., 347.

powers. "We, who are without weapons or riches or a stake in this world, are become a danger to the masters of the kingdom of death."[18]

Bayard Rustin, in many ways, felt likewise, although he did have an appreciation for the "finer things" that is not so evident in the lives of the Berrigans. Though he was raised in a poor family and never graduated from college, Rustin had a sophisticated taste in everything from food to music. However, Rustin's life is a testament to the fact that he was more concerned about causes than consumption, and elevated people over prestige. Rustin, by necessity or choice, ended up as primarily a background figure of the civil rights movement and midcentury antiwar efforts. Yet it was he who most clearly articulated the theological and practical foundations on which these movements were erected. He taught Martin Luther King Jr. nonviolent civil disobedience, organized the famous 1963 March for Jobs and Freedom in Washington, DC, and gave direction to the protests against the war in Vietnam. It is widely agreed that Rustin was the brains of these movements, yet he stepped aside, or more precisely, allowed himself to be pushed to the background, to let folks like King shine.

As a Black gay pacifist during a time of high racial tension, a contentious war, and the Stonewall riots, Rustin had a lot to be angry about, but rather than let that anger lead to hate, Rustin chose to follow the way of Jesus, which demands respect for personality. Respect for personality is made possible by simplicity because one's vision is not blurred by multiplicity or consumer-driven greed and gluttony, and therefore one more clearly sees the personhood of the other. In fact, respecting personality is an act of simplicity itself because it is the choice to treat others with dignity regardless of circumstance. In this way, Rustin exemplified Christian simplicity.

It is not the case, however, that most Christians living in America embrace these forms of simplicity embodied by Rustin and the Berrigans. Indeed, American Christians seem to look more American than Christian. And as Bacevich reminds us,

> Americans [have come] to count on an ever-larger economic pie to anesthetize the unruly and ameliorate tensions related to class, race, religion, and ethnicity. Money [has become] the preferred lubricant for keeping social and political friction within tolerable limits. Americans, Reinhold Niebuhr once observed, "seek a solution for practically every problem of life in quantitative terms," certain that more is better.[19]

We want not only more, but more choices—more varieties of more—which complicates our lives, clouds our moral vision, inhibits our spiritual growth, and separates us from each other. Christians ought to know better. After all, Jesus spoke

---

[18] Stringfellow and Towne, *Suspect Tenderness*, 9.
[19] Bacevich, *Limits of Power*, 23.

repeatedly about the dangers of such a view. It is this illusory "more" that keeps folks from entering the kingdom (Matthew 19:24).

The situation American Christians must confront is further complicated by the fact that it is precisely our demand for more that both perpetuates war and destroys healthy economic systems. Bacevich writes, "Here is the central paradox of our time: While the defense of American freedom seems to demand that US troops fight in places like Iraq and Afghanistan, the exercise of that freedom at home undermines the nation's capacity to fight. A grand bazaar provides an inadequate basis upon which to erect a vast empire."[20] The church, however, has no need to build an empire, because we are to be satisfied with the simplicity of God's kingdom, willing only to please the One whose salvation is our joy. We believe in a community of communities making up the family of God rather than an empire competing to make consumption a cause for which we are willing to kill.

Community: The Fellowship of Humanity

There is perhaps an irony that simplicity seems increasingly less easy to achieve. If we are not careful, we may view the endeavor as a private and personal one. However, the best engine for simple living is community. Community takes investment. Like a Jackson Pollock painting, it is simultaneously remarkably simple and messy. While people seem to long for community, many of us have subjugated our need for it to our desire for more. Again, Bacevich offers insight on this point: "As individuals, Americans never cease to expect more. As members of a community, especially as members of a national community, they choose to contribute less."[21] This is true in the American church as well. Thus, we need a reversal, precisely the sort of reversal that Jesus inaugurated in his ministry, where we are willing to contribute more to our communities and expect less as individuals.

Here again, we approach a paradox, because this mentality does not deprive individuals but enriches and supports them, even as it is often strenuous and demanding. Daniel Berrigan once again serves as an example of this truth. As his friend Don Moore wrote,

> Dan helps us to confront the demands that community life should be making upon each one of us... . He will not let us keep private our disappointments or problems or discouragements. It is a failure of community, in Dan's mind, if someone is shouldering a burden alone... . If someone is reluctant to speak out, perhaps the commun-

---

[20] Ibid., 11.
[21] Ibid., 10.

ity is at fault. Perhaps the community has not manifested to one of its own a loving openness and acceptance. This demands that the community, or better, that each member of the community carefully nourishes with the others a spirit of concern, friendship, trust, and sense of presence.[22]

Yet Moore continues, "It is almost a matter of routine now within the community that each Jesuit's problems and predicaments are, to the extent that he wishes it, the community's problems and predicaments. This is as it should be; we are not alone, and we are all, in St. Paul's terms, ministers of reconciliation."[23]

It is precisely ministers of reconciliation that a world consumed by consumption and driven by the business of war needs urgently. As Daniel Berrigan alluded to, Christian community teaches us about conflict resolution, the redemptive power of inconvenience for the sake of another, and especially the truth that we are not our own. It teaches us to draw close to God, the One who resolves conflict by giving himself, the One who, from the time of creation to the time of the eschaton, continues to volunteer to be inconvenienced for the sake of humanity and has even given himself up to us as One who, though self-sufficient and necessary, made himself dependent in the incarnation and expendable on the cross. Jesus is not his own; he belongs to the Father and the Spirit. The Father belongs to the Son and the Spirit, and the Spirit likewise belongs to the Father and the Son. This is what the community of the Trinity teaches us.

In line with this core Christian doctrine, Bayard Rustin's vision of community flowed from his belief that the teachings of Jesus pointed to what Rustin referred to "the brotherhood of man," and what we might term the fellowship of humanity. Biographer Jervis Anderson wrote that "Bayard seemed to envelop people with his sense of the oneness of humanity."[24] This belief compelled Rustin to work with virtually anyone who offered to share in his struggle against oppression. Furthermore, Rustin wrote that "segregation, separation, according to Jesus, is the basis of continual violence. That which separates man from his brother is evil and must be resisted."[25] Often it is our hoarding of seemingly scarce goods that keeps us apart, and thus whenever we share those goods or sacrifice our supposed allotment for the sake of others, we undermine violence. For Rustin, it was bringing people together that was perhaps the greatest threat to the war machine, which sought—and still seeks—to keep people apart. This is something that the military-industrial complex relies on as its puppeteers seek

---

[22] Don Moore, "Life in Community with Dan," in *Apostle of Peace: Essays in Honor of Daniel Berrigan*, ed. John Dear (Maryknoll, NY: Orbis, 1996), 141.

[23] Ibid., 142.

[24] Jervis Anderson, *Bayard Rustin: Troubles I've Seen; a Biography* (New York: HarperCollins, 1997), 5.

[25] Long, *I Must Resist*, 12.

to maintain economic divisions so as to have a limitless stream of soldiers flowing in from the ongoing economic draft, on one hand, and an ever-growing constituency of well-educated, well-paid contractors, weapons designers, engineers, and public relations experts, on the other. Unfortunately, even supposed political liberals are complicit in this enterprise, as their various ideas of government social engineering often bolster economic systems that lead people to rely on political and military structures to make ends meet. Rustin saw this as he argued that it was poor (Black) folks, even as a result of the best intentions of liberal White elites, that were drawn into the most dangerous fighting positions in any given war. Furthermore, even though Rustin adamantly opposed war, he saw segregation in the military as problematic. It perpetuated injustice on a number of levels, in the United States and abroad.[26]

Jesus, too, was confronted by the temptation to sacrifice community for the sake of expediency, or prestige, or comfort. The clearest example of this is, of course, Jesus's encounter with Satan (recorded in all of the Synoptic Gospels), who offered Jesus each of these enticements, but at the cost of sacrificing his community with Father and Spirit, along with the community of the coming peaceable kingdom that Jesus made possible on the cross. Scripture has other examples as well, including the time recorded in John 6, when the crowd tried to make Jesus king by force after he had miraculously fed thousands, but Jesus, we are told, withdrew to be by himself. It might seem odd, in a discussion about community, to point to a passage in which Jesus withdrew from a crowd to be alone, but I want to suggest that Jesus knew that a community built merely on feeding people was a false community, and that the power dynamics of such a relationship would prevent the full flourishing of the members of this crowd.

This understanding became evident the next day, after Jesus literally walked on water to get back to his disciples, when Jesus told the crowd that full stomachs do not provide sufficient basis for forming a community of disciples. Rather, such a community must be built on spiritual nourishment as well. Jesus offered himself as spiritual nourishment, changing the power dynamic by making it clear that he was not merely interested in giving stuff to people but rather would not settle for less than giving the fullness of himself to them. Upon realizing that receiving such a gift, the gift of God's friendship, would also entail the demands of a deeper relationship than merely that of provider and consumer, many people deserted him. This, however, clarified who was up to the task of practicing community and who only wanted to be fed. In all this, we see that Jesus rejected a system set up on the basis of earthly power, which seems to be related here to satanic power, and authority that settled for making consumption —even perhaps overconsumption (as the story tells us that everyone ate their fill)—the raison d'être of human existence. Satan wants us to settle for bread

---

[26] Ibid., 110–26.

from a stone, but Jesus tells us that the only bread sufficient for life eternal is the bread of his flesh, the bread of communion shared with God and all those who have been called to eat the body broken for us.

It seems, then, that Jesus is sustained by community, both with the Father and the Spirit and, to some degree, with his disciples, while also making it possible for others to join this community, one that negates the separations caused by wealth inequity, race, artificial borders of nation-states, and patriotic allegiances. Jesus's time with the Father and the Spirit in eternity and with his disciples on earth made possible his sacrifice on the cross, even when he felt abandoned by everyone. In this way, community is vital for followers of Christ as well because it prepares Christians for the lonely times that will likely result from opposition to economic injustice and war.

Rustin knew well, in his own life and the lives of others, the pain of being ostracized and abused because of outspokenness about economic injustice and militarism, among other issues, but Rustin also knew the value of the respect for personality, that is, the care for unique individuals as such. Thus, as Michael Long notes, "Unlike some Radicals who focused merely on systems—the military-industrial complex, capitalism, and racism, for example—Rustin often made heartfelt appeals on behalf of individuals in dire straits."[27] In a letter to President Kennedy from 1962, Rustin recounts the story of an elderly man who had been a conscientious objector since before World War I, and who had quit paying taxes after the atomic bomb was dropped on Hiroshima because "he could not conscientiously pay for weapons of destruction any longer."[28] As a result, this man, Max Sandin, had his social security payment and his union pension garnished, leaving him destitute. While Rustin acknowledged that he, unlike the Berrigans, believed in the principle that "conscientious objectors should be willing, when [they] resist the state, to accept the penalties that the state imposes," he argues that this case has "extenuating circumstances because of [Sandin's] sincerity and his age and his health."[29] The appeal here is not made on the basis of a commitment to ideas of justice and nonviolence but a commitment to a person, one whose decisions of conscience had proven to be costly. Rustin, along with the community at the Peace Action Center, where Sandin was staying at the time because he had no income, demonstrated the sustaining power of fidelity in the face of hardship brought on by one's rejection of the business of war. Our loneliness, the loneliness caused by violence and greed and consumerism, is most powerfully assuaged by belonging to a community committed to sustaining each of its members, to full human flourishing, and to continually drawing the connections between economics and war so that injustices may be resisted together.

---

[27] Ibid., 251.
[28] Ibid., 252.
[29] Ibid., 252.

Furthermore, Christians need community because opposition to injustice and war must be taught. For instance, it was from his Quaker predecessors that Bayard Rustin learned the social teachings of Jesus and the particular frame of understanding them as a demand for nonviolent action. Rustin, in turn, along with his friend Glenn Smiley, taught these lessons to Martin Luther King Jr. during the Montgomery bus boycott. According to Anderson, at the beginning of the boycott, King kept guns and had armed guards, but Rustin talked King into giving those up and embracing nonviolence fully. Rustin said to King, "If in the heat and flow of battle a leader's house is bombed and he shoots back, then that is an encouragement to his followers to pick up guns. If, on the other hand, he has no guns around him, and his followers know it, then they will rise to the nonviolent occasion."[30] Similarly, and no doubt historically connected, Rustin was making essentially the same arguments against World War II that King would later level against the war in Vietnam, and likewise Rustin, even before King's ascendency, had named the connection that King would call the "triple evils" of racism, militarism, and materialism. In short, King was surrounded by a community, of which Rustin was a key member, that taught him about faithfully naming and opposing these evils.

As Christians look to the witness of Jesus and previous generations of the faithful, they learn to be a marker for future generations of goodness rather than evil. Bacevich writes, "History will not judge kindly a people who find nothing amiss in the prospect of endless armed conflict so long as they themselves are spared the effects. Nor will it view with favor an electorate that delivers political power into the hands of leaders unable to envision any alternative to perpetual war."[31] Yet this is where we find ourselves, and the Christian church in America and elsewhere must decide without delay to live otherwise, to refuse to support unjust war and to protest political powers hell-bent on keeping the war machine moving along, leaving destruction in its wake. The church ought to be leading the way as a people who do indeed find something amiss with endless armed conflicts and who recognize the proper human telos that enables us to envision another way of life and the Spirit that empowers us to do so.

Rather than settle for perpetual armed conflict and the unjust economic systems that demand more blood so long as it is someone else's, Christians envision another world, and we live as if it is already here because we know it is and that it is coming. Jesus tells the apostles that he gives them his peace and leaves it with them (John 14:27). It is in our participation in the Eucharist that our actions most resemble and conform to Christ's nonviolent form of life. Followers of Christ give so that others may have peace and abundance, rather than take so that we may indulge.

---

[30] Anderson, *Bayard Rustin*, 188.

[31] Bacevich, *Limits of Power*, 13.

Charity: Service as the *Summum Bonum*

In my first youth ministry position, the youth group was made up almost entirely of students from low-income families. Some of them wanted to go to college but felt it was out of their reach financially. So some went into the military, hoping that they could get an education during or after their military stint. Rustin drew attention to this reality several decades ago:

> And even during this horrible Vietnam war, many Negro young men who would have no alternative but to stand on street corners ... are convinced that by joining the armed forces they can learn a trade, earn a salary, and be in a position to enter the job market on their return.... All this means that thousands of Negroes, in order to rehabilitate themselves, are forced to take a stand beyond morality and exploit the opportunities presented to them by their country's military involvement. I myself can afford the luxury of drawing those moral lines, but it is more difficult to suggest to people who are hungry, jobless, or living in slums that they turn their backs on opportunities that promise them a measure of economic betterment.... If this attitude on the part of thousands of Negroes horrifies the peace movement, then perhaps the peace movement might well conclude that it must give a large part of its energy to the struggle to secure the social and economic uplift of the Negro community.[32]

This quote represents the crux of my argument. If we are to be against war, we are to be against the business of war, that is, we must oppose and undermine all the ways that war becomes financially attractive to various socioeconomic groups. It is not enough simply to argue that war is wrong or that people should not participate in unjust wars; it is the church's responsibility to see to it that those whose hunger and poverty limit their choices, and prevent them from considering the morality of war, are provided enough economic stability that they are at least able to weigh the various moral claims and make the decision themselves, rather than having it made for them by their abjection. Likewise, it is the Christian call to put ourselves, as much as possible, into their experience of hunger and suffering, and so better understand their predicament and offer a more convincing witness.

Rustin played a significant role in shaping Martin Luther King Jr.'s understanding of the triple evils. For instance, Rustin suggested that economic and other social issues kept many African American folks from joining the peace movement of his day. Yet he also wrote, "It may well be that the solution to one problem has implications for the solution of another."[33] This suggests that meeting economic needs, through a variety of charity and justice activities, is one

---

[32] Bayard Rustin, *Time on Two Crosses: The Collected Writings of Bayard Rustin*, ed. Devon W. Carbado and Donald Weise (San Francisco: Cleis, 2003), 149–50.
[33] Ibid., 148.

way to grow the peace movement and prevent the military-industrial complex from so successfully recruiting people, because the poor, when their economic needs are met, will be perhaps less inclined to capitulate to the war machine, since they will have more freedom to do otherwise; and the rich, when their time and money are devoted to causes of peace and justice, rather than ensuring their own success by either actively or passively supporting the violent status quo, will consider the moral implications of a job in lieu of a lucrative salary.[34]

It is evident in the lives of the Berrigans and Rustin that a deep spirituality— the Berrigans' from their Catholic commitments, Rustin's from his Quaker roots —guided and sustained their continued actions for community and against injustice, as well as the times of incarceration they often faced for those actions. As it was for the Berrigans and Rustin along with their compatriots, so it is for all followers of Christ: to sustain a healthy, loving, Christian community requires a robust and ever-developing practice of Christian spirituality. It is in fact Christian spirituality, which I am broadly defining as intentional and disciplined openness and obedience to the Holy Spirit, that undergirds and informs the practices of simplicity, community, and charity.

Spirituality: Overcoming Evil with Good

Bacevich claims, along with Niebuhr, that it is hubris and sanctimony that keep the American military-industrial, empire-seeking, shopping-and-spending machine going, at least for now. The response, as I see it, is to produce a spirituality in people that encourages humility and sincerity. If we are to follow Jesus's command to overcome evil with good, then we ought to have some understanding of what constitutes good, and we ought to have at least some of that good present in our own lives before we can rightly expect it of others. Dan Berrigan suggests that "it is in the Word of God one finds the resources to keep going in such times as these."[35]

The Berrigans, McClendon, and Rustin all agree that there is an order to the way goodness spreads. It must begin in individuals and communities, especially the church community, then move outward to society. As this process relates to war, Rustin writes, "The truth is that war is wrong. It is then our duty to make war impossible, first in us, then in society."[36] Rustin had in mind a spirituality that first shaped him so that he could play a part in shaping the social order. He, like McClendon, was interested in the church's witness, especially the consisten-

---

[34] For example, see Kara N. Slade, "The Military-Educational Complex," in McCarty, Tapie, and Barringer, *The Business of War*, 141–60.
[35] Quoted in Stringfellow and Towne, *Suspect Tenderness*, 5.
[36] Long, *I Must Resist*, 2.

cy, or lack thereof, between the church's preaching and its actions. Rustin was quick to call out incongruities, saying, for instance, that segregation in the church continued to crucify Christ.[37] For Rustin, it was paramount that Christian spirituality form the church to be a body that first demonstrated goodness within so that it could faithfully call those outside the church to repentance as well.

To cultivate such a spirituality that shapes individuals and communities to eliminate warring in their own hearts, then to bear witness to the reality of God's shalom in the world, Christians must be disciplined. We see this in the Plowshares movement, for example, whose members Dan Berrigan described as "spiritually disciplined and well-prepared people who can do these things and who can take the heat."[38] And no doubt those who oppose warmaking powers—whether those powers be governments, economic systems, or hedonistic philosophies—will face some heat as they seek to enact a different sort of community, one that seeks to shape all of society to be more peaceful and just.

Of course, the Christian telos goes beyond simply shaping society; it centers on the shalom brought about by friendship with YHWH. If we are to show the way, to teach warmaking powers and ordinary citizens about their responsibilities, then we must have a clear sense of what God is doing in the world. Then we can begin to see how both the church and state fit into fulfilling the *missio Dei*. According to McClendon, "For Christians, questions about lasting peace can never be separated from eschatology... . Our eschatology and our peacemaking are two sides of a single coin." And by including eschatology in discussions about peacemaking, Christians can rightly critique "pacifists who [believe] in 'the brotherhood of man,' [and thus think] that world peace [is] just around the corner."[39] For Rustin, the idea of "the brotherhood of man" did not lead to the naïve pacifism of many advocates of the Social Gospel, but instead it led to a lifelong commitment to working for peace and justice, even if they were not soon coming. Even World War II, which notably turned Reinhold Niebuhr from his earlier pacifism, did not deter Rustin, who, although given a religious exemption for conscientious objection, "chose imprisonment over the protections to which he was entitled as a religious conscientious objector."[40]

Anderson goes on to quote Rustin's response to the summons from the draft board for his physical examination in preparation to send him to a civilian work camp:

---

[37] Ibid., 179.
[38] Quoted in Polner and O'Grady, *Disarmed and Dangerous*, 350.
[39] McClendon, *Ethics*, 318.
[40] Anderson, *Bayard Rustin*, 98.

I cannot voluntarily submit to an order stemming from the selective service act. War is wrong. Conscription is a concomitant of modern war.... Conscription for war is inconsistent with freedom of conscience which is not merely the right to believe but to act on the degree of truth one receives, to follow a vocation which is God-inspired and God-directed.... Though joyfully following the will of God, I regret that I must break the law of the State. I am prepared for whatever may follow.[41]

On the other side of this time in prison, Rustin continued to speak and act as a pacifist, speaking and working against every one of America's wars during his lifetime. In short, Rustin exemplifies not the naïve pacifist of Niebuhr's famous critique but one who recognizes God's work in the world and who joins in that work, no matter the cost or the length of the journey to peaceful resolution. A commitment to the fellowship of humanity need not entail naiveté but rather demands working faithfully to bear witness to the way God is bringing about that reality. We see such work, of course, in the early church, even with all its problems, as the first Christians discerned together God's work among them and in the wider world.

Conclusion: Acts 2 Community

Bacevich recounts a speech by Jimmy Carter that, despite its unpopularity then and now, rings truer today than when Carter first delivered it, in July 1979.

> In a nation that was proud of hard work, strong families, close-knit communities, and our faith in God too many of us now tend to worship self-indulgence and consumption. Human identity is no longer defined by what one does, but by what one owns. But we've discovered that owning things and consuming things does not satisfy our longing for meaning. We've learned that piling up material goods cannot fill the emptiness of lives which have no confidence or purpose.[42]

Bacevich expounds, "In other words, the spreading American crisis of confidence was an outward manifestation of an underlying crisis of values."[43]

If this is the case, then it is the Christian church that is best positioned to lead the movement of reversing the crisis. It is followers of Christ whose collective story and moral formation equip them with the tools needed to respond and lead others in the right direction. The above practices seek to strike at the root causes of the problem rather than settling for treating symptoms and merely

---

[41] Ibid., 98.
[42] Quoted in Bacevich, *Limits of Power*, 33.
[43] Ibid., 33.

changing policies in hopes that a change of heart will follow. Even as recent wars have lost popular support, few have decried the underlying causes and presuppositions necessary to make the venture possible and seemingly necessary in the first place. How many today are speaking up against greed as attendant to violence? Very few, it seems. Thus, we the church must point to those causes, the sins that are most acutely dominating American consciousness and lifestyles, and we must practice a different way of life. This way of life is outlined at the end of Acts 2:

> They devoted themselves to the apostles' teaching and to fellowship, to the breaking of bread and to prayer. Everyone was filled with awe at the many wonders and signs performed by the apostles. All the believers were together and had everything in common. They sold property and possessions to give to anyone who had need. Every day they continued to meet together in the temple courts. They broke bread in their homes and ate together with glad and sincere hearts, praising God and enjoying the favor of all the people. And the Lord added to their number daily those who were being saved. (2:42–47)

Contributors

Dr. Justin Bronson Barringer is Lecturer in Religious Ethics at Southern Methodist University, Dallas, Texas.

Dr. Jochen Cornelius-Bundschuh is Adjunct Professor at the University of Heidelberg and former Regional Bishop for the Baden Region in the Evangelische Landeskirche.

Dr. Angelika Dörfler-Dierken is Professor at the Institute for Church and Dogmatics History, University of Hamburg, Germany.

Dr. Martin Elbe, an economist and sociologist, is a researcher at the Zentrum für Militärgeschichte und Sozialwissenschaften der Bundeswehr (Center for Military History and Social Sciences of the Bundeswehr) in Potsdam, Germany.

Dr. Marco Hofheinz is Professor of Systematic Theology at Leibniz University, Hannover, Germany.

Dr. Keith Joseph is Bishop of North Queensland in the Anglican Church of Australia.

Dr. Isolde Karle is Professor of Practical Theology and Director of the Institute of Religion and Society at Ruhr University, Bochum, Germany.

Dr. Torsten Meireis is Professor of Ethics and Hermeneutics and Director of the Berlin Institute for Public Theology at Humboldt University, Berlin.

Dr. Seumas Miller is Professor of Philosophy in the Australian Graduate School of Policing and Security at Charles Sturt University Canberra, Australia, and Senior Research Fellow in Philosophy at the Uehiro Centre for Practical Ethics, University of Oxford.

Contributors

Dr. Niklas Peuckmann is Chair of Practical Theology in the Faculty of Protestant Theology at Ruhr University, Bochum, Germany.

Dr. Stephen Pickard, a retired Anglican bishop, is Adjunct Professor of Theology at the Australian Centre for Christianity and Culture, Charles Sturt University, Australia.

Dr. Gerd Theißen is Professor Emeritus of New Testament Theology at Heidelberg University.

Dr. Sylvie Thonak is Senior Instructor at a high school in Baden-Württemberg, Germany.

Dr. Jürgen von Hagen is Professor of Economics and Director of the Institute for International Economic Policy at the University of Bonn.

Dr. Hartwig von Schubert is a former Senior Research Fellow at the German Institute for Defense and Strategic Studies in Hamburg, and currently a Lecturer at International University Hamburg.

Dr. Michael Welker is Senior Professor of Systematic Theology and Director of the FIIT–Research Center for International and Interdisciplinary Theology at the Ruprecht Karl University of Heidelberg.

Dr. John Witte Jr. is the Robert W. Woodruff Professor of Law, McDonald Distinguished Professor of Religion, and Director of the Center for the Study of Law and Religion at Emory University, Atlanta, USA.

Printed in the USA
CPSIA information can be obtained
at www.ICGtesting.com
LVHW022135041023
760082LV00002B/75